Preface

Your kind of selling is different.

When you read a book about salesmanship, it seems to apply to selling life insurance, or automobiles, or machine tools, but not to your kind of selling (unless you happen to be selling life insurance or automobiles or machine tools). Different types of selling require quite different techniques and methods. Selling encyclopedias to parents of school children is about as different from selling promotions to a supermarket chain as dentistry is from airline piloting.

The salesperson selling a million-dollar CAT scanner to a hospital may have two or three hours to make the presentation to a buying group; the pharmaceutical representative has about 3 minutes to introduce a new product and resell a couple of older ones.

The territory may vary in size from a single national account to the entire United States.

The number of sales calls per week can vary, literally, from one to a hundred.

True, the basic principles of selling may be the same, but their applications are so different in different types of selling that it's almost like learning a foreign language. This book shows how these basic principles are applied in different kinds of selling.

Moreover, the nature of the selling task is changing rapidly. One of our contributors, Gourdin Sirles, division sales manager for AT&T, points out that because of the increasing cost of the face-to-face sales call, many types of selling formerly done in person are now handled by telemarketing or by direct-mail or direct-response marketing. The businesses in which in-person selling still predominates are the complex, high-tech fields like health care and information management.

iii

Still other forces are shifting the emphasis back to the salesperson. The vice president of marketing for a leading manufacturer of branded consumer products observes that the importance of the sales force decreased some years ago, when three major networks dominated television and a few supermarket chains controlled the most important retail outlets. Today, he notes, with cable TV, VCRs, the growing independence of local TV and radio stations, and a proliferation of fast-food outlets, the importance of the field sales force is increasing.

Have automation and high-tech communications methods reduced the need for flesh-and-blood salespeople? In the 20-year period from 1954 to 1974, according to the Bureau of Labor Statistics, the percentage of employed persons engaged in selling fluctuated between 6 percent and 6.6 percent. According to the 1980 census, there were 11.8 million salespeople in a work force of 100.8 million—about 11.7 percent. The increase is probably due to a change in census-taking methods rather than to an increase in the percentage of workers engaged in selling.

The 11.8 million sales workers were subdivided as follows:

Supervisors and proprietors	2,958,000
Sales reps, financial and business services	1,853,000
Sales reps, commodities (other than retail)	1,442,000
Sales reps, retail and personal services	5,500,000
Sales-related occupations	54,000
Total	11,807,000

How This Book Was Written

No matter how many books you may have read about selling, you'll find this one different.

First of all, each chapter starts with a concise summary of one basic principle of selling that has been known since the serpent sold Eve the forbidden fruit by promising her the benefit of knowledge.

Second, each chapter then gives examples of how these general principles are applied specifically in various types of selling.

Third, and most important, these actual applications were not dreamed up by some ivory-tower theorist but have been contributed by working salespeople who are the stars of their companies and their industries.

The gee-whiz type of salesmanship book often describes sales methods one can hardly imagine a real-life sales rep using on a real-life buyer. That can't be said of these suggestions. They're right off the firing line.

Through the cooperation of the National Society of Sales Training Executives and of *Sales and Marketing Management* magazine, leading companies in a number of fields were asked to select their outstanding sales representatives to serve as contributing editors. Some of them are top-rated sales reps for their companies; others, after a distinguished career in selling, have moved on to positions in sales training and sales management. Their biographies appear at the end of the book.

Their response was wholehearted. They have given you the secrets of successful salesmanship, as they have developed and perfected them the hard way, in their kinds of selling. One cannot help but be impressed by their willingness to share their valuable know-how with all sellers everywhere—including their competitors!

The companies they represent have been selected to give a cross-section of many different types of selling (except over-the-counter retail sales).

The contributors represent four basic types of selling:

Selling to business and industry. These salespeople sell equipment, components, and supplies to manufacturers and business establishments. They may sell intangibles, such as workers' compensation insurance or motivational programs; or equipment, such as machine tools or packaging machinery; or supplies, such as business forms; or parts or ingredients of the manufacturer's products.

Selling for resale. These are the salespeople of the manufacturer, selling to wholesalers, distributors, or retailers; or the salespeople of the wholesaler or distributor, selling to retailers. In this type of selling, the emphasis is not so much on the benefits of the product to the end user as it is on the benefits to the merchant: markup, turnover, new customers, low inventory, marketing services, and the like.

Selling to the consumer. In this category are the people selling real estate, automobiles, life insurance, securities, household services, and so on.

Selling to doctors and hospitals. This is a highly specialized type of selling. Representatives of pharmaceutical manufacturers are one of the physician's major sources of information about new pharmaceuticals and their applications. Sales representatives selling to hospitals may be selling pharmaceuticals and other hospital supplies, or they may be selling specialized equipment costing millions of dollars.

This book contains about 850 specific ideas that have proved useful and practical in various kinds of selling. The sales representative reading this book may get valuable ideas from other salespeople in the same industry, or from those in different industries selling to the same types of customers, or even from salespeople in entirely different industries.

For example, Cevin Melezoglu of American Greetings sometimes gets an appointment with a hard-to-see prospect by sending the prospect a greeting card with a written note that she will telephone on such-and-such a date. Greeting cards happen to be the product she sells, but a sales rep in a totally different type of selling might find an unusual greeting card a way to get the attention of a crusty purchasing agent.

Here, with my heartfelt thanks, are the names of the sales pros who have written most of this book.

Selling to Business and Industry

American Express (Travel Management Services), Greg Deming
AMP, Inc., John Kulp
AT&T, Gourdin Sirles
Automatic Data Processing, Paul Lentz
Dun's Marketing Service, Steven Rand
GTE Mobilnet, Inc., Roland M. Charles, Jr.
Los Angeles Times, Janis Drew
Maritz Motivation, Bruce White
McGraw-Hill, Walter W. Patten, Jr.
Monsanto, John Paul Jones
Occidental Chemical Corporation, John Heitzenroder
Pitney Bowes, Charlotte Jacobs
Turner Construction, Michael Ciarcia
Unisys Corporation, Nick Debronsky
Wausau Insurance Companies, William O'Neill

Selling for Resale

Alberto Culver, A. R. Flores
American Greetings, Cevin Melezoglu
Cooper Tire & Rubber Company, William Clark
The Dial Corporation, Edward J. Lahue
Dr Pepper, Dave Pitzer
The Drackett Company, Richard Ziegler
Eastman Kodak, Larry Nonnamaker
Hewlett-Packard Company, Paul Sanders
McKesson Drug Company, Bob Chargin
Nabisco Brands, Jonathan Vitarius and Patricia Markley
Simmons USA, David Clark
Whirlpool Corporation, Gary Rucker
Zenith, Carl Unger

Selling to the Consumer

Allstate Insurance, Jack Hallberg
Chrysler Motors, Gordon Wallace
Coldwell Banker, Suzanne DeNoyior
Encyclopaedia Britannica, Tom DeLaMater and David Van Tosh
Mary Kay Cosmetics, Judie McCoy
Merrill Lynch, Betty Cinq-Mars
Northwestern Mutual, John O. Todd
Terminix International, Hal Kessler
Tupperware Home Parties, Denise Kaluzna

Selling to Doctors and Hospitals

Baxter Travenol, Doug Haynie
CIBA-Geigy, Peter C. Pappas
GE Medical Systems, J. M. Garcia
Roerig Division of Pfizer, Ralph Eubanks

I also wish to express my appreciation to Charles ("Chuck") Strother, who taped incoming phone contributions while I was out of town, and to my wife, Marty, who patiently permitted her dining-room table to become a mail center.

Contents

Part Four: After the Call   239

Part One
A Career in Selling

1
What's It Like?

The authors of this book are a group of highly successful salesmen and saleswomen in many different kinds of selling. It seems logical to start by asking them:

- What do you feel about selling as a career?
- What is the work like?
- What does it take to be a successful salesperson?
- How can you maintain an "up" attitude in the face of the inevitable rejections?

Here are some of their answers:

Selling As a Career

"Few occupations offer such satisfying and instant rewards as does selling," says Bruce White of Maritz Motivation Company. "Behaviorists stress the importance of immediate feedback and positive reinforcement as necessary consequences to shape our actions. Salespeople are reinforced constantly, and closing a sale is definitely the tangible result of successful effort. And since most salespeople receive commissions or bonuses in relation to their sales, incentive increases with the rate of success.

"All of us want to be recognized for our achievements. We need and seek the honor and praise of others. Nowhere is our psyche stroked better than in selling. We receive plaudits from our company and our customers as well.

"Because the days of personal, inspirational leadership are gone—our role models and bosses have too much to do and too many to lead—the gap is being filled with motivational 'programs': communications campaigns, motivation and incentive programs, honor and recognition awards, presidents' clubs and top performers' councils, and so on. Nowhere is this more evident than for salespeople. They get all the glory! (But that's what the factory workers have always said anyway.)

"New or aspiring salespeople should look for their own best 'niche' in the selling field. The daily regimen differs widely by type of selling; witness the following chapters in this book. Don't be afraid to change companies in order to try a different type of selling. That used to be called 'job jumping' and was considered a black mark on one's résumé. Not anymore! The *experienced* sales rep, the proven performer in many situations—big-ticket items, multiple distribution channels, retail, wholesale, consumer sales, and so on—is a valuable commodity.

"Once you've found the selling climate you most enjoy and the company to back you up, then dig in, learn the business and the politics, start taking risks, and reap the benefits.

"I know many sales reps who have opted to make a career out of selling with no thought of promotion. They enjoy what they do, the people they call on, the location of their work, and the fact that they're practically their own bosses. They enjoy a fine standard of living and aspire to a future unencumbered with extra paperwork, responsibility and ulcers."

Janis Drew of the *Los Angeles Times* summarizes the sacrifices and rewards of a sales career. First, the sacrifices:

You will never be without pressure in the form of a quota. Sales is a career that carries a defined measurement of performance. You had better be emotionally stable with a strong self-image, because there will be times when your production goes down no matter what you may or may not do.

You will always work hard. You need to constantly motivate yourself, or you will fail. The measurement of success against the quota is so visible that you can never afford to be lazy. The competition is stiff, and you'll lose your margins if you don't give 100 percent.

You cannot express your "down" moods. I have never seen a successful salesperson with a negative attitude. We all have a few moments when it's rough, and we may briefly allow it to show. But our overall attitude must be constantly positive. We entertain a lot and take business trips regularly, so this means staying "up" both in and out of the office—on the road, during meals, and so on.

You will give up a portion of your private life. Often the best business deals are made over luncheon or dinner. All magazine sales reps are given expense accounts for entertainment. You are expected to go far beyond an 8-to-5 day or a 40-hour week.

Next the rewards:

You have tremendous freedom. You regulate your own time. You are out of the office on a schedule you design for yourself. It is almost like being in business for yourself. You don't sit at a desk under someone's supervision. You will also schedule trips to various cities or territories where there often isn't an office to go into at the end of the day.

You gain strong self-respect. As you realize the freedom and responsibility of dictating and managing your own time, you develop a strong sense of self-respect. And when your performance translates into sales, your self-respect increases.

You can expect good earnings. Sales is a career that provides an above-average income. Even for those not on an incentive or commission basis, salary plus expense account and automobile allowance make for a very good financial package.

Your work is exciting. Sales is a diverse experience. The people you call on change, and the advertising categories or territories are constantly evolving. This forces you to adjust and provides a degree of excitement and challenge unknown to the person with a secure desk job.

"As I look back on my career choice," says Dave Pitzer of Dr Pepper, "I am convinced that selling was the only choice I would have been happy with. Here's my philosophy as to why:

"Growing up with a sports background, I was always involved in some type of team or individual sport. In high school I played three sports, and in college I narrowed it down to two. Therefore, during a 12-year span, I became accustomed to daily competition via athletics.

"Suddenly I found myself graduated from college, and since nobody was going to pay me for shooting baskets or scoring touchdowns, I had to find a real job. Although I did not realize it at the time, selling provides that daily dosage of competition that frustrated athletes like myself thrive on. Without it, we shrivel up and die mentally. I honestly can't imagine being a banker or office worker with no apparent daily competition.

"When recruiting, I always consider a sports background as a positive asset because of my own experience. So when a recruiter asks you why you are interested in sales, don't reply that it is because you get along well with people; say it's because you can't live without the recommended daily dose of *competition!*"

"The successful salesperson spends his time making something happen," says John Paul Jones of Monsanto. "He uses initiative, creativity, and some degree of aggressiveness to fill a need or desire of another person.

"Looking back over these 30 years, I would choose no other career. My only regret is that I spent seven years in manufacturing before realizing I had some of the qualities for success in selling.

"I consider myself at the apex of the structural triangle. To my customers I am the company, for better or worse."

To John O. Todd of Northwestern Mutual, it's selling that makes the world go around.

"Too often when people think of selling, they are thinking about the kind personified in *The Music Man.* But just think about it as persuasiveness. How long would a lawyer last if he were not able to persuade his clients that he could serve their interests? How can a doctor build a practice if he can't sell his patients on taking his advice?

"Several years ago I wrote these verses to indicate my belief that the act of selling is service to mankind, is in fact the lubricant for much of human happiness:

The Salesperson Makes the World Go Round

Remember when they used to say
  "That man's a selling fool"?
What did they mean? I think it's safe
  To say that as a rule

They meant the man could con someone
  To buy what he would sell
Without regard to whether he
  Who bought could even tell

Just why he bought the proffered wares
  From such a wily one;
He may have had no need for them
  When all is said and done.

Think now instead of all the things
  That people do enjoy
Because someone with avid zeal
  His talents did employ

To teach or tell, persuade or sell
  The benefits to see,
Which without help the chance would pass
  And people such as we

Could go through life with ox and cart
  And never would we see
The glories of full color on
  The big broad-screen TV.

Or better still, recall we will
  Our lives without insurance.
We all know how this boon to man
  Has called for sales endurance.

So if you will as seller serve
  And by the Golden Rule
You join the greats who preach or teach
  In church or in the school,

And as you do, with follow-through
  To tend your client's needs
You know full well that you could tell
  Of countless helpful deeds,

Of people served and made secure,
  Of children sent to college,
Of mothers who maintain their homes
  Secure within the knowledge

That every month the mailman comes,
  He brings their bread and board
To keep the family on the road
  That father headed toward.

> Salesmanship they call it—
> To teach and to persuade.
> I think it's quite a role in life
> Good salesmanship has played.

To David Van Tosh, Executive Vice President, Sales, Encyclopaedia Britannica USA, the three principal advantages of being a salesperson are: (1) the independence, the feeling of being in charge of your own career, (2) the tangible measurements of progress from year to year with financial rewards in proportion, and (3) the development of a lifelong habit of entrepreneurial thinking. The only disadvantage, he feels, is that it's up to the individual to pick himself up by the scruff of the neck, turn off that televised ball game, and get out into the field.

What's the Work Like?

"Fun!" says Denise Kaluzna of Tupperware Home Parties. "Many times I have to pinch myself. It's hard to believe I get paid for having fun, talking and eating on the job—that's what many people are fired for. It requires a tremendous amount of effort if you want to stay on top, but the rewards are well worth it."

Speaking recently to a salesmanship class at a university, Richard Ziegler of The Drackett Company told the students that if they were ever to be successful in sales, they would need to do the following:

1. Get up at 6 A.M. almost every working day of their selling career, not because they had to but because they wanted to "go the extra mile."
2. Spend time at night and on weekends improving their presentations and their product knowledge.
3. Be willing to relocate.
4. Smile when they wanted to frown (something like show business).
5. Accept the fact that they would have to travel and be away from the family.
6. Spend time in buying offices waiting on buyers who had their own problems and couldn't care less about theirs.
7. Dress meticulously—hair combed (if they had any), shoes shined, blouse pressed, shirt clean, tie on, and absolutely no runs in their stockings.

Finally, he told them, they would get a sales budget, and they'd *better* make it—and it would *never* decrease. Throughout their whole career, they'd be expected to do more next year than this year.

"My gawd," one of the students exclaimed, "why would anyone want to be a salesperson?" Rich's reply:

1. If you're good, you'll make a comfortable living.
2. If you're *good*, that's real job security.
3. You'll have status in the company you work for. Remember, no sales, no company.
4. Finally, you'll get a company car and expenses, and you'll occasionally be whisked away to plush hotels in exotic places for sales meetings—and that's not bad, is it?

"Our work is unique in two ways," says Jack Hallberg of Allstate Insurance. "First, how many jobs are there where somebody doesn't put a limit on what you can earn? The amount of money that can be made in selling is absolutely incredible. It's one of the few jobs in which you can really get out of it exactly what you put into it.

"Second, it's flexible. In what other jobs can you take the morning off if you want to, and work in the evening to make it up? A lot of doctors live in my area, and not one of them has ever had the time available to coach one of the school sports teams. When my children played high-school sports, I never had to miss a game. The flexibility is one of the greatest advantages."

"What's the job like?" reflects Carl Unger of Zenith. "Well, it's both rewarding and exasperating. One day you can't seem to do anything wrong, and the next you can't seem to do anything right. You have highs and lows, but the overall picture is a feeling of winning, of doing something worthwhile.

"I once heard a speaker say that what salespeople want most is not money (although they love it) but recognition. You win this recognition by servicing your customers in a very professional way, by doing unto them as you would be treated yourself, by looking for ways of helping them become better at what they do, to see themselves as successful. When all this is done, you will find the rewards to be fantastic. As they become successful, you will too. Because of the quality of your work you will both share in the good times, and that is what makes it all worth doing. To me, that sums up everything.''

Judie McCoy of Mary Kay Cosmetics feels that a salesperson, even when promoted into management, should still do some selling. "I could never be completely out of personal selling," she says. "I don't feel I can train effectively unless I'm out there. You have to be fresh. I know every objection. I don't 'buy it' when salespeople tell me something can't be done, because I'm doing it. In the last two days I have earned $300 from two appointments and some phone orders, and this is only one source of income for me. My unit is No. 1 in the country, not because I'm directing my salespeople, but because they're following my example.''

"What's the job like? Whatever we make it," says Tom DeLa-Mater of Encyclopaedia Britannica. "If you don't prepare, don't maintain a schedule, the job can be horrendous. But when you do prepare, learn, study, build enthusiasm, it can be the most exhilarating, fulfilling experience in the world. I believe with Zig Ziglar that we can get anything in the world we want if we help enough other people get what they want.''

An amusing portrait of what it's like to be a real estate agent is painted by Kathleen Young, a licensed real estate sales agent and a free-lance writer. See Figure 1-1 on pages 12-13.

What Does It Take to Succeed in Selling?

What kind of person is most likely to succeed at selling? Is there such a thing as a "sales personality"? Are top salespeople born or made?

Jake Kulp of AMP says, "I have had many discussions with professionals concerning the question, 'Are good salespersons born or made?' I am sure we all have had customers who would respond that they are hatched.

"There are certain intangible qualities with which good salespeople are instilled at an early age; I also believe that we can influence our sales qualities through introspective experience, training, and natural maturing. As in any profession, willingness to work hard will overcome many shortcomings.''

"I truly believe that all self-motivated, goal-oriented persons can succeed if they believe they can, and if they believe in the benefits of what they are selling," says Denise Kaluzna of Tupperware Home Parties.

"Good sales reps are not born," says Bill O'Neill of Wausau Insurance Companies. "No way! Salespeople are forged by the obstacles they overcome, by the failures they have learned from, and by the successes that have spurred them on their way. They have to want to work hard and work smart."

"A successful media salesperson," says Janis Drew of the *Los Angeles Times*, "should be committed, focused, responsible, organized, positive, creative, intelligent, and hardworking—even driven. Yet, more important, the best salespeople are those who are good with *people*. Successful sales is a matter of motivating another individual or group to respond favorably to, and then buy, your medium.

"To realize the most effective method for attaining a goal, the smart salesperson will listen and aggressively observe the buyer. Sensitivity is the key, and everything you do matters. The relationship you build and maintain must be handled with great care. No matter how intelligent, hardworking, or organized you are, you'll fall flat without good people skills."

"Good sales reps," says John Heitzenroder of Occidental Chemical Corporation, "end up being the type of people you like to be with: considerate, courteous, honest, loyal, dependable, tolerant, empathetic, with self-respect and a pleasing personality.

"Good sellers are creative—they produce ideas, solve problems, make things happen. If you lose creativity, you lose enthusiasm and the job becomes boring."

Comments John Paul Jones of Monsanto: "The successful salesperson must have all the qualities we learned as Boy Scouts—honesty, loyalty, courtesy, and so on—and yet be able to go it alone and be totally responsible for the ups and downs each day. He must be prepared to face more downs than ups, but when the latter happens, what a great feeling!"

"It takes a special kind of person to sell effectively," in the opinion of Larry Nonnamaker of Eastman Kodak. "It also takes a tremendous amount of dedication and sacrifice to spend the extra hours necessary to be a cut above average.

"I believe salespeople are created and not born, although certain characteristics may be inherent. I believe what has made me successful is a determination to be the best. I am a perfectionist with a very competitive nature. I hate to lose at anything, especially when my career is at stake. I have always been willing to spend whatever time is needed to achieve whatever goal I have set for myself.

Figure 1-1.   *What the work is like for one real estate agent.*

So you wanna be in pictures? You wanna work flexible hours, deal directly with the public and earn high commissions? You think you might like to join the crowded roll of licensed real-estate agents?

The ads are certainly enticing. Those testimonials of million-dollar producers make it sound so easy. They're always smiling in the photos we see.

What nobody tells you about is the hard work, the stress and the rejection that drive so many agents from the streets. The years it takes to build a solid client/customer base require the adaptability of being available weekends and nights year 'round. Holidays, birthdays and anniversaries are special only to us, not to my customers. Rain, sleet and snow, we are on call, much like our family physician or mail carrier. We only complain among ourselves about customers who call about ads and rudely hang up. We steam along despite having set aside precious time only to discover that the afternoon is spent waiting for "no shows." It's sometimes as lonely here as the life of the Maytag repairman.

Home phones suddenly become an open line for customers, especially the one who wants to see that "spectacular" house you told him wouldn't last. Right in the middle of dinner, he wants to meet you at 7 P.M.

How about the dental appointment you've waited three weeks to get, the one you have to cancel at the last minute because a homeowner would like to speak to you about selling his home. Vacations, oh those vacations! Agents invariably have a big deal in the works right at departure time.

What keeps us going, you ask? The fun! The excitement! The addictive feeling of triumph! Frankly, selling real estate is similar to social work. We are mediators. We are counselors. We negotiate, with buyer, with seller and with attorney.

I've been in real estate now for three years. I've watered plants, brought in mail, taken out trash barrels and mopped kitchen floors for absentee homeowners. I've baked apple pies, arranged flowers and selected soothing music in homes where I sponsor an open house. I've waited hours in empty, cold homes for meter readers who never show. I've coordinated the services of roofing companies, cleaning services and lawn maintenance. I've left guests at home in order to present an offer on Christmas Eve, and I've even had a binder signed at my kitchen table at 1 o'clock in the morning. I very regrettably missed my nephew's wedding because a transferee had only one weekend to find a home. (I had a very irate sister-in-law.)

At times there's been domestic turmoil over my schedule. I have found myself apologizing to my children for missed school concerts and Saturday soccer games. I've testified, and won, in County Court over an unpaid commission, ending up 20 months later with only half after legal fees.

But the pros far outweigh the

cons. I am home if my kids are really sick. I can run down to Philadelphia to see my mother for a few days now and then. We've gone on nice vacations that would otherwise not have been. The kids wear the latest in sneakers and we've had two new cars lately. My daughter's teeth are $3,000 straighter and I might be sporting a mink next year. My husband is finally pleased with the mounting balance in the college fund.

I could have gone to law school or received my degree in medicine to earn a more lucrative income for the hours I keep. But I didn't, and I kick myself on alternate Wednesdays only. The highs of each transaction make up for it all.

My college psychology courses have sure come in handy. I can anticipate the reactions of people who are about to buy or sell their shelter. They often go through excruciating decision-making, and I am there to guide and advise.

I've had some lost deals, deals that have died a slow death weeks before the scheduled closing. I agonize with the sellers and often feel I should have been aware of trouble brewing. But, a psychic I am not. On the other hand, I have had a wonderful success rate. The compliments and letters received, the friends I have made—these are worth a thousand more days of my time. I've had the reward of almost winning Agent of the Month twice in three months.

Getting my license was a piece of cake compared to the on-the-job training. The 45-hour state sales course only touched on the essentials of field work. My company's training sessions were only homework for the real world of real estate. There are more books available to us on stress and rejection management than there are remedies for the common cold. But it takes sales to develop and grow. Sales and satisfied customers build a network of referrals for years to come.

The chances of making enough to live on the first year are very slim. On the average, it takes six months to see the first penny. The light at the end of the tunnel is far off for the neophyte. The path to the first sale may be 80 showings. There are no jackpots for the timid, no rewards for the introvert.

After time I have learned how to teach the lesson of compromise. I have learned to grit my teeth behind the smile when parents of the first-time buyer look at me in disdain. They think I control the price of real estate. I pray when a deal reaches the attorneys. I breathe a sigh of relief when an engineer's report comes in clean.

I've come a long way these thousand days. I don't stop my life anymore. I simply put it on hold when I choose that business warrants my time. I don't go berserk when I must share a client, and thus a commission, with a co-broker. I've learned to turn the ringer off after 10 P.M.

We threaten to quit the business at least once a year, after just one more deal. We've learned not to take rejection personally and have more stamina for it.

Source: Kathleen Young, ''Despite Dinners Gone Cold, I'm an Agent for Fun of It,'' *Newsday*, Nov. 29, 1986. Reprinted with permission of *Newsday*.

"I believe you have to work hard, be very persistent but flexible, be very personable with such qualities as sincerity and honesty, be organized and, unfortunately, be willing to sacrifice some of your personal life. There are few people willing to put in 8 to 12 hours a day and still work on weekends. But I truly believe that people like myself who are willing to make this commitment love the work."

Are any particular personality traits needed to succeed in selling? Says David Van Tosh of Britannica: "I started with this company back in 1962 and I must tell you that the answer is no. I've been around thousands of successful salespeople and they all have different philosophies, like different things, and do different things—that's what makes it fun.

"What they have in common is work habits. If you develop successful work habits you'll succeed, because most of the activities in selling are procedural. People will say 'He's a born closer.' I don't believe that. A closer is someone who has learned the techniques of closing. The only difference between two salespeople is that one might learn those techniques a little more quickly than the other. But if I were to leave this planet tomorrow, I would go to my Maker knowing that there is no such thing as a stereotypical salesman."

"Outstanding salespeople have that extra intestinal fortitude, that willingness to go the extra mile, like staying in the office until seven o'clock while most salespeople are relaxing," says Charlotte Jacobs of Pitney Bowes. "When I was starting, I didn't care what it took, working weekends, whatever. It's a certain gut feeling, hard to explain to others, that you're going to do whatever it takes to succeed, no matter what the expense.

"The successful salesperson is very goal-oriented, constantly setting goals, even small goals set daily. Whenever your company announces an award, it becomes your goal to win that award. The successful salesperson is very competitive. If the company announces a contest with a VCR as first prize, the successful sales rep doesn't say, 'To heck with it, I already have a VCR.' The rep wants to win the contest just for the sake of winning; the prize is secondary."

"What does it take to be a star?" asks Bruce White of Maritz Motivation. "Hard work certainly; you get out of it what you put in. Some good luck assuredly: right time, right place. Knowing your place (to thine own self be true)—some of us Midwestern types simply don't belong in New York City, and vice versa. That's not to say that good salespeople can't succeed anywhere in the world, but the consummate professional feels comfortable in his surroundings and exudes the confidence and the appreciation for that special environment he calls home.''

''There are no secrets to sales success,'' declares Denise Kaluzna of Tupperware Home Parties. ''You don't need gimmicks, just honesty, sincerity, lots of personal goals, and solid business practices like these:

1. Have a good plan.
2. Work it consistently every day.
3. Organize yourself.
4. Hire others to do your busywork so you can be out in the field.
5. Love what you do—if you're not happy, it will show.
6. At the end of each week, examine what worked and change what didn't.

''The harder you work, the luckier you get. Tough times don't last, but tough people do!''

A graphic picture of what it takes to succeed is given by Betty Cinq-Mars of Merrill Lynch in describing her own career:

''Am I a great salesperson? Probably not. I really admire sales talent and can clearly see it in people. I know that I am not really the very best, although probably better than average.

''I rank 70th out of 13,000 at Merrill Lynch. What is truly surprising is that I do it in the small community of Kalamazoo, Michigan. How come, if I am merely 'better than average' in selling? I think I know the answer.

''I am organized, disciplined, determined, and hardworking, and hire the very best people to work for me. These five attributes can make the 'just better than average' salesperson one of the best.

''When I started working in this business 11 years ago, I decided that I needed a plan to get where I wanted to be. My success is not accidental. I worked long hours—12 hours each work day and five hours on Saturday and Sunday. Until recently I worked every holiday, including Christmas and New Year's Day.

''A great salesperson would not have needed to do this. A better-than-average salesperson in Boston or Chicago might not have needed to do this. But I was in Kalamazoo, Michigan, with a goal.

''My discipline to stick to this arduous schedule was one of the biggest ingredients in my success. I also taught myself to be productive each minute that I worked. If I was going to sacrifice, I wasn't going to waste my time at work when I could be making chocolate chip cookies in my kitchen at home while watching a movie on TV.

"I critically examined everything I did each day. In the beginning I would even look at how I folded letters that needed to be stuffed. What was the fastest way? Then I decided that not only was there a faster way to fold, but that I could pay someone to stuff them in a fast way. I was on my way.

"Learning whom to hire to help me was a long and difficult process. I was fortunate in that many of my assistants quit. As I replaced them, I noticed what qualities were more compatible with the type of work I needed done and with my personality. I now have seven assistants working with me, all of whom share the same virtues. They are strong, independent, sharing women who are honest, direct, loyal, and committed to doing the best job. I hire only assistants who are more intelligent than I. My success is very much all of our success. I appreciate them. They are an important part of our business, and I try to make them feel that way each day.

"Organizational skills can be learned. In my case, I believe, it is generic. My father is the most organized man I know. Walk into his garage, and you see nuts and bolts and screws all labeled and deposited in small drawers. His record collection is alphabetized and cross-filed by type of music. (He is, by the way, a great salesman.)

"Like my father, I am organized to a fault. I have every client's stock listed in my personal computer by group. All my clients can be generated from my computer by group: IRAs, money markets, clients who buy tax-free bonds, clients in low tax brackets, etc. I have trades posted daily, card files kept up daily, lists of 'Clients to work with this week,' 'Clients to work with next week'; it goes on and on. My desk is as neat as can be. I can find a report or statement in seconds."

What Is the Role of Self-Improvement or Self-Development?

"Self-improvement should be a continual process," says Bill O'Neill of Wausau Insurance Companies—"informally by learning from other account reps, formally through courses on sales skills and product knowledge."

"I believe self-improvement is a natural progression for the searching personality of salespeople," says Bruce White of Maritz. "They want to know more and are always on the lookout for techniques that will sharpen their skills and improve their sales results."

"One of the biggest factors in sales success," says Jack Hallberg of Allstate, "is up-to-date product knowledge. You have to keep abreast of change, whether through a continuing education course or just everyday reading. I'm astounded at the lack of product knowledge on the part of some people in sales. They have no one to blame but themselves, because in any sales job the material is always there, and all you have to do is take the time to study it."

"My method of self-improvement is always to compete against myself," says Bob Chargin of McKesson. "Every month I try to produce more than I did that month last year. I might add that employers can do a lot by offering incentives. It doesn't hurt to wave that carrot!"

How Important Is a Positive Attitude— And How Do You Maintain It?

"With the right attitude you can conquer all," says Denise Kaluzna of Tupperware Home Parties. "Before I walk into a group, I look in the mirror and say, 'You're good, Kaluzna.' At each demonstration I look for people whom I can talk with about the Tupperware opportunity. If I've given my best and they decide not to join, well, it's their loss, and I go on to the next person."

"Attitude and motivation go hand in hand," points out Bruce White of Maritz. "They feed each other. Prospects want to deal with highly charged, 'up' salespeople. And sales successes recharge batteries and stimulate positive mental attitudes."

"I think the No. 1 key to being successful in selling is your positive attitude," says Bill O'Neill of Wausau Insurance Companies. "Along with positive attitude comes the enthusiasm that becomes contagious. If you maintain a positive attitude in your work and in your personal life, you'll more likely get the results you're hoping to achieve. If you maintain your positive attitude and your enthusiasm, you will overcome any obstacle.

"How do you maintain a positive attitude? The first thing is to believe in yourself and your product. Don't sell just for the commission. If you start thinking about 4 percent here and 5 percent there, you'll be found out by the policyholder. He or she will know you're not genuine. You have to always let your policyholders know that you are trying to provide the best service for them. Just write the business and the dollars will come.

"If you hit a slump, change your style. If you've been prospecting by phone, try prospecting in person. Change the order of your presentation. If you've been talking workers' compensation first, then general liability, auto, property and so forth, try quoting property first. It will make you more alert.

"Go all out every time. If you put 110 percent on every presentation, you'll never have to doubt yourself. Even if you lose, you know that you did your best.

"And don't forget to charge your batteries now and then by taking some leisure time."

"I think your attitude has everything to do with success in selling," says Judie McCoy of Mary Kay Cosmetics. "My attitude is that I'm going to the top in my career. I know how to release rejection. I don't allow myself to take rejection personally. If I feel that happening, I stop in my tracks and have a little miniconference with myself. I tell myself: 'Release it, get rid of it, don't take it personally. Love 'em and leave 'em and move on.' I'd rather go out and see a new prospect than beat a dead horse. I don't feel that I have to sell everybody I contact, because not everyone is interested in my product, but there are thousands of women out there who want what I have to offer, so rather than focus on the ones who don't, I focus on the ones who do."

"Attitude is extremely important, regardless of your job," says Bob Chargin of McKesson Drug Co. "Naturally, we all have our down days. You cannot, however, let personal problems carry over into your job. Do whatever it takes to keep an 'up' attitude. Some people get it by music, others by a joke. Find out what makes you happy, then do it every day, whether you're feeling down or not."

"In new business development," says Steve Rand of Dun's Marketing Services, "I work with an attitude that I must give it all I have, knowing in the back of my mind that not every deal comes through. However, every deal that goes nowhere brings me one step closer to the one that will go my way."

John Heitzenroder of Occidental Chemical suggests that when a rep feels demotivated, he or she should ask for some help from the sales manager, who can lend stability and control to the sales force. Often the manager can motivate the rep by helping the rep generate good new solutions to the rep's sales problems.

Cevin Melezoglu of American Greetings agrees that maintaining an "up" attitude is very important in selling, and adds that a career in selling offers a number of different motivating factors that vary in importance as salespeople develop their skills and abilities.

"When I first started selling, I liked the unstructured work environment and the personal contacts," she writes. "Later, since organization and time management have always been my strongest points, the challenge of structuring my own systems for efficiently running my territory was extremely important.

"Contrary to what others say about needing 70-hour work weeks, I have found that I can achieve more by working smarter rather than simply working longer. Granted, there will be peak seasons when salespeople have to work long hours and weekends; but if that becomes chronic, perhaps there are opportunities for greater efficiency. After all, how productive are the last few hours of a 70-hour work week when repeated week after week?

"After selling in the field for a while, I began to develop a certain entrepreneurial attitude. I began to feel a degree of ownership of my market. I had to manage my territory like a business, making my own decisions without the daily supervision of a manager.

"The most exciting aspect of managing my territory was the fact that there was no limit on the amount of money I could earn. To have all this opportunity, coupled with the full support of my company—no wonder selling is such a wonderful and satisfying profession!"

Jack Hallberg of Allstate Insurance also feels that attitude is vitally important to the sales rep. "The rep has to realize that sales business is similar to life," he says. "You're going to have hills and valleys in life, and you're surely going to have them in this business. You have to be prepared for real highs on the hills and real lows in the valleys, but beyond every valley there's another hill.

"Whenever I get discouraged, just mention one name to me. That fellow's name is Terry. He sells shoes door-to-door and office-to-office, and he's completely crippled with cerebral palsy. It's an effort for him to stand up straight, yet still he has the ability to drag himself out of bed and go up and down Western Avenue selling shoes to businessmen from office to office.

"So whenever I feel down, I just think about him and say to myself, 'If he can get up, go out in the work force, sell shoes, tell jokes, and do it every day when it's an effort for him to walk, I certainly don't have anything to feel down about.' "

Part Two
Before the Call

2
Finding Prospects

It's a lot more pleasant to call on known, friendly customers than it is to face that potentially cold world of unknown prospects. But some amount of prospecting—calling on strangers or nonbuyers—is a necessity in all types of sales work.

Successful salespeople of consumer products such as autos, real estate, or securities spend a substantial part of their time adding to their lists of customers. To sales reps selling for resale to wholesalers, distributors, or retailers, prospecting consists mainly in calling on known buyers who are not now buying, and in spotting newly established businesses. To the seller of industrial products, prospecting often means calling on other people within the customer corporation, trying to sell additional products or additional applications of products now being purchased.

As Jake Kulp of AMP puts it, "Prospecting is planting the seeds; developing the business relationship is cultivation; and obtaining an order is the harvest. Any farmer knows that there is little to harvest if he neglected to plant the seeds."

This chapter discusses methods of identifying, finding, or getting the names of prospects—all sources except referrals, which are covered in a later chapter because referrals are usually obtained after the sales call. Methods of getting to see the prospect are covered in the next chapter.

Methods of prospecting vary widely in different kinds of selling, but most successful sales reps have this in common:

1. They set prospecting targets for themselves—a certain percentage of time to be spent on prospecting, for example, or a certain number of prospecting calls per week. They also know the best times for prospecting and the best times for selling.
2. They give this function a high priority, rather than letting it slide until there's nothing else to do.
3. They use several prospecting methods and, for their own information, keep records on the number of leads and sales resulting from each method.

Adds Walter W. Patten, Jr., of McGraw-Hill: "And they discipline themselves to do what they know is not easy—for without careful planning, prospecting can at times be a magnificent waste of time, but with care, a new customer from this source can be the most rewarding!"

As a means of making sure that no good prospecting method is being overlooked, you may want to use Figure 2–1. Simply put checkmarks in the boxes listing prospecting methods you are now using and question marks by methods that might be worth trying.

Selling to Business and Industry

For the men and women who sell American Express Travel Management Services to major corporations, a key tool is the "target list," reports Greg Deming of American Express.

"A target list," he explains, "is simply a comprehensive listing of all companies which have the profile of a company likely to have the potential travel volume the salesperson is looking for. Every salesperson has different sources for compiling this list: Dun's Million Dollar Directory, Dun's State Sales Guides, National Register Publishing's Directory of Corporate Affiliations, state manufacturer's registers, and the listings published by the Chambers of Commerce of most cities and counties. We have developed client models by SIC code that help the salesperson determine the probable potential of a prospect based on the industry and the number of employees.

"The objective of the salesperson is to turn the names on these target lists into clients by moving them, one by one, from the target list to a first presentation. The sales skills that contribute to this process are (1) telephonics, (2) mail marketing, (3) industry networking, and (4) trade affiliations."

Figure 2-1. A checklist of prospecting methods.

	How Contacted			
Source of Name	Personal Call	Letter	Phone	Combination of Methods

1. Publications
  a. Inquiries from ads
  b. Inquiries from news stories
  c. News stories about new business, personnel changes, etc.				

2. Personal contacts
  a. Friends
  b. Business associates
  c. Members of service clubs, such as Rotary, Kiwanis, etc.
  d. Members of rep's church, sports, professional, or other organization				

3. "Radiation" or "endless chain" leads—getting names from a customer or even from a prospect who didn't buy				

4. Lists and data banks*
  a. Telephone directories
  b. City and state directories
  c. Industry directories
  d. Membership lists
  e. Mailing lists				

*Steven Rand of Dun's Marketing Services points out that his organization lists 6.5 million businesses selected by type of business, size, headquarters or branch, rate of growth, and so on, and that Donnelley Marketing has 70 million consumer households listed by income, car ownership, family makeup, and so forth.

(Figure continues on the following page.)

5. Using ''bird dogs'' who are in a position to spot prospects; many sales reps give them part of any resulting commission				
6. Eyeballing: observing new stores, factories, buildings				
7. Leads from trade shows, conventions, fairs, displays, ''take one'' boxes, etc.				
8. Leads from speeches made by rep				
9. Cold calls; canvassing				

For salespeople selling equipment, ingredients, or supplies to manufacturers and business firms, prospecting is not the same as it is in other types of selling.

''Prospecting is an absolute must in my type of selling,'' explains John Paul Jones of Monsanto, ''although it may differ somewhat from selling direct to the consumer. I am not searching so much for new buyers but for new applications in initial stages of development within existing accounts.

''My business brings me into contact with manufacturers of power tools, household appliances, and electronic equipment, all of which are constantly developing new products. Therefore, I must maintain contact with new research-and-development groups to position Monsanto for the future while closing on projects introduced 12 or more months in the past.

''As for quotas, I usually set aside a minimum of 30 minutes during a two-hour call to contact engineers and project managers responsible for future applications.

''My best sources are persons within companies where I have had successful contacts in the past, followed by leads from technical publications, also successful product innovations by others in the same market.''

Another seller of industrial chemicals is John Heitzenroder of

Occidental Chemical Corporation, until recently the chemical division of Diamond Shamrock. He makes three appointments per day with customers and spends the intervening time making cold calls on companies he has "eyeballed"—a process known for years as "smokestacking." His first call is simply a fact-gathering and qualifying call to find out about the company's products and to get the name and phone number of the person to phone later for an appointment.

He still recalls making a call on one of these eyeball prospects, early in his career, with his boss. The buyer said, "Sonny, we're already buying that product in carload lots from one of your competitors." This was a real surprise to both John and his boss, since none of their records indicated the prospect company was a major purchaser. Diamond Shamrock later became an important second source for this company.

Says Jake Kulp of AMP: "Since I'm selling to two major defense contractors encompassing about 15 million square feet, my prospecting occurs 'on site.' I make it a point to ask for three additional names from every new contact I make. This pyramid method of finding prospects is also a good way to initiate the closing phase of the sales call; for example, 'Before I summarize the action items, could I have the names of other engineers who could benefit from our offering, or who have responsibilities similar to yours?'

"Industry friendships are also an important source of leads. Much information is exchanged or even bartered in reception areas by reps whose products don't compete but are integrated into the same systems your products are. In some instances, when competing reps can't fill a customer need, they will suggest that I give the customer a call.

"Start a file on each prospect, detailing relevant information. There are times when your initial impressions about a prospect are incorrect, or change. The prospect who at first appeared to be a nice, low-level person may turn up as a program manager three months later. The least your prospect file should contain is important information about each individual, such as phone number and mailing address."

"And don't forget," adds Walter Patten of McGraw-Hill, "to find out who besides the person you are talking to is involved in 'sourcing.' In many cases your current contact may be only one of a team which makes the final decisions. If you know who the other team members are, you can send them copies of your follow-up letters, thus reminding them of the fact that you want to be a supplier.''

Steven Rand, senior account executive with Dun's Marketing Services, points out that it's important to prospect within existing accounts as well as look for new opportunities. A beginning salesperson, he feels, usually starts calling on smaller firms to learn the business without blowing any large-potential accounts, and gradually works up to the larger prospects with more complicated needs and longer selling spans.

"Eventually," he points out, "a good salesperson must be selective to get the best return on time spent prospecting by concentrating on applications the sales rep knows best and feels most comfortable with.''

An unusual source of new business consists of a present customer who goes to a different company. "Cover your back at the original account," he advises, "and contact your old customer in his new position.''

The importance of investing prospecting time for maximum payoff was also stressed by Paul Lentz of Automatic Data Processing. "Prioritize leads, by industry, size, or geographic location, who have provided the most business, and concentrate a proportionately greater percentage of time calling on them.''

Bruce White of Maritz Motivation Company stresses the importance of getting referrals within a major corporate client, as well as getting referrals from one customer to a counterpart in another company. Since his firm sells incentive travel, he makes it a point to strike up acquaintances with fellow travelers on planes, trains, and ships. "These fellow travelers," he notes, "will tell me what kind of travel incentives their companies use and whom to contact, and may even provide information about your competitors or suggest selling strategies.''

Gourdin Sirles sells several hundred million dollars worth of AT&T's services to ten major international insurance and financial organizations. To him, each customer represents a market, and prospects can be found throughout the company and at all levels of management. "Prospects can be found among several hundred similar but geographically dispersed branches of a customer company, or within different lines of business," he points out. "The key is to develop applications and then 'migrate' them across lines of business and geographically. Use existing contacts to find new prospects within the same or different companies, at different locations or lines of business.''

He would add to the table of lead sources: employees and officers of your own company, including installation and service organizations; other suppliers to the customer; influential industry contacts; and even members of the board of directors of prospect companies.

Charlotte Jacobs, who represents Pitney Bowes in Cincinnati, has a territory consisting solely of the national headquarters of 16 companies. Prospecting, for her, consists in finding applications for Pitney Bowes's wide line of products in other departments of these customers. She stresses the importance of maintaining good rapport with the present users so that they will not only suggest applications elsewhere in the company but also serve as "satisfied users" in recommending the products to others.

Janis Drew, a top advertising salesperson for the *Los Angeles Times,* says, "A good print salesperson is constantly on the lookout for new business prospects. There is a continual attrition rate in advertising sales, and it is the new prospect that offsets that attrition."

Her guidelines for making "credible and intelligent choices for a prospect list" can profitably be adapted to other industries:

1. Find out who is spending money, but not with you. "If you're hungry, it's more efficient to get a piece of an existing pie than to start one from scratch."
2. Determine where this money is being spent, whether on TV, radio, outdoor, direct mail, magazines, or newspapers.
3. Focus on other print users first, as it is more difficult to switch an advertiser from one medium to another than it is to switch him from one print medium to another.
4. Use all the resources of your newspaper's marketing research department: major accounts, their expenditures, where spent.
5. Subscribe to or manage to see all major weekly and monthly consumer and trade magazines and newspapers within your given industry responsibility. Comb through them carefully for leads.
6. Keep the prospect list tight and focus 80 percent of your time on the top 20 percent of your list's potential. If you achieve four new pieces of business out of 20, you're doing well.
7. Allot no less than 50 percent of your time to prospecting for new business (including increases in current advertising schedules). New business is at the center of productive sales

efforts. Servicing current accounts is important and must be attended to, but it is business that has already been sold. If you rely on it, you are not selling. Selling is new growth, and progress is measured that way.

8. Join local professional advertising organizations to maintain a high profile within the advertising community. The more people you know, the greater your opportunity to hear about a new available budget.

9. Keep your integrity with *everyone*. This is the most important advice I can give to anyone who is considering sales or who is in sales. If you are trusted, you will learn about prospective business before others, giving you the edge over your competition.

Walter Patten, an account manager for *BusinessWeek* magazine, advises: "Sell your publication's values in meaningful terms to your customers and prospects. Advertising in publications is bought (not sold) based on perceptions of value, real or otherwise, as these values fill a perceived need."

Selling for Resale

Salespeople selling to retail stores (or selling to wholesalers or distributors) usually spend most of their time servicing existing customers, but the smaller part of their time spent on prospecting is critically important.

"Selling drugs and sundries is different from many other kinds of selling because there are only so many pharmacies," says Bob Chargin of McKesson Drug. "The bulk of my time is spent servicing current clients, but I make it a point to spend no less than eight hours a month on new prospects. How do I find them? Believe it or not, the phone book is a great source of information. So are current customers—they have to know about their competition."

"Prospecting is important but takes only a very small percentage of the time of our nonfood sales reps, because 99 percent of their work is with stores already stocking our products," reports Rich Ziegler of The Drackett Company, which sells household cleaning products such as Windex, Drano, Vanish, O-Cedar handle goods, Renuzit, Endust, and Behold furniture polish. "One type of prospecting they have been doing in recent years is getting our products into all nongrocery outlets like drugstores, hardware stores, mass merchandisers, and service merchandisers or 'rack jobbers.' We also get an occasional tip on a new account as a result of inquiries coming into our customer service department."

"Prospecting ranks very close to the top in order of importance of all my duties," says David Clark of Simmons Beautyrest. "Unlike most sales reps, I enjoy prospecting, because I feel it is an all-win situation no matter what the outcome of the sales call. Even if a new account isn't signed immediately, a wealth of knowledge is gained in a very short time. This is one of the few situations in which a rep gets to share the company's products, promotions, and merchandising plans against those of competition. It often provides applicable new ideas."

Carl Unger of Zenith thinks about how much business he is losing if he is *not* selling to a dealer in a particular market. Each day, each month, each year, he feels, someone is doing business, lots of it. He wants it for himself. He is always on the alert for new accounts, or for technicians whom he might make into new dealers, which is how he started many of his current accounts.

Larry Nonnamaker of Eastman Kodak Company reports that 95 percent of his time is spent with existing dealers, but that in the 5 percent of his time spent on prospecting, he is looking mostly for "nontraditional" channels of distribution. "I get many of my prospects by looking for announcements in the newspapers talking about new retail concepts and layouts. While even a single outlet is a prospect and may do a large volume, I tend to look for chains with multiple locations, especially when dealing with a business not accustomed to selling photographic supplies.

"While the majority of our products are sold directly to retailers, we continue to look for wholesalers servicing accounts that we may not have found, or covering large geographic areas we can't afford to cover ourselves. Tobacco wholesalers have often worked well for me. Many wholesalers find that once they are servicing an account, it's to their advantage to sell a multitude of the retailer's needs.

"As I see it, anyone who opens the doors of a retail store has the potential to sell a roll of film, a camera, batteries, or photofinishing, and you never know if they're willing to do so until you ask."

Similarly, Ed Lahue of The Dial Corporation (Armour meat products, Dial soaps, Old Dutch Cleanser, and others) reports that most of his business comes from existing customers. "If a new chain store is about to open up, we'll be told about it by chain headquarters; if it's an independent, we learn of it from a wholesaler. I do some eyeballing to spot small independent stores opening up, and sometimes the other sales reps you talk with while doing a reset in a retail store will tell you about new outlets."

Jonathan Vitarius, who sells Nabisco Brands products in New Jersey, is motivated to seek new outlets because his salary-plus-incentive income is based on meeting specific objectives in existing accounts, and "all new accounts are gravy." He suggests three methods of finding new outlets:

1. Seasonal opportunities: placing Oreo and Chips Ahoy! cookies in ice cream stores during the summer.
2. New products to new types of customers: selling Ritz crackers in tins to gourmet food outlets; when Nabisco Brands introduced Super Girl cookies a few years back, he sold them to movie theaters where the Super Girl movie was playing.
3. Eyeballing the territory for new retail outlets being built— "It's important to be first in."

Pat Markley, who sells for Nabisco Brands on Long Island, says one never can tell where a new outlet may be found. "One day I was driving to work when my car broke down in a busy intersection during a pouring rain. Several gentlemen pushed me into a gas station, where I used the phone to call the company mechanic. The owner of a station asked what company would provide a company mechanic, and when I told him I worked for Nabisco Brands, he asked if we could supply him with cookies and crackers. Of course we could."

Advertising can be another source of leads, Pat says. "We ran a full-page ad in *Convenience Store News* for our 'single sleeve' line— one sleeve of a cookie instead of a box or bag. The ad listed a number to circle on the reader's service card. We got a tremendous response. I would simply phone the buyers who responded and say, 'I'm responding to your request for more information about our single-sleeve line.' I'd make an appointment to see them—it was almost as if they felt under an obligation to buy."

Small accounts like this are handled by telephone. When Pat opens a small account, it's a challenge to convince the storekeeper that he's important to Nabisco, but will be serviced by telephone because the potential volume does not justify regular in-person sales calls.

A. R. Flores of Alberto Culver says that many sales reps in the consumer packaged-goods field feel that they have no responsibility for prospecting, since accounts and territories are assigned to them. "While it is true that they need not prospect for new customers," he notes, "the area where prospecting is necessary is for *new product usage* within the account—when the account moves into a new product, to advertise, feature, or display it to attract new customers. An example would be a drug chain moving into food products on a seasonal basis and featuring them at a deep discount as a customer draw."

Cevin Melezoglu of American Greetings puts it this way: "If we went for seven years without adding a new customer, we'd be out of business. So prospecting is one of the most important functions of the sales rep. We require each rep to make four *planned* prospect calls a week—actual presentations, not just drop-in calls."

Two sources of information about new store openings she has found valuable are the distributors who sell to pharmacies, and salespeople selling other kinds of products to the pharmacies and gift shops that are major outlets for American Greetings.

Dave Pitzer, regional vice president of Dr Pepper, says that for his company, prospecting is the fastest way to build sales volume and absorbs the lion's share of salespersons' time. A typical Dr Pepper rep makes ten to twelve calls a day, of which 60 percent are prospect calls.

"Although prospecting is very important," he adds, "emphasis should also be placed on coverage or maintenance calls. It's less exciting, but we preach, 'Maintain first, sell second.' If you lose one account, you need to sell two additional accounts to show growth."

He also makes a point that several others stressed: While prospecting, keep a record of all pertinent information for future use. "Our sales force uses call books. Each call book has information about each account the rep has called on, whether they use Dr Pepper or not. The information can be reviewed by the rep before a sales call, and also becomes a data base a new rep can inherit if the current rep is transferred or leaves."

Gary Rucker of Whirlpool reports that his salespeople do not call on potential new retail outlets unless their existing dealers are failing to give them the desired market penetration. If they do decide to go after a new dealer, the territory manager gets complete information about that dealer: size, sales volume, inventory size, credit rating, product lines handled, and so on. This comes from such sources as D&B, credit checks, and other salespeople calling on that store. For Whirlpool reps selling appliances directly to builders, two sources of information are new building permits and new applications for utility meters.

William Clark of Cooper Tire & Rubber sells to tire dealers, who in turn sell to service stations. He makes it a point to use different roads in driving to his existing customers. In this way he may find a possible outlet on some back road that he would never have known about if he stayed on the main highways. He makes it a point to try to call on at least one new prospect each week.

Bill finds that competitors' sales reps often inadvertently give out useful information. "If you pick their brains a bit, you'll find out how they are doing with various accounts, and if their sales are down at one outlet, this might be one you'd plan to call on."

Cooper Tire does not open a new outlet within ten or 15 miles of a successful dealer. However, sales reps make drop-in "get acquainted" calls on the competitors of their present dealers, with no attempt to sell anything. "We'll know where to find a new dealer if our present one needs replacing," he points out, "and besides, it does have a tendency to keep our present dealers on their toes."

Bill also underscored the importance of checking with the company's credit department before wasting time calling on a dealer who can't pass a credit check.

Paul Sanders sells Hewlett-Packard computers to only four retailers in San Francisco, three of which have multiple branches. Since his role is primarily to support these customers in their selling efforts, his "prospecting" consists of establishing and maintaining contacts at all levels in these huge retailers: president or CEO, accounts payable and receivable, marketing, advertising, merchandising, inventory control, warehouse and distributing, service and maintenance, retail store managers, MIS directors. "I try to become familiar with everybody, inquire about new people, try to be helpful to everyone," he says.

Selling to the Consumer

In many types of consumer selling, repeat business from the same customer is either long deferred (as in autos) or practically nonexistent (as in encyclopedias). Hence prospecting is the cornerstone of the selling process.

"This whole book could be written on the subject of prospecting methods," comments John O. Todd of Northwestern Mutual. "The real point is that in most selling jobs of a type where the salesperson must find and go to the prospect, if he or she does not find ways to prospect, nothing happens. That would be like a merchant who opens a store without merchandise.

"Using that analogy, I have always sought to maintain a *prospect inventory*. This is a constantly revised list of *qualified* prospects, meaning people I have seen and whose possible needs I've been able to determine approximately, and whom I think I can make an attempt to close within 30 days. I have learned that for the inventory to be valid, it must contain a prospective volume of possible sales that is approximately six times my desired volume for the month."

(John's methods of getting referrals are discussed in Chapter 15.)

Jack Hallberg is also in the insurance business, with Allstate. Before joining Allstate, he sold gas ranges door-to-door for People's Gas of Chicago. "When I joined Allstate," he recalls, "I found that just knocking on doors was sort of foreign to most people in the insurance business, but it was my modus operandi for the first couple of years in the insurance business. After 18 years I now have a book of business that exceeds 5,000 accounts, so most of my business is through referral. I don't have to go looking for prospects, they come to me.

"The biggest difficulty today's salespeople have in finding prospects, I think, is getting themselves into the routine of looking for new prospects all the time. They just don't devote time to building up what we call an 'ex bank'—the dates on which people's automobile insurance policies are going to expire. That way they can contact them at the right time.

"This principle applies in all sorts of industries—you build up a list of when buying seasons open or supply contracts expire."

Carefully planned prospecting has been one of the keynotes in the success of Betty Cinq-Mars, Merrill Lynch vice president in Kalamazoo, Michigan. "I spend a good deal of time contacting prospects," she says, "but I never feel that I have to make cold calls. Over the last 11 years I have targeted a market, and every month these 7,000 or so prospects receive a card or note from me. I also have a radio comment I do daily, so many people know me now,

Figure 2-2. Sample card messages.

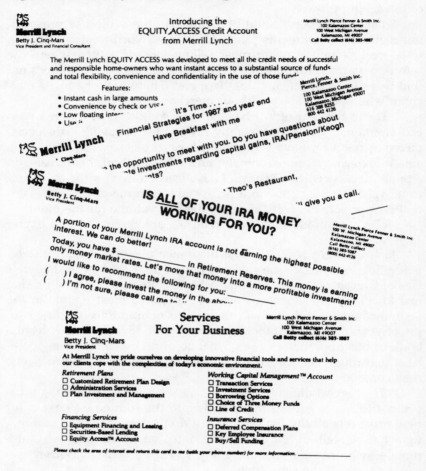

Courtesy of Betty Cinq-Mars of Merrill Lynch

although I knew no one in the community when I started 11 years ago.

"I try to find the most time-efficient method of getting clients and prospects to phone me. Making up cards works best for me. I print a concise message on 3½" × 8½" cards and send them out to the target market (see Figure 2–2). Even those who would not read a long letter are likely to glance at a small card. That glance will get their attention, and they may call me or do what I suggest that they do. The card, of course, is only the appetizer; the main course starts when they call me and I write or call them back. I often get great desserts!

"I spend a lot of time thinking about the format, style, and wording of the messages to be printed. When you have a limited space, you have to choose every word very carefully.

"For example, I use cards to

- Invite people to breakfast, asking them to call me for an appointment.
- Send them current CD rates when their old CDs are maturing.
- Invite people to investment seminars.
- Introduce new products.

"I use cards to ask people for referrals, but in this case I use a greeting card format to make it look more personal." (More about this in Chapter 15.)

"I do not put stamps on these cards and mail them. Instead, I enclose them in window envelopes. A computer-printed address ticker is attached to another blank card and enclosed so that the address will show through the window. This may seem time-consuming, but the effect on people is better than if they had received a naked card or a computer-printed sticker on the envelope itself.

"Let me elaborate on this point a bit, because it is important. Whenever I receive direct-mail letters, I sort them into two piles: one that I feel like opening and another that I would throw away without opening. I then check each pile and think what made the difference in my reaction. Does a personal stamp or a typed label make the difference? Does a name on the corner make it more inviting?

"In the same way, I look at everything critically. I examine conversations I have with salespeople. When I buy a dress or a car, I find myself wondering what I liked and disliked about the experience."

Suzanne DeNoyior, branch manager of the Coldwell Banker real estate office in Huntington, Long Island, points out that in the real estate business one can't afford to wait until someone decides to sell his or her home; one must reach the homeowners before they have made that decision, so that they will give Coldwell Banker the listing when they do decide to sell.

She and her sales reps "farm" specified neighborhoods, contacting homeowners by face-to-face house calls, monthly newsletters, and telephone follow-up. When a home is listed through their office, and again when it is sold, notification is sent to at least 100 homes in the neighborhood.

"The best prospecting story I have heard," she reports, "is when one of my sales reps was in the operating room of a local hospital for elective surgery. The doctor suggested that the patient concentrate on an object on the wall in order to remain calm during surgery.

"She mentioned that she wanted to come back in the next life as a man, because women have to put up with so much adversity. The doctor said he wanted to come back as a rich housewife and life in a million-dollar home. The patient replied that he needn't wait that long, as she had plenty of million-dollar houses to sell. She described several she had recently inspected—and ultimately sold him one. That's prospecting in an unusual place!"

"Encyclopaedia Britannica went out of the direct canvassing business years ago," reports David Van Tosh, Executive Vice President, Sales. "We advertise our products, and people respond seeking information about our products; they know that a representative will call on them because that's printed right on the response card.

"About 50 percent of our business comes from direct-response advertising in television, magazines, and direct mail. The other half is generated locally. Our reps literally create their own direct-response advertising at the local level. They put 'take one' boxes in high-traffic locations, coding the response postcards so that the leads come back to the rep after being mailed to our Chicago headquarters. We also use unattended counter displays.

"We also do a lot of business at counters set up in fairs and conventions. We're the world's largest exhibitor, booking well over 3,000 events a year. We're also largest in total space booked. General Motors has a lot of space at a few auto shows, but if you add up all our 300 square-foot booths at 3,000 events, we book more space than they do.

"We're the world's largest medical exhibitor. We go to virtually all the medical shows, dental shows, lawyers' conventions, home shows, boat shows, camper shows, sports and fishing shows, Oktoberfests, every tiny little fair.

"We're also big in malls. We have a temporary tenancy plan enabling us to put up a portable kiosk. We also have traffic-building mall promotions. We're very proud of our newest one, 'A Century of Fashion.' This is a museum-quality exhibit that took three years and $250,000 to produce, consisting of 23 mannequins displaying the past hundred years of fashions. We have a special truck and driver to take it around. We display it in a mall, and place a selling location near it.

"We're not as diligent in getting referrals as we should be—there are just so many other things for our reps to do. If some sales rep phones you and says he got your name from someone else, you're likely to say, 'He had no business giving you my name.' So our reps are used to getting little pieces of paper saying, 'Please have your representative visit me to explain how I can purchase this set.'

"Our people are a little spoiled. When they can go to a place like the Texas State Fair and write 15 or 20 orders in a two-day period, it's difficult to get them to call on someone who didn't initiate the response.

"We don't stress referrals as much as we should. We have about 2,000 salespeople; if I could get each of them to write one referral lead every two months, we'd have enough money to display Britannica in the Rose Bowl."

Judie McCoy of Waukesha, Wisconsin, one of the top sales producers for Mary Kay Cosmetics, started out by selling to her friends and relatives, but soon realized that she would never win one of the famous Mary Kay pink Cadillacs by selling just to friends and relatives.

"So," she says, "I asked people I knew, whose opinions I respected, for their opinions of my product. Women don't want to be sold, so I created an atmosphere in which they would try the product first-hand with a small group of their friends, get their friends' reaction to their new appearance, and ultimately purchase the product.

"So then I asked them for the names of other people they knew who could give me an objective opinion of the product. Because this is a service business, we get back to our customers, and this gives us an opportunity to obtain referrals.

"In my business, image is extremely important. You need a professional image. I have found that if you look the part of a professional skin care consultant, you will attract people to you.

Wherever I go, I make it a point to look the part of a Mary Kay beauty consultant. People notice. I like to wear a diamond bumble bee or some other pin I've won from Mary Kay. People will say, 'That's an interesting pin,' and I say, 'Oh, yes, I got that from Mary Kay.'

"Most of my business has come from casual contacts. Five of my eight consultants who have gone on to win pink Cadillacs were the result of these casual encounters."

When there's not a lot of traffic in the showroom, Gordon Wallace of Spitzer Dodge Motors in Columbus, Ohio, uses the phone book Yellow Pages to call construction companies, printers, businesses of all kinds to ask if they need a van or a truck.

He also has "bird dogs" working for him in most of the biggest factories in Columbus. The bird dog gets $25 to $50 for each car sold to a prospect the bird dog sends to the dealership.

"Whenever I go into a store to buy something," Gordon says, "whether it's a florist, service station, grocery, or whatever, I always leave a business card and try to make a favorable impression.

"I've been with Spitzer Dodge three years now, so I'm beginning to get repeat business. I keep in contact with my customers, phoning them when their cars are due for an oil change, asking them if everything is all right. Nine times out of ten I'll have a good rapport with the customer. At that time I'll ask them, 'Do you know of anyone else who might be in the market for an automobile or a truck?' and I'll get three or four names from them."

Hal Kessler of Terminix International in Brookfield Center, Connecticut, uses the "crisscross" phone directory to phone neighbors of customers with whom Terminix has pest control contracts. (Terminix sells a residential contract for a monthly treatment for $30.) "If we have an active customer who lives at No. 10 Railroad Street," he explains, "we go into the street-reference phone book and call the people who live at Nos. 8 and 12 Railroad Street, and those across the way at Nos. 9 and 11 Railroad Street. If one person has a pest problem, the people nearby are probably going to have the same problem. The phone conversation goes like this:

" 'Hi, I'm Hal Kessler from Terminix. The reason I'm calling is that we've experienced a bit of a rodent problem (or a roach problem or ant problem or termite problem) in your neighborhood. We would like to come by and give you a free inspection, with no obligation or expense at all, to see if you have the same problem and to see if we can help you in any way.'

"We try not to give the name of the original customer, because people are sometimes sensitive about letting their neighbors know that they have a pest problem, but if the prospect insists on knowing who in her neighborhood had a problem, I will usually give the name. I try to avoid it, but sometimes I can't.

"The homeowner says one of two things: either 'Sure, come by and give me the free inspection,' or 'No, I'm not interested. I have no problem.' In that case I say, 'If you ever do have a problem, remember to phone Hal Kessler at Terminix.'

"For example, we did some termite work for a customer on Bridge Street. I phoned all the houses on the same block and explained that termite colonies tend to move anywhere from a quarter mile to a half mile under the ground, and can come up into a house in many different ways. 'We would like the opportunity to come into your house and check it for you,' I explained, 'because termites can cause substantial structural damage. They can eat your house up.' I closed ten additional contracts on that block.

"I've given out more than 3,000 of my business cards. I put them everywhere. I tape four or five cards to the phone in a public telephone booth. A lot of people are always looking for something to write on, so if my card is there, they'll write somebody's phone number on the back of it and put it in their pocket. Can't hurt.

"I wear my Terminix uniform a lot, even outside working hours. I get a lot of exposure. I sometimes wear my uniform to the bowling alley. Where else could I get 200 men to know who I am and what I do? If they have a problem, it comes into their heads to say, 'I'll get hold of that Hal fellow I see at the bowling league.' I get a lot of business that way.

"I do my supermarket shopping in my uniform; it brings in a lot of business. I constantly talk about Terminix. I really enjoy my job and feel that if I enjoy it, I might as well tell people what I do. Everybody in town knows what Hal Kessler does.

"For commercial account leads, I ask the Health Department in each town to send me a computerized printout of every restaurant in their town. They have that list available because they must inspect each restaurant four times a year. That list is worth gold to me—diamonds. I send a letter to every restaurant and then follow up with a phone call. The only three answers I get are 'Yes, you can come in and make an inspection' or 'No, we don't have any problems' or 'We have an exterminator, and we're happy with him.' "

Selling to Doctors and Hospitals

J. M. Garcia, now in charge of sales training for the GE Medical Systems Business Group, was previously an ace sales rep for Diacon Computer Systems of Columbus, Ohio, which provides computer services for doctors and dentists. Other than referrals, his best source of leads when selling computer services was the phone book, because the prefixes of phone numbers enabled him to concentrate on one section of a city at a time.

Doug Haynie of the Baxter Travenol Division of American Hospital Supply Corporation observes that although a hospital is assigned to a rep, within that hospital there will be anywhere from five to 15 customers.

"The successful rep does not call just on the Purchasing Agent, but learns about the power structure within the hospital and how purchasing decisions are made. The most important single factor in successful selling to the hospital is finding an individual who is sold on your company's products and philosophy, and nurturing that person's relationship with other key decision makers within the hospital. To state this in another way, there is nothing positive about cold calling that would not be helped by having a referral."

Peter C. Pappas of CIBA-Geigy, who calls on doctors rather than hospitals, explains that "we don't have to prospect for new accounts in the pharmaceutical business, as we have more than we can handle. The average sales territory has about 300 to 500 physicians. If the rep wants to call on the important prescribers at least every six weeks, and if he averages six calls a day or 30 calls a week, he will see 180 doctors in a six-week cycle. That means he must identify the 120 doctors who are elderly, semiretired, or low prescribers whom he will see only rarely. A new rep may spin his wheels for a year or so before learning that it's physically impossible to call on all his doctors, and learning which ones to call on. Information gained from the doctor, his nurse or receptionist, and the retail pharmacist is a must."

Peter enjoys the challenge of meeting a new doctor for the first time—the equivalent of the "cold call" in other types of selling. "On this first call," he says, "you learn as much as you can about the doctor, his interest, his methods of practice, the pharmaceuticals he prefers to use. In future calls you build on this information and add to it, always working toward the objective that he or she will prescribe your products because of their advantages over the competition.''

He recalls a former district manager who said that each doctor is like a bank, and each sales call is a deposit of additional information about your products. No deposits, no returns.

3

Getting to See
the Prospect

There are basically only three ways of getting to see a new prospect. Successful sales reps experiment with variations of these methods to find out which one, or which combination of methods, is best suited to their personality and their kinds of prospects. The basic methods are: (1) cold calls (in person), (2) telephoning for an appointment, and (3) a letter, usually with a follow-up phone call.

Making Cold Calls

The phrase ''cold call'' is used here to refer to an unannounced call on a total stranger, although it is sometimes used to refer to unscheduled calls on known customers. In some forms of selling it is the primary prospecting method. In other types, cold calls are often used to fill in idle time between two appointments.

The sales rep simply approaches the receptionist and asks to see ''Mr. Jones'' (if he knows the prospect's name) or ''the president'' or ''the purchasing agent'' or whatever other executive the rep's past experience has shown it is best to contact.

Some receptionists, especially in larger firms, will try to screen out unwelcome visitors. ''What did you want to see him about?'' they will ask.

The worst thing the sales rep can do is to say, "I represent the Little Giant Widget Company." This is merely another way of saying, "I want to try to sell him some widgets." The receptionist is likely to reply that the firm doesn't buy widgets, or that the firm is already well supplied with them, or to ask the rep simply to mail some literature.

Instead, when the rep is asked what he wants to see the prospect about, he uses a carefully prepared and very brief benefit statement that also arouses curiosity—and immediately asks again to see the prospect.

"It's about a new method of reducing your rejects—is he in?"

Telephoning for an Appointment

The advantages of making appointments are: (1) they enable the sales rep to schedule his time more efficiently, (2) they make the call seem more important, (3) they are more likely to give the rep some uninterrupted time with the prospect, and (4) they avoid wasting time by going to the prospect's office only to find that he's out of town.

Even when calling on regular customers, if the rep does not have a fixed schedule of calls, it's a good idea to phone ahead to set up the call. This again avoids the "Sorry, he's out of town" problem.

The key to making appointments by phone is to remember that the rep is not asking for some of the prospect's time—he is offering him a benefit that will make it worthwhile for the buyer to learn more about it.

"Mr. Jones, we've developed a method that will reduce your maintenance costs by as much as 20 percent. When will it be convenient for you to learn about it?"

Some reps like to use the alternative question: "Would it be convenient for you to see me at ten o'clock tomorrow morning, or would the afternoon be better?"

The most common resistance is, "No thanks. We're satisfied with our present (supplier, arrangements, whatever)."

Best response: "Fine! It's nice to meet loyal customers. I certainly wouldn't think of asking you to take all your business away from them. But by learning something about our methods, you'll have a valuable yardstick to use in judging the performance of your present supplier."

Writing a Letter and Following Up with a Phone Call

Letters to prospects rarely result in a request for more information, but they do pave the way by making it a bit easier to get past the receptionist (by phone or in person) or to make an appointment.

"What did you want to see him about?"

"It's about that letter he received last week about reducing rejects. Is he in?"

Selling to Business and Industry

To sales reps calling on manufacturers, a major point of difference seems to be: "Should I make cold calls or not?"

Definitely among the anti-cold-call faction is John Paul Jones of Monsanto.

"Cold calls are very unproductive and a waste of time for both parties. They should not be used, even to fill in time gaps. This time can be better used in planning the next scheduled call.

"In industrial selling I use the telephone to introduce myself, my company, and the relevant products. I follow this up with a letter and product data, if requested, and then phone for an appointment after the prospect has had time to scan the information. I have used the cold call, or 'smokestacking,' as we used to call it, on rare occasions. About the only time it got me past the receptionist was when someone was curious to find out what a real live John Paul Jones looked like."

Steven Rand of Dun's Marketing Services believes that the cold call and the eventual sales presentation are such different disciplines that they should be assigned to two different sales forces.

"I believe," he says, "that a sales rep should do what he or she does best—sell! Not all salespeople can deal effectively with the continual debilitating rejection associated with cold calling. You need to do it when you're getting started, for no other reason than to get the 'feel' of your market, but after you've achieved a certain level of production, cold calling can be counterproductive.

"I believe in using a formalized, inside telemarketing operation to canvass accounts, build a profile of potential, and make appointments. This provides sales reps with more selling opportunities faster, and should increase their sales by putting them in front of more people ready to buy.

"Somebody is out there ready to buy today. By using techniques up front that are different from those the sales rep needs to close the deal, telemarketing can find the hot prospects faster and get the salesman there quicker. Two different disciplines: why not two different sales forces?"

Dun's Marketing Services offers a prospecting method called "Sales Tracker." The clients specify what sort of prospect companies they wish to reach, and what types of executive in these companies. Dun's then sends a Sales Tracker sheet (see Figure 3-1) for each prospect company, complete with peel-off mailing labels, information about the company, and spaces in which the sales rep enters additional information as he or she obtains it.

Steve does recall an early cold-calling experience that was a turning point in his selling career. "It was late one Friday afternoon before Labor Day," he remembers, "after I had been with Dun's just four months. First off I didn't 'know' that in the summer you didn't 'work' Friday afternoons. In this case it was even after 5 P.M.

"I was in an office building on lower Fifth Avenue in New York City and had just finished getting my brains beaten in on an unsuccessful call. I was tired and beat, and pressed the wrong button in the elevator. When the doors opened, it wasn't the lobby but rather the second floor, which was taken up by an office products company. I thought, 'What the heck—let's do one more call.'

"When I walked in, I saw this very strange fellow with Brillo for hair, a full beard, his shirt open to his waist, dripping gold and wearing an earring (remember, this was in 1970) and with a crazed look in his eye. Nevertheless, I asked for the owner, who, of course, turned out to be this individual. He asked what I wanted.

"I blurted out, 'I'm with D&B and we sell leads!'

"He stared at me for about 30 seconds and responded, 'I'll buy everything.' And for the next three or four years, he almost did.

"So much for all the sophisticated, state-of-the-art selling seminars I had attended. The chemistry between us worked instantly. Here I was, a raw, hungry recruit wearing a tie and jacket, and this unusual entrepreneur who had an encyclopedic memory on businesses and recognized immediately a new resource that could help him be successful faster than he had been so far."

William O'Neill, who sells business and commercial insurance for Wausau Insurance Companies, relied upon cold calls almost exclusively when getting started, although he does less of it now that he is billing $12 million a year, largely from referrals.

Figure 3-1. Dun's "Sales Tracker" form.

DUN'S SALES TRACKER™

PRODUCED EXCLUSIVELY FOR USE BY: OFFICE EQUIPMENT DEALER

D-U-N-S NO. 01-050-0108	DATE 06/15/87	JOB NO. A1234	SEQUENCE NO. 342	SALESPERSON

COMPANY NAME CASTLE CORP	STATUS HQ	INITIAL CONTACT DATE

ADDRESS 549 OLDHAM ST	COUNTY ERIE	USER/INFLUENCER NAME/TITLE

CITY, STATE, ZIP OUTWAY NY 10498	DECISION MAKER/TITLE

CONTACT/TITLE

C.E.O.   R T DREWERY PR
          MICHAEL W. WEINSTEIN   VP FINANCE

OVERALL EVALUATION

☐ HIGH POTENTIAL   ☐ MEDIUM POTENTIAL
☐ LOW POTENTIAL   ☐

EMPL. HERE 61	TOTAL EMPLS. 140	SALES VOLUME $7,730,000	PRODUCTS:

QUOTE:

PRIMARY SIC 3552	SECONDARY SICS 3566 3562	COMMENTS

LINE OF BUSINESS MFG IND MACHY	TELEPHONE NO. (317) 435-0041	

PARENT: THE OUTWAY CO.
COMPANY AFFILIATION: B & J MACHINERY CORP

SURVEY DATA	COMPETITIVE INFORMATION

1 FROM WHOM DID YOU PURCHASE YOUR PRESENT EQUIPMENT?

2 HOW LONG HAS PRESENT EQUIPMENT BEEN INSTALLED?

3 DEGREE SATISFACTION/DISSATISFACTION WITH EQUIPMENT?

4 WHAT FEATURES ARE IMPORTANT FOR PURCHASE DECISION?

5 LIST DECISION TIMEFRAME/LEASE RENT OR PURCHASE?

← FOLD HERE AND PEEL BACK

DATE NO. 1   R T DREWERY PR   MICHAEL WEINSTEIN   VP FINANCE   DATE NO. 3
               CASTLE CORP   CASTLE CORP
               PO BOX 3537   PO BOX 3537
               OUTWAY NY 10498   OUTWAY NY 10498

DATE NO. 2   DIRECTOR OF PURCHASING   OFFICE MANAGER   DATE NO. 4
               CASTLE CORP   CASTLE CORP
               PO BOX 3537   PO BOX 3537
               OUTWAY NY 10498   OUTWAY NY 10498

* 1987 Dun & Bradstreet, Inc.   **DUN'S MARKETING SERVICES**   PRINTED IN USA

DUN'S SALES TRACKER™

DATE	CONTACT	STATUS

FOLLOW UP ☐ 30 DAYS ☐ 60 DAYS ☐ 6 MONTHS ☐ _____
ACTIVITY ☐ PRESENTATION ☐ DEMO ☐ PROPOSAL ☐ NO INTEREST
EST. TIME OF PCHSE ☐ 30 DAYS ☐ 60 DAYS ☐ 6 MONTHS ☐ 1 YEAR

FOLLOW UP ☐ 30 DAYS ☐ 60 DAYS ☐ 6 MONTHS ☐ _____
ACTIVITY ☐ PRESENTATION ☐ DEMO ☐ PROPOSAL ☐ NO INTEREST
EST. TIME OF PCHSE ☐ 30 DAYS ☐ 60 DAYS ☐ 6 MONTHS ☐ 1 YEAR

FOLLOW UP ☐ 30 DAYS ☐ 60 DAYS ☐ 6 MONTHS ☐ _____
ACTIVITY ☐ PRESENTATION ☐ DEMO ☐ PROPOSAL ☐ NO INTEREST
EST. TIME OF PCHSE ☐ 30 DAYS ☐ 60 DAYS ☐ 6 MONTHS ☐ 1 YEAR

COMMENTS

PURCHASE _____

DATE _____

COMMENTS _____

Courtesy of Dun's Marketing Services. Used by permission.

His calls were not 100 percent "cold." He used to spend about two minutes per prospect getting information about the company from industry directories, trade journals, and Dun & Bradstreet reports. Before entering the company's offices, he looked at the parking areas and loading docks, and inside he noted whether there was a sprinkler system.

"Even if I didn't succeed in seeing the buyer," he explains, "on a later phone call I could say, 'I see that your building is a one-story, fire-resistant masonry-brick structure with sprinklers. We have something you might be interested in, in the way of property and fire insurance.' "

Although Bill prefers cold calls, Wausau reps are free to use whatever approach system works for them. "Some reps have absolutely tremendous phone techniques," he reports. "They have honed this craft until it is really not worth it for them to go out on the road."

The beginning sales rep usually has to overcome "glass door fever" and screw up his or her courage before making cold calls—particularly that first one each day. "One day when my first manager was making calls with me," Bill recalls, "I had this list of companies we were going to call on. When we got to the first place, I spent about ten minutes driving around the parking lot looking for the ideal place to stop, when finally the boss asked, 'Are we ever going to park this car, or what?' "

At first it's difficult and uncomfortable for the average sales rep—unless he or she is a brash extrovert—to ask to see some total stranger and face the unknown consequences. After the first call of the day, each subsequent call becomes a bit easier.

The first cold call is less menacing, suggests Walter Patten of McGraw-Hill, if the rep views it as an opportunity that might very well turn up a sizable customer. "Make it a challenge!" he says. (In the field of consumer selling, Encyclopaedia Britannica suggests that its sales reps, when calling on a home, look up at the top of the chimney. This forces them to take a heads-up, shoulders-back posture which is impressive to any resident who may be looking out the window at them.)

"You have to take the long view of it," adds Walter Patten. "Out of your first 100 cold calls, you may get two or three good interviews. Out of the next 200, because you know your product and your prospects better, you might get eight or ten interviews. I recall one time making 20 or 30 calls a day for an entire week without getting anywhere. Next day I set out to make another 20 but only got to make three, because everybody wanted to speak to me that day."

Roland M. Charles, Jr., major account executive for GTE Mobilnet, Inc., says that "in dealing with top executives of *Fortune* 1000 companies, the primary method I use in contacting a new prospect is a letter plus a follow-up phone call. This method affords me three advantages:

1. It gets my foot in the door of a major corporation with a decision maker.
2. It supplies the prospect with information about my company and product (company annual report, product information, third-party testimonials, and so on). This, I feel, reduces the anxiety level of 'should I buy or not?'
3. It allows me to follow up with the decision maker, set an appointment, and give him the opportunity to buy."

Similarly, Bruce White of Maritz Motivation, when assigned to a field office in a new city, identified more than 100 prospective buyers from directories and lists, and set his objective at 20 letters with follow-up phone calls, ten sales calls, and five presentations each month. (The presentation is usually a detailed recommendation for a specific type of sales contest, based on information gathered during the initial sales call.) This method generated enough sales, with their associated service responsibilities, to reduce time for prospecting drastically.

"I prefer the letter-plus-phone-call method," Bruce says, "unless it's a referral within a client company, in which case it's either a phone call or a drop-in visit while at the client's offices.

"In one selling situation, when I was unable to secure an appointment with the decision maker over the phone, I had to resort to the cold call, dropping into the reception office once a week and asking the receptionist to phone *anybody* in sales or marketing with whom I could speak. No success. But each time, I left behind a different brochure or case history, which eventually got to the right place. Soon I was able to speak to a prospective buyer in the lobby, then in his office, and finally was introduced to the decision-making group and secured an invitation to make a sales presentation. Persistence pays!"

Walter Patten of McGraw-Hill (publisher of *BusinessWeek*) clips stories from *BusinessWeek* about the prospect's industry or competitors and mails them to him. "It takes but a moment of my time," he explains, "and when I do phone, the prospect invariably recognizes my name. Making an appointment is no problem, because the prospect automatically thinks of me in terms of someone calling to offer assistance."

Some industrial sales reps find it fairly easy to see new prospects. Nick Debronsky, who sells Unisys computers and software in the Denver area, usually works one industry at a time, getting the names of prospects from industry directories. He phones the prospect and says, "My name is Nick Debronsky, and I'm your Unisys account executive in this territory. No matter what sort of equipment you're using now, my 20 years' experience in the industry might help you solve some of your problems. When can we get together over a cup of coffee?"

If the prospect says he has IBM hardware, Nick says, "Fine. But no one vendor has equipment that can do everything. Perhaps there's something in our very complete line of hardware and software that will be valuable to you."

Similarly, Charlotte Jacobs of Pitney Bowes, whose entire territory consists of 16 national headquarters in the Cincinnati area, finds it easy to see new prospective users within these companies. She tries to contact the highest possible executive, finding that decisions are easier and faster with upper management.

Paul Lentz, who sells ADP's computerized payroll and other data processing services to major accounts in the Chicago area, says that if you ask the receptionist if you can see a prospect, you give the receptionist a chance to screen you. Instead, he puts it in the form of an instruction: "Hello, my name is Paul Lentz. Please tell the controller I am here to see him." Or, if he has phone-canvassed the company in advance, "Please tell Mr. Koldize I'm here to see him."

"In selling computer services," he says, "I do not try to be elusive about the product I am selling. If the prospect is not interested, I want to terminate the conversation and get onto the next call.

"Therefore, I usually start out by *briefly* introducing myself and my services, then shut up and let the prospect do the talking. If he is not interested but I still feel there is a need or a potential sale, I ask him a few questions to update my file on him and ask permission for the opportunity to 'touch base' with him some time in the future. The next time I call, he knows me, and I can tailor my product presentation to those specific needs I uncovered on the previous call.''

Janis Drew of the *Los Angeles Times* says one must always have an appointment when calling on an advertiser or advertising agency. In magazine and newspaper print sales, she says, you would be perceived as unprofessional on any drop-in call and would not be admitted. Her suggestions for making appointments:

- Make your phone calls between 9 and 11 A.M. and/or 3 and 5 P.M. If the person doesn't take your call, leave a message saying when you will call back. On the second call, if he doesn't take it, leave a message for him to call you and specify a time.

- Persevere and call as many times as it takes. Most clients and agencies will take your call by the third attempt. If not, don't give up and don't take it personally. Your prospect is busy, and you should respect his time. Just be sure you call back when you say you will. Your credibility is all you have in the business, and it's built on your word.

- Once the prospect has answered, introduce yourself and your company very briefly and with enthusiasm. Give him a clear picture of your purpose and why he'll benefit, but keep it short. Offer him a minimum of three time choices so it's not a yes-or-no, open-or-shut proposition, but rather a question of which particular time is appropriate.

- Promise you'll need only 10 or 15 minutes, and keep your promise. Not many people will say no to 10 minutes. If he is busy the week you want to see him, be very agreeable and upbeat, moving into the following week or weeks to pick a time. Try never to hang up without an appointment or time when you'll call back to schedule one.

- If it gets tough, drop a sentence that you're seeing, or have seen, his peers within his industry, that they're interested, and that you don't want him to be left out of the offer. Stay friendly. Don't pressure.

"Since we meet with prospects by appointment only," says Greg Deming of American Express, "the key skill is using the telephone to get that appointment. The important point here is that the phone is used to set an appointment, not to sell the product.

"The first 25 seconds make or break the call. The salesperson must identify himself or herself and the company, give a brief but powerful benefit statement, and end by testing the prospect's receptivity to an appointment.

"The key technique here is to put the receiver of the call at ease, feeling assured that there is no risk in setting an appointment. If this is not done correctly, the salesperson must be prepared to handle a myriad of objections: 'Send me a brochure,' 'I don't have time,' 'I'm not the person you must see'—the list goes on and on.

"If you encounter an objection, the objective is not to win an argument but to address the objection, eliminate any risk in seeing you, and close on the appointment."

Gourdin E. Sirles of AT&T offers a dozen tips on getting to see the prospect:

1. Do your homework prior to contacting the prospect.
2. Determine the decision makers and influencers key to this sales situation.
3. The approach must be customer-focused, not internally focused, and must provide enough motivation for the customer to see you.
4. The approach must be tailored to the level of the person you are attempting to visit. The purchasing agent or analyst has a different set of criteria than the executive or senior vice president. This advice applies not only to the method of contacting the prospect but also to what you say and do.
5. The approach also differs depending upon how you identified the prospect. Was it a referral, another contact in the same company, a friend, or who?
6. A fourth way of getting to see a new prospect is a third-party introduction.
7. Don't forget to use success stories from other customers, often competitors of the prospect in the same industry, to develop interest.
8. An effective sales force serves as an information communications conduit between competing customers.
9. Cold calls should be used only to fill time or as a last resort. Sales calls now cost $394 each!
10. Telephoning for an appointment may be more effectively done by an in-house telemarketing person specializing in this area.
11. Make friends with secretaries and other "gatekeepers." Build a relationship.
12. I have used all the suggested methods, but generally leverage my existing contacts to move up the decision-making tree of my customers.

Selling for Resale

Getting to see the retail store manager is usually not too difficult, as he is readily available on the floor or in his office. But here again, there is disagreement about the relative value of cold calls vs. appointments.

"By far the most important method in our business is the cold call made in person," says Jon Vitarius of Nabisco Brands. "Often store managers are too busy to accept phone calls. One retailer told me, 'If I'm good enough to be here, you better be here too.'

"It is always important to be prepared with a plan of attack. In calling on a new outlet, visual props are a plus. Numbers don't always tell the entire story. A picture of all your products in a display will sell the entire line instead of a few single products."

Jonathan points out that many of the suggestions on getting past the receptionist, summarized in the introduction to this chapter, apply also to the telephone call for an appointment.

"I develop a written outline for major appointment calls to be made by phone," he says. "By anticipating negative responses, you will be ready to overcome most objections and secure the appointment—but don't let it sound canned."

For larger accounts, he uses a two-call sales pattern. This enables him to assure the decision maker, when asking for an appointment, that this will be a fact-finding, nonselling call. With difficult buyers, it's easier to set up a fact-finding call than a sales presentation call. He often sends a follow-up letter confirming the appointment, since busy store managers sometimes forget to write down the appointment.

On the other hand, Dave Pitzer of Dr Pepper says, "We try to limit cold calls to the smaller-volume accounts—'down the street' or 'mom and pop' stores, in our vernacular. By walking in unannounced on a large-volume account, you risk losing credibility. The buyer might think, 'If his product is so good, why didn't he call for an appointment?' But we always fill in the gaps between appointment calls with cold calls, both prospecting and coverage calls."

"In most cases," says Dave Clark of Simmons, "it is possible to see a buyer without an appointment, although the larger the retailer, the more difficult it is to do this. In the retail business, the bottom line for the buyer is to increase business. Therefore, the key to establishing a rapport with the buyer is to show him that you can increase his volume, no matter what size his business, and do it profitably. If you can establish this, I feel there is not a buyer in business who will not see you. If you can't do this, there is no reason for him to see you."

"Once I discover a new retailer," says Bob Chargin of Mc-Kesson, "I make it a point to find out the owner's name. I then stop by the store and introduce myself. My main objective is to find out if the owner is happy with his current supplier. I learn a lot from the reply. If he's happy, I thank him and leave, making a note to stop by again in two months. If, however, he shows even the slightest sign of unhappiness, I try to set up an initial meeting.

"I always try to set up my first sales meeting over breakfast, lunch, or dinner. Don't get me wrong, I'm not trying to impress the potential client. I have found, however, that if I can get him away from his place of business, I can have his undivided attention. It's extremely difficult to make a sales presentation when someone is constantly being interrupted by phone calls or questions from employees. Even if I don't get the account, I make it a point to stop by at least once a month to introduce myself.

"Our warehouse and sales office is located in a large Northern California city, where I also happen to live. Several years ago, part of my territory was located in the foothills some 40 miles away. The area is rural, with several small towns scattered over 40 miles. The salesman for our main competitor lived in one of these small towns. He was a nice fellow and a favorite with the ladies. His local ties made him an able foe.

"One day our sales manager decided to ride along with me. After our third stop, the sales manager suggested we make a cold call. We called on a good-sized drugstore that was the private domain of our competition. We walked into the store and handed our business cards to a clerk. The owner, an elderly fellow, was standing behind an elevated pharmacy case, reading some kind of document. Once he saw our cards, he flew into a rage.

"His language was so foul that two female clerks rushed to the back of the store. For the next ten minutes that store owner called us every dirty name ever uttered. Finally, when he stopped out of exhaustion, I asked, 'Why are you so upset with us?' He stared at me, waved the document, and yelled, 'You bastards are all the same. Look at this bill. The SOBs screwed me out of my 2-percent discount.'

"I looked at the bill. He was wrong, but he was right. His bill was less than $2 short of the amount required for the discount. 'If you were my account,' I said, handing the bill back to him, 'I'd write you a credit on the spot.'

"I turned and headed for the door. Pausing for a moment, I turned back and said, 'If you ever want to change wholesalers, give me a call.'

"Outside, the sales manager, who had almost lost his cool, said, 'I don't care if you never call on that blankety-blank again.' I looked at him and asked, 'Where would you like to make the next cold call?'

"A month later, the irate owner phoned my home—at 11:30 P.M., no less—and asked me to stop by his store next time I was in the area. We had lunch. Within two months he became one of my top accounts in the area.

"There's a moral to this anecdote: Always leave the door open."

Bill Clark of Cooper Tire also uses the first call on a prospective dealer to set up an appointment for a later call to present the line. "Tire dealers own their own businesses, for the most part," he explains. "If they are successful, they are busy. Trying to squeeze in your presentation on a cold-turkey call between retail customers, phone calls, and people dropping in, it just loses its entire punch. If you are interrupted five or six times during a presentation, you have wasted your time.

"So we set up a future appointment, and when we walk in at that time, we can say, 'Let's get out of here and have a cup of coffee, where we won't be interrupted.'

"However, we have to be prepared to make the presentation on the first call. When we ask for an appointment at a later date, the dealer may say, 'I have the time right now,' and if you're not prepared to give your presentation, you've lost a whole lot."

Bill sends not only a reminder letter in advance of the appointment but also a follow-up letter afterward to thank the dealer for giving them the time.

Many reps selling for resale find it easy to contact prospects. When Whirlpool decides to take on a new dealer, reports Gary Rucker, the sales rep shows the prospect a five-year forecast of his Whirlpool business—projected volume, costs, recommended remodeling, advertising plans, the works. The rep gets the statistics from headquarters but writes them up personally rather than using a computer printout.

Larry Nonnamaker of Eastman Kodak rarely makes cold calls, because he gets many leads from trade shows or from phone calls generated by Kodak's national advertising in trade journals. Most dealers are eager for the Kodak rep to show them how to display, merchandise, and sell the products.

Cevin Melezoglu of American Greetings says that "in very difficult cases I send them one of our greeting cards, writing on it that I'll be in the area on such-and-such date and will call in advance to set up an appointment. I may add a note about the card itself; sometimes that gets their attention."

Simple persistence is another way to get to hard-to-see prospects, she reports. "I've had several Hallmark stores tell me they see me more often than their Hallmark representative."

Carl Unger, who sells Zenith VCRs and TVs, says that when he's satisfied that this is the kind of outlet he wants, he simply walks in with a big smile, introduces himself, and tells the owner or manager what he has to offer. Often he has asked other good customers to put in a good word for him with the prospect. If it seems that there's some possibility of converting the prospect to a customer, Carl makes sure to see the prospect often enough to get on a first-name basis as soon as possible.

Richard Ziegler of Drackett suggests that the rep send a telegram as a last-ditch effort to get an appointment with a difficult buyer.

Few sales reps become as desperate as a travel agent in Pennsylvania. Unable to see the decision maker in an important business travel account, he borrowed a homing pigeon from a friend who raised them as a hobby. The surprised executive received a box containing a live pigeon and bearing a note saying, "If you're ready to let me tell you about the advantages of letting us handle your travel needs, just toss this pigeon out of your window." What else could he do?

Selling to the Consumer

In some types of consumer selling, phoning for the appointment is easy. "For me," says Hal Kessler of Terminix, "it's just a question of phoning the prospect and offering a free inspection."

Similarly, David Van Tosh of Encyclopaedia Brittanica says, "In phoning for an appointment we don't use overly complicated techniques because we're not dealing with a cold prospect whose name we got from a directory or from a neighbor—we're responding to people who asked us to call on them to tell them about our product. Ideally we make appointments, generally by phone, and drop in only if the prospect has an unlisted number. But we make more than half of our appointments over the counter, at fairs, malls, and other high-traffic locations.''

Judie McCoy of Mary Kay Cosmetics finds it is easier to get appointments with women when she explains that she wants to get the woman's opinion about her cosmetics. ''I believe very strongly that women don't want to be sold but like to give advice,'' she says, ''so I'm a very soft sell. I let the product sell itself by teaching how to use it. I rarely make a cold phone call to a stranger to get an appointment; there has usually been some kind of contact or referral.''

''In my career as a life insurance salesman, broadly speaking, there have been two basic phases,'' reports John O. Todd of Northwestern Mutual.

''During the early years, I made it my function to be the 'gopher.' This meant that the function of my first call was to sell the expertise of my more experienced associate. This is much easier than to sell life insurance itself, for I could sing the praises of my very competent associate in helping the prospect save taxes, make more money, and improve his financial position. That build-up almost literally put a halo around the head of my experienced associate, so that when he came with me, our prospect was eager to be helped.

''The second phase was when I could be classified as the expert because of all the things I had learned as an apprentice to my former mentor. This solved my prospecting problem in the second phase, for success breeds success. As my record of selling accomplishments grew, many young associates found that they too could be more successful by joining up with greater experience.''

Gordon Wallace of Spitzer Dodge in Columbus, Ohio, simply phones prospects and asks them to come into the showroom. Part of his success is undoubtedly due to his enthusiastic belief in his product. ''The Caravan is the best-selling van on the market today,'' he explains; ''the Dodge Aries is rated by Motor Trend as the best subcompact car on the market; the Dodge Omni, for $7,500, there's not a car on the market that can compete with it.''

Suzanne DeNoyior, branch manager of Coldwell Banker Real Estate on Long Island, urges her sales reps to contact homeowners before they have decided to sell. Most potential homeowners will not admit that they are ready to have their homes marketed; they say they are "thinking about it" and then interview four or more real estate brokers in the area. In these competitive situations, Coldwell Banker offers buyers or sellers a book of saving coupons on goods and services at Sears, the parent company of Coldwell Banker.

Many homeowners try to sell their homes themselves without enlisting the services of a real estate agent. Their ads often specify "No broker calls." Suzanne's reps make cold calls on these people to point out that the "For Sale by Owner" strategy reaches the bottom segment of the market: bargain hunters and nonserious shoppers. Furthermore, buyers who need a house in a hurry trust a licensed broker to price the home competitively, which the owner often does not do.

"One of my most unusual appointments was procured through a cold phone call to a 'For Sale by Owner,' " she recalls. "When the homeowner answered the phone and I explained that I was answering his ad, he replied in astonishment, 'Oh, no! She's finally done it—she's selling my house from under me.' When I offered some sympathy, he invited me to inspect his home while his wife was out shopping at the supermarket.

"When I arrived, this gentleman offered me a tour of the house and then invited me to have a cup of coffee. We discussed all the ramifications of selling his home, and I was about to leave, when his wife arrived and seemed curious to find a strange woman so early on Sunday morning.

"When I explained why I had come, she insisted that she had never placed an ad in the newspaper. We checked the ad and discovered that I had dialed the wrong number.

"I prepared the necessary market analysis, and although they were not good prospects at the time, they became clients within the next two years. Even a wrong number can be a lead!"

Betty Cinq-Mars of Merrill Lynch explains that after 11 years in business, she doesn't knock on strangers' doors and seldom makes cold phone calls.

"There are, however, 'call-ins' who just happen to phone the office when it's my turn to pick up the phone. When I talk to prospects the first time, I get their addresses and phone numbers and send out a follow-up letter within 24 hours. If the clients wish to make an appointment to see me, I could encourage them to do so, but it is not necessary. Much of our business is done over the phone.

"Breakfast appointments work very well for me because we can talk in a relaxed atmosphere. Clients appreciate the fact that I am going out of my way to accommodate them. It is important to impress them that I am offering them a valuable service for their own interest, not trying to sell them anything they don't want to buy. I talk with my clients as a consultant, not a salesperson.''

Selling to Doctors and Hospitals

The sales rep for the GE Medical Systems Group, reports J. M. Garcia, usually has only about 25 hospitals in the territory, so it doesn't take long to get acquainted with key doctors and hospital administrators.

When he was selling computers to doctors and dentists, he found that the best approach was an initial phone call, ''always exploratory, very low key, very informal—'Hi, how are you, are you busy these days? Any problems handling the accounts receivable or the medical records?' These calls simply qualified the doctor for an in-person visit.''

Peter Pappas of CIBA-Geigy, like other pharmaceutical sales reps, makes regular calls on a universe of doctors. The only new prospect is a doctor who has just hung up his shingle.

''One must either stop in and wait, or make an appointment for the next time you'll be in the area,'' he says. ''This first visit is usually an information-gathering event. What's his specialty? How old is he? Who is his nurse? His receptionist? And do get to know the receptionist well—she is usually the key to seeing the doctor in the future.''

Sometimes a busy specialist is difficult to see. ''Recently when we introduced a new transdermal drug delivery system (a skin patch which delivers medication through the skin), I knew I would have some problem seeing the busiest of this particular specialty. I had to come up with something that would pique their interest.

''I came up with what I call my silver bullet, my door opener. I placed a placebo-filled patch on a slightly larger piece of plexiglass and handed it to the nurse to give to the doctor. There wasn't one instance in which I failed to see the specialist. The door opener aroused their interest to such an extent that they just had to see me to learn the rest of the story. One physician was so excited, he kept me talking about the product for 30 minutes—the average call is three to ten minutes. When I checked back, I found he had prescribed it twice that morning.''

"Some physicians," reports Ralph Eubanks of Roerig, "refuse to see sales reps. In these instances, I've been successful in using a humorous letter. To surgeons who won't see me, I send a letter saying, 'I'm considering having you remove my gall bladder under a local anesthetic so I can tell you about our new products.' To pulmonary specialists, the letter said, 'I'm considering having you do a bronchoscopy so I can gurgle to you about our new products.'

"In one such situation, when I called on the surgeon, the nurse had my card pinned to the bulletin board and said, 'Boy! Is he waiting to see you!' I'd never been able to see this surgeon before, but this time he really played it to the hilt. She said, 'The doctor will see you now.' I went into his office, and he had on his surgical mask and his scalpel in his hand. But I did establish some rapport with him.

"It's very easy for a doctor to sit in his office and have his nurse or receptionist refuse to let you see him, but it's hard for him to do it face to face. So we learn their routines—where they park, when they come into the office, what elevators they use, and then try to set up an 'accidental' meeting. For example, he's going up in an elevator. You say, 'Gee, I've really been trying to see you—is there any chance of seeing you for a couple of minutes before you get started with your patients?' It's difficult for him to say no face-to-face.

"It's not too difficult to learn physicians' habitual schedules. The nurse will tell you, 'The doctor comes in at ten, but he doesn't see sales reps.' When you have a hospital display, you have plenty of time, while standing at your display, to notice when the hard-to-see doctors come and go.

"Many doctors have offices near the hospital, and walk from the hospital to their offices. You can meet them and explain that you've been trying to see them before they get started on their practice. Many doctors will say, 'Okay, come along.' Others will say, 'I really don't have the time, but show me what you have,' and you get a chance to present your product while walking toward his office. We call this 'clotheslining.' Doctors would resent these 'accidental' contacts if you started talking about your product, but not if you merely ask for a few minutes of their time.

Although calls on doctors are usually of the "cold call" variety, Doug Haynie, who sells to hospitals for Baxter Travenol, says that doesn't apply to hospitals. "My personal philosophy," he said, "is that cold calls are a no-no. People don't like to be interrupted at their work, especially by a sales rep. All I am doing by showing up unannounced is stating that his time must not be very valuable, and that he should be able to drop whatever he is doing and talk to me."

At the end of each call, Doug makes an appointment for the next call. If that is not possible, he makes an appointment by phone at least three days in advance, and confirms it two or three hours before the appointment by using his car phone.

"This gives the customer a few hours' reminder that I am coming in, so he has time to reflect on what I want to discuss. I call this 'maintaining control of the customer's mind.' I want him to be thinking about me and what I have to say, and the more times I contact him, the better."

4
Planning the Call

Most experienced sales reps discovered long ago that one minute of itinerary planning can save a half-hour of driving time; one minute of planning the call can save ten minutes of floundering about while making the presentation.

Call planning consists primarily of setting an objective for the call, then planning the sales strategy to attain it. In some types of selling the call objective is clear and simple: Make the sale and get out. But in more complicated types of sales calls, results are better if the sales rep sets a very clear-cut objective (or clear-cut objectives) before making the call. For example, a wholesaler or distributor sales rep calling on a retailer will often have, in addition to the objective of filling the regular order, a set of objectives like: sell ten cases of new product X; schedule a display of product Y; get one more shelf facing for product Z. In complicated industrial or technical sales, involving a long series of calls on different buying influences, the buying cycle will be completed faster if each call has a specific objective that advances the process one step closer to the goal.

The nature of the objective is very important and is often ignored in books on selling. The objective should be stated not in terms of what the sales rep intends to do but in terms of what he wants the prospect to do, or agree to do, as a result.

The call objective is never "to tell him about our new product" but instead "to get him to buy a truckload of our new product." What the sales rep says or shows is only the *means* toward the goal; the goal is some action taken by the prospect as a result.

Sometimes a salesman will set an objective he hopes to reach, but will have a secondary "fallback" objective if the first one isn't attainable. A travel agent, for example, may call on a small firm with the objective of getting all its travel business; if the firm is happy with its existing agency, the seller switches to a secondary objective of getting part of the firm's travel business, using the "yardstick" approach.

Selling to Business and Industry

Walter W. Patten, Jr., of McGraw-Hill maintains that there is no such thing as a call without a specific purpose (or at least there shouldn't be). "And the purpose," he adds, "must be a carefully thought-out benefit for the prospect or customer. Call with some benefit that is useful to them, and the next time you call you will be a welcome visitor."

Jake Kulp of AMP points out that call planning is a circular process consisting of five steps:

1. Set the call objective.
2. Gather any information that will help you attain it (what Jake calls the "G-2 step").
3. Plan the call.
4. Make the call.
5. Very important: review the call. If you did not achieve your objective, why not? What did you learn from this call that will be useful on the next call? And that gets you back to step 1 for the next call.

Call planning for American Express Travel Management Systems is shaped by the fact that the division's complicated selling process involves six clearly defined steps.

"How long does it take before a name on a prospect list becomes a client?" asks Greg Deming of American Express. "What percentage of names on the prospect list will become clients this year?

"The answers within each sales organization will vary with the sales skills of each salesperson. However, the one thing that is usually the same is the key events that take place when a prospect is transformed into a client, and the best salespeople know these events. That's the difference between a 'presenter' and a 'sales manager.' A sales manager knows where he stands and exactly what the next objective is.

"Our experience shows that when a sale is consummated, the sales manager was successful in guiding the client through a cycle of six key sales events. These are key events, not particular calls. For companies with simple and well-understood needs, the first presentation and needs analysis can be achieved on one call. For larger companies with complicated hidden needs, several months of work may be required to complete a needs analysis."

The six key events are:

1. Target list
2. First presentation
3. Needs analysis
4. Formal presentation/proposal
5. Decision
6. Implementation

Greg, as director of sales, tracks the progress of his sales reps on his personal computer and can tell you exactly which rep is best at each of the six events.

"My goal is to develop two or three new major accounts per year (that's about all time will permit)," says Steve Rand of Dun's Marketing Services. "Since my sales cycle can require multiple calls and frequently must coincide with new budget cycles, it can take six to nine months to develop any meaningful business. Therefore, I want to be sure I'm investing my time on a target account that can give me the return I need to make my new sales accountability.

"A typical sales cycle includes the following elements: (1) initial contact, (2) information gathering, (3) face-to-face meeting, (4) general presentation, (5) product demonstration, (6) specific proposal, and (7) close. Different stages of the cycle require different levels of preparation.

"For example, when I identify a prospect I wish to call on, I initially contact two or three different departments within the target company: marketing, advertising, sales, and (in a small company) the CEO. I must find out who has the budget and who has the responsibility, determine their method of selling (direct sales force, distributors, telemarketing, and so on) and their short-term sales objectives.

"To get a measure of their potential, I'll also speak with their competitors, with trade organization sources, get an annual report if it's a public company or at least pull a D&B on them, as well as speak to other suppliers to develop a well-rounded picture of the company and the people I would have to deal with.

"Based on the target profile I've developed, I make a determination rather quickly whether to proceed or to shelve this prospect until some future date. Although the company may be in a high-potential industry in which I'm presently doing business and in which I have had some success, if it doesn't 'smell right,' I'll move on to another. Not every company is ready for what we have to offer. Sometimes, when I can afford to, I'll wait for the players to change or the company goals to change before giving it my best shot."

Expanding on the methods used by American Express in its pre-call fact finding, B. Robert Greenfield, vice president–sales of its Travel Management Services, says, "Since our offer is of interest to senior management, usually the chief financial officer, it is important for us to present ourselves as professionals.

"We therefore gather as much information as possible about the company and the individuals involved prior to making the initial contact, so that we can have a better understanding of the company and how we can best position our offer in the light of what we learn about their specific needs.

"For example, we will obtain an annual report (if available) and try to relate to a statement made in the chairman's comments, as well as extract useful information about the industry and the company's position in it. We also use our existing client base to review how companies in the same industry use our service, so we can better inform our prospects about usages that apply to them."

"Your basic objective," writes Janis Drew of the *Los Angeles Times*, "is always the same: to sell. But the intermediate or 'mini-objectives' will vary with the stage of the selling process. What is important is that you stick with the objective during the call and maintain control of the focus.

"Your calls on advertising agencies will always be different from those made on the advertiser, and within each group, calls will vary with the level and status of the individual you are seeing. A suggestion would be to follow a format similar to this:

"Start with the agency. Call first on the media department (which buys the space or time), in this order:

1. Media planner
2. Media supervisor
3. Associate media director
4. Media director

"Your first call on the media planner will be a fact-finding mission to learn the marketing target of their client's product, the fiscal planning and scheduling times, the key personnel involved, and the breakdown of the budget between print and broadcast media. Once you have this information, you can build a presentation tailored to the account so that you don't waste your time or theirs. You would then work forward on the list, seeing everyone and explaining why you feel your newspaper or magazine should be on their schedule.

"After having seen the media department, move on to the account (creative) group and progress as follows:

1. Account executive
2. Account supervisor
3. Management supervisor

"Your discussions with the account group won't be as specific as to dates and figures, but more general as to how you can help attain the client's marketing objectives.

"Finally, be sure to meet the client. The agency can recommend your publication, but the client can always cancel you if he doesn't understand your value. However, see the client less frequently, as he has hired the agency primarily for the purpose of buying advertising."

John Paul Jones of Monsanto explains that "the objectives or goals are developed in the account strategies we write for all major industrial customers. These are nothing more than a blueprint for sales production. Included are the goal, primary and secondary objectives, timetable for each accomplishment, and a checklist to determine each result."

Bruce White of Maritz Motivation has a "sales action plan" for each account. This plan specifies the sales volume, the product lines involved in the motivational programs, timetables, and presentation activities. This is the long-term strategy; each individual call has its own tactical objective, which may be to get acquainted with a potential buyer, get to know the prospect better, or establish common ground for future sales. Sometimes the purpose of the call is to handle a customer complaint and reaffirm the business agreement. "This is nonetheless a sales call in support of the action plan," he points out.

"There is considerable behind-the-scenes work done by the home-office sales support team in developing sales strategy and preparing for a key sales presentation. In the incentive industry, 'dog and pony shows' (elaborate presentations) consisting of everything from film, video, and live narration to performers such as Hawaiian dancers, Western bands, mariachi trios, and so on, and rooms full of flipcharts and layouts, are used as sales aids.

"The preparation of these presentations requires significant time and talent, not to mention money. The sales rep must be rehearsed on the effective use of these elements. Many times we'll videotape the rehearsal in order to critique our 'pitch.' Internal support personnel will play the roles of clients and ask questions. The more time spent on preparation, the better the end result.

"On difficult problem-solving calls, I'll work out the scenario in my head, often practicing answering questions aloud. Sometimes I'll prepare a written script just to think through important points. At times I've even had to refer to my 'notes' in addressing a client's difficult service complaint. Playing out the sales call interview before the call is an excellent preparation tool—and will usually be tougher than the call itself!"

Paul Lentz of ADP says that his objective on a first call is to get a portion of the business if he can't get the entire account immediately. If there is little or no current interest, he sets the stage for future visits, knowing that the prospect's needs may change.

"The first call," he says, "is usually a brief overview of my services, but primarily an analysis of the client's needs. I attempt to pique interest and set the stage for a more in-depth analysis on the next call."

Charlotte Jacobs of Pitney Bowes always knows, before a call, what she wants to accomplish and what she wants the customer to do. "Even if it's a cold call within one of my accounts, and I've never met this individual before, I always have something I want to accomplish."

In calling on a new prospect, she has found the problem-solving approach very successful. "I explain that I'm with Pitney Bowes and would like to tell them about some of my new systems," she explains, " 'but before I do that, are you having any problems with our equipment or any other equipment?' If you show an interest in solving their problems instead of trying to sell them everything in your briefcase, you've become a hero to them and established a consultative relationship.''

Gourdin Sirles of AT&T believes that the larger and more complex the potential sale, the more important it is that the objective of each call be clear and well thought out.

Each type of sale, he comments, requires its own strategy: (1) the small, upgrade sale can be handled by phone or on the first visit; (2) larger sales may require more than two visits and involve various influencers and decision makers; (3) large sales (over $500,000 in his business) frequently require many sales calls.

Possible call objectives, Gourdin points out, can include:

1. To start the development of a long-term relationship.
2. To get a second appointment.
3. To initiate a study.
4. To get an appointment at a higher or lower level.
5. To position another member of the team.
6. To solve an immediate problem, thus reducing frustration, gaining goodwill, and achieving status on a longer-term problem.
7. To have the customer attend training.
8. To get the customer off premises and onto your own turf for an executive briefing.
9. To discuss potential problems with competitors, current systems, or the like.
10. To raise interest in changing the course of action.
11. To play golf or go to dinner with the client (and often the spouse).
12. To meet other officers within the company.
13. To provide information on industry trends, issues, concerns.
14. To close a sale, of course.
15. To collect a bill or shorten the payment cycle.

Gourdin summarizes the importance of clear-cut call objectives by recalling that ''if you don't know where you're going, any road will take you there.''

''Preplanning cold calls is essential because of the very limited time you can actually spend in front of the prospect,'' says John Heitzenroder of Occidental Chemical. ''Before ever making a call on a prospect I try to qualify him/her as much as possible by consulting business directories, D&B reports, trade journals, and the business sections of local newspapers, as well as calling on the prospect's competitors. I will even drive by the prospect's place of business without going in, just to get a feel for his operation. The more I can learn about the prospect, the greater my chance of a successful cold call. I jot down an outline of the facts I have uncovered and review it before making my first call.

"On that call, I try to formulate an approach such as emphasizing a particular line of coverage or benefit that may be important in his or her business. Often I don't even discuss my product with the prospect on the first call. It's better to ask a lot of questions about his or her business—after all, the prospect is the best reference source for information about the firm. I usually take my lead from the prospect in shaping my approach.

"I think a buyer appreciates it when you can discuss his business and his industry. He realizes that you've done some research and that you're genuinely interested in his company.

"I use an index-card file to maintain updated information about my prospects. The whole idea is to make as much of an impact as possible within the time limitation. I've watched and learned from really good salespeople—they don't make cold calls, they make hot ones!"

Selling for Resale

To Larry Nonnamaker of Eastman Kodak Company, pre-call planning is one of the most important aspects of selling. "Making a quality sales call does not happen by chance," he says. "Being successful does not happen by chance."

Larry spends two or three times more time planning the call than he does on the call.

"When I go into a call," he says, "I know what I want to sell, how much I want to sell, what the benefits to the retailer are, what objections he will have, how I will address those objections, a complete plan from shipping to merchandising to advertising the product, the margins the dealer will receive, and my anticipated reorders after the initial sell-through.

"All sales reps have to deal with the unexpected, but by planning thoroughly before they ever enter the dealer's office, they minimize the chances of failing to attain their objective.

"I always tell the dealer, right at the outset, my reason for being there. After getting the dealer's approval, I leave something in writing for his or her reference, and then send a follow-up letter restating our objectives to make sure that the plan is followed through."

"One of the main purposes of a sales call to an existing account," says Dave Clark of Simmons, "is to help the retailer fine-tune his business plans. To enable you to achieve this objective, you need to know which of your products or promotions are working and which are not. Only at this point can you suggest plans for the future. If you are not prepared, your competition will do it for you.

"I personally feel that the more prepared you are, the more the buyer will feel that you take his business seriously and that you are the individual who can get the job done. The buyer is buying you as well as the products or ideas you are selling."

At Hewlett-Packard, Paul Sanders is usually making support, problem-solving, or expediting calls on retail executives and salespeople. "I'm talking to them because there's usually something that could be better," he explains. "I have a mental list of five or six items I want to cover, and always come away from an interview feeling that I've accomplished something."

Dr Pepper has an interesting way of getting the sales rep into the habit of setting specific call objectives. While a manager is working with the rep, the rep must state the objective on each call before contacting the account. Dr Pepper uses the "SMAC" formula for defining a good objective—it must be:

Specific in nature
Measurable
Achievable
Compatible with the company's objective

Cevin Melezoglu of American Greetings is another who stresses the importance of setting the call objective in *measurable* terms (how could one measure an objective like "getting acquainted" or "establishing rapport"?).

"Prior to each call," she reports, "I decide what product I am going to present, how much of the account can reasonably be expected to sell through, my recommended delivery date, and how the merchandising will be handled—that is, would store personnel or American Greetings put up the merchandise? And part of my measurable objective would be two backup plans in case the first objective proved unattainable.''

The Drackett Company and the Dial Corporation, like many other firms selling to retailers, use call records to maintain up-to-date information on each account.

Says Ed Lahue of Dial: ''The sales rep has a card for each account in a small ring binder. During a call, if he notes a major objective to be accomplished on the next call, he notes it on that account's card. He'll also list a number of minor objectives on the card: get this brand of soap between the other two, get this product up to eye level, etc. Also, the rep is alert to spot objectives while making the call; for example, if the store is overstocked on crackers, suggest a display of crackers with Armour's chili.''

Rich Ziegler of Drackett says that the overriding piece of advice he can offer sales reps is that ''time spent in planning a particular call should be proportional to the expected result of the call.'' In calling on a store, Drackett reps prepare a five-step sales presentation:

1. The attention step (opener)
2. The interest step (benefit statement)
3. FAB (features, advantages, benefits)
4. Trial close (open-ended question asking buyer's opinion)
5. The close

Drackett salespeople do much of their call planning the evening before, reviewing the call records for the scheduled stops, noting any long-term objectives (usually distribution, shelving, or pricing objectives) that have not yet been attained, listing merchandising opportunities, and making sure they have an adequate supply of point-of-sale materials to place in the stores. During the call, Drackett nonfoods sales reps also note a major volume or merchandising objective for the next call on the account.

Says Ziegler: ''I don't believe in stretch objectives—that is, if 20 cases is what the store needs, suggesting 30 cases on the assumption that the dealer will cut it down and end up with the recommended amount. I believe the sales rep should recommend exactly what's right for the buyer and the account, and soon the buyer will learn he can take the sales rep's word on business recommendations.''

Jon Vitarius of Nabisco Brands sees the setting of objectives as a kind of trickle-down operation. He submitted the chart shown in Figure 4-1, indicating that the CEO establishes an overall volume objective for product X, the sales manager creates an incentive for sales reps to push the product, and the reps set volume objectives for the different stores that will add up to the territory objective.

His colleague at Nabisco Brands, Pat Markley, says that 99 percent of the time, one of her objectives on a store call is to get a display (usually an additional display). Sometimes she'll obtain a copy of the store's plans and fit her display suggestions into them. For example, if there's going to be a sale of grape juice or grape jelly, she'll suggest an accompanying easel display of cookies. Sometimes she spots opportunities for a display by walking around in the store before talking with the manager.

"An interesting part of my sales preparation is that since I'll have only five minutes or so with the manager of a large chain store, I have to know in advance practically the verbatim script of my presentation so I won't waste any time. The quicker I can give him the information he wants, the better it is for me, because he'll find me a competent and pleasant person to deal with. At the end of the call I have about ten seconds to say, in essence, 'Buy or cry.'

"Sometimes the best you'll get from a manager is 'Whadaya got?' meaning what items am I featuring, what's 'on deal.' I have a couple of seconds to say, 'I have OREOs,' and he'll ask 'How much do I make?' I need to have the figures in my head, or at the tip of my fingers in the sales book. 'Well, at $1.99, let's say, you'll make 10 percent, and at $2.09 you'll make 15 percent.' And that's often the end of that call."

Carl Unger of Zenith keeps a card file on each customer and updates it as items of interest cross his desk. He's always prepared to discuss performance, inventory, back orders, product to be shipped, product to be advertised, how it's to be advertised, financing plans, and so on.

"Our industry," he says, "has a grade card or report card available to it, called 'Share of Industry.' It gives me an idea of how I am doing in relation to the rest of the TV industry. It shows my strengths as well as my weaknesses.

"My call objective is usually to correct some weakness. Because of all the information in my customer file, I can achieve the objective without wasting anyone's time. Sometimes the only way to correct a weakness is to appoint a new dealer."

Figure 4-1.   The "chain of objectives."

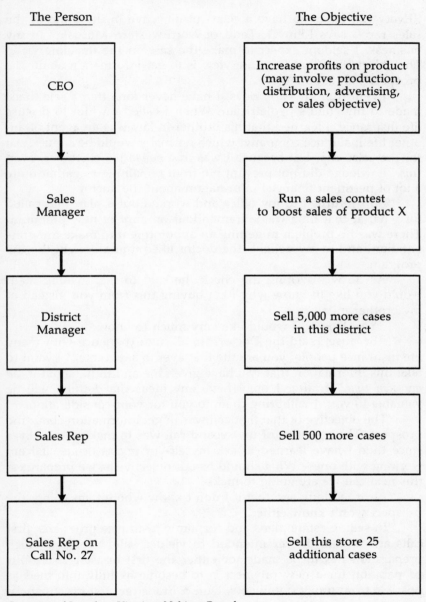

The Person	The Objective
CEO	Increase profits on product (may involve production, distribution, advertising, or sales objective)
Sales Manager	Run a sales contest to boost sales of product X
District Manager	Sell 5,000 more cases in this district
Sales Rep	Sell 500 more cases
Sales Rep on Call No. 27	Sell this store 25 additional cases

Courtesy of Jonathan Vitarius, Nabisco Brands

Selling to the Consumer

"Every call needs to have a clear-cut objective in the mind of the sales rep," says John O. Todd of Northwestern Mutual. "In my business, I seldom expect to make the sale on the first interview. The objective of that first interview is to get information about the prospect's situation.

"Even from my early days, I have never forgotten a sale that I made to my child's pediatrician. When I called on him to discuss life insurance, I learned that his brother-in-law was an agent of another life insurance company, which normally would be a quick exit for the sales rep. But because I was in a sense his customer, even this knowledge did not prevent me from remaining to gather quite a lot of pertinent financial information about the doctor.

"So I returned to my office and worked out a plan that called for what at that time was a tremendous amount of new premium. There was no problem in getting an appointment to make my presentation, and to my delight, the doctor liked it and bought the full program.

"As he was writing the check, he said to me, 'Young man, would you like to know why I am buying this from you instead of my brother-in-law?'

" 'Yes, Doctor, I would like very much to know.'

" 'Because,' said the Doctor, 'in all my experience with many life insurance people, you are the first ever to say to me, "I want to take this information that you have given me and think about it, *on my own time*. If, after I do, I have any ideas that I think will be valuable to you, I will bring them to you for your consideration." '

"The objective of that first call was to get information about the prospect. The objective of my second call was to make a sale. Ever since then I have learned to ask myself—or my associate, if I am working with one—'What should be our objective as we prepare for this next call we are going to make?'

"I learned long ago that if I don't know where I am going, the prospect won't know either.

"In selling estate plans and corporate insurance programs, first calls are seldom if ever intended to yield a sale. Even so, much preparation has to be made for either the first or later calls. Our preparation for a new prospect is to become as fully informed as possible from proxy statements, Dun & Bradstreet reports, financial statements, and reference sources.

"Our preparation may include the use of overhead transparencies, with hard-copy handouts that we may or may not allow the prospect to retain. We mark these copies: 'This information is proprietary and will be given to the client upon authorization to proceed.'

"Even if we are presenting a finished plan based on the prospect's own information, the preparation will often call for many hours of work. So preparation, preparation, preparation is the watchword of great importance to anyone's success in selling."

"For crucial calls," says Betty Cinq-Mars of Merrill Lynch, "I get all the positions of the related accounts, figure out what the clients' total investment needs are, and have my recommendations ready before making the call.

"I usually submit written proposals to the clients, let them think about it, and then call them if they don't phone me. I do not use a planning form, but the written proposal serves as the outline of our conversation.

"This sequence of phone call–written proposal–phone call works well. In many cases I get the order on the second phone call, but sometimes I may have to repeat the sequence one or two more times. There is no reason to give up just because a client does not like my first recommendation.

"Regarding pre-approach fact finding, when I talk with a prospect the first time, I try to find out as much about him or her as possible: age, income, net worth, line of business, history of previous investments, and many other things that are not related to the investment per se. This enables me to picture the kind of person the prospect is, what kind of investment is suitable for his situation, and what he will be willing and able to do. It is always easier to sell what the clients want to buy."

A different type of planning is used by Mary Kay Cosmetics sales director Judie McCoy, after she has arranged for a small group of women to attend one of her demonstrations of skin care and makeup. "I contact everyone who's going to be at this appointment in advance," she explains, "and ask them pointed questions. I want to know why they're coming. Are they curious about the product? Do they want to learn more about makeup techniques? Are they interested in hygiene and skin care? Or are they just coming to be nice to their friend who is hostess for the appointment? An advantage of phoning ahead of time is that you avoid postponements or 'no shows.' "

In selling real estate, Suzanne DeNoyior of Coldwell Banker sets call objectives based on the needs of the individual prospect, but listens for clues that may indicate a change in objectives and the need for a "personal touch." "The yardstick in real estate sales is flexibility," she adds.

Selling to Doctors and Hospitals

Call objectives are as important in the pharmaceutical business as they are in other types of selling, reports Peter Pappas of CIBA-Geigy. "If you just walk into a physician's office and show him a promotional sales piece, your time runs out and you're out the door without accomplishing anything."

On a typical doctor call, the objective is to make a sales presentation on a primary product, a briefer presentation on a secondary product, and a reminder on a third product—all these within the usual five- to ten-minute time limit. Beginning sales reps find it difficult to cover three products in such a short time, but Peter finds that careful planning the night before makes it possible.

Because of the time limitation, it may take three or four calls, each with its own interim objective, to attain the final objective. Peter calls this the "building block" approach.

"For example," he explains, "from notes taken on previous calls, you know that this doctor is concerned about your Product Z because his colleagues and your competitors tell him it is not effective over a 24-hour period. This is a legitimate concern which must be answered before you can eventually get him to prescribe your product.

"So on the next visit you show him third-party research papers by other doctors indicating that blood levels of Product Z do in fact maintain therapeutic levels for 24 hours, and that he might consider using it for his nocturnal angina patients. If he agrees, fine; if not, you have an objective for your next visit. In either event, by using a clever bridge, you can easily get into a secondary product or a third product.

"Of course, there are times when your planned objectives go right down the tube. If the doctor wants to devote the time to talking about a fishing trip or an upcoming medical meeting, you'd best discuss these and not business. Somebody once told me you have to be flexible in the medical business, and it couldn't be truer!"

J. M. Garcia, in selling computer systems to doctors, used a pattern of three calls, each with a specific objective:

On call No. 1, scheduled by a previous phone call, the objective was primarily fact gathering: qualifying the account, determining if there was a need, identifying the decision makers and, more important, the influencers—office manager, nurse, sometimes a spouse or relative.

Call No. 2 was a sales presentation of the benefits of the computer system, the objective being to arrange for a demonstration.

Call No. 3 was a demonstration with the objective of a signed contract.

He finds that setting call objectives is even more important now that he is with General Electric, selling imaging equipment (X-ray, CAT scanners, ultrasound, magnetic resonance) to hospitals.

"The sales cycle can run from a minimum of three months up to a year. The objectives on initial calls would be to determine if there is a budget and how it is established, whether the existing equipment is becoming obsolete or is simply nearing the end of its life span, and, above all, who are the decision makers. This will vary from hospital to hospital: technicians, radiologists, chief of radiology, administrators, controllers, legal department, chief of staff, and so on.

"Each subsequent call has the objective of moving the long, complicated decision-making process one step nearer to the close."

Doug Haynie, selling to hospitals for Baxter Travenol, stresses the importance of being aware of the customer's objectives as well as the sales rep's.

"One of the most difficult aspects in this type of selling," he notes, "is to determine the best position between what the company tells you to do and the way the customer tells you he wants things done. You are representing your company, but the customer's purchases are paying your income. If you can walk that fine line between generating the profit the company wants and fulfilling the needs of the customer, you become a valuable asset to both sides and the customer is always willing to listen to your ideas."

Doug likes to start a call by making it perfectly clear to the customer what his objective is on that call: to review a prior discussion, provide additional data, or discuss a procedural question. He follows up with frequent reminders of what has been determined so far and what needs to be done in the future within the time limit the customer has set.

Figure 4-2. Call planning form used by Roerig Division of Pfizer.

ROERIG

SALES CALL GUIDE

Physician's name _DR. SMITH_   Date _11/13/87_

Specialty _INTERNAL MEDICINE_

Objective of this call? GET DR. SMITH TO PUT FIVE TYPE II DIABETICS ON _____ FOR SIX WEEKS TO EVALUATE EFFICACY

If objective is achieved how will you recognize it on this call? DR. SMITH WILL AGREE AND PLACE DOSAGE CARDS IN FIVE PATIENT'S FOLDERS.

What is your strategy; what do you plan to do? (opening, features, benefits, sales aids, etc.)

USE VISUAL AID OPENER "TIMING IS EVERYTHING"

STRESS ① LOWERING GLUCOSE LEVELS WITHOUT THE RISK OF hypoglycemia.

② SHOW CLINICAL FROM JOSLIN CLINIC STATING _____ IS THE ONLY ORAL AGENT THAT CONTINUES TO PROVIDE EFFECTIVE GLUCOSE CONTROL FOR OVER FIVE YEAS WITHOUT HAVING TO BUMP UP THE DOSE

③ EMPHASIZE ONE A DAY DOSING FOR CONVENIENCE

What objections do you anticipate? _____ IS NOT AS POTENT AS _____ IN LOWERING BLOOD SUGAR LEVELS.

DID YOU ACHIEVE THE CALL OBJECTIVE? Yes ☑ No ☐

If "yes" describe how you recognized it. (what did customer say or do?) If "no" what will you do to achieve it next time?
DR. SMITH THOUGHT OF _SEVEN_ PATIENTS TO TRY ____ ON & ASKED THE NURSE TO BRING IN THE PATIENTS FILE FOLDERS. HE PLACED DOSAGE CARDS & FILE CARDS IN FOLDERS.

Salesperson _Ralph Eubanks_

Courtesy of Ralph Eubanks, Roerig Division of Pfizer

"If you remind them of the answers they have given you," he says, "and they take ownership in the decision-making process, it is almost impossible to fail."

Ralph Eubanks reports that the Roerig Division of Pfizer encourages its reps to use the form shown in Figure 4-2 for planning important calls.

Part Three
The Sales Call

5

Relaxers and Openers: The First Impression

"You never get a second chance to make a first impression."

It's a familiar old saying, but it underlines the importance of the first few seconds of the interview. Even if the customer is an old friend, the approach can establish the mood.

A story frequently told at sales conventions is about the sales manager who invited a Broadway drama coach to teach his salespeople how to smile in a warm and friendly fashion—even when they didn't feel much like smiling. There was a marked increase in sales thereafter.

The first part of the interview usually consists of two steps: the "relaxer" and the "opener."

The Relaxer

On most sales calls, it's customary for the conversation to open with a minute or so of friendly chitchat not directly related to the sales call. Encyclopedia salesmen call this the relaxer, and it does indeed overcome initial tension and put the prospect more at ease.

The topic of this chitchat, like every other aspect of the sales call, will be more successful if it is planned. The topic should be one that is interesting and pleasant to the prospect, won't take up too much time, and hopefully can "bridge" into the sales presentation. Typical relaxer topics include:

- A sincere compliment about something the sales rep has observed about the prospect's office or home.
- Reference to anything the sales rep and the prospect have in common, such as a mutual friend, interest in some sport, membership in some club or church.
- Any current news the sales rep has learned about the prospect, such as a promotion or election to an office in an organization.
- Any interesting bit of news about the prospect's business or industry.

The Opener

The sales presentation itself usually starts with some kind of opener or "hook" designed to grab the prospect's attention. The reason: We've all learned to fake interest. The prospect may be chatting about some current topic, or nodding in agreement from time to time, when in fact his mind is miles away: There's a labor negotiation coming up, or a problem with the spouse, or an appointment with the dentist.

The attention-getter, or opener, can be:

- A statement of a benefit. "Mr. Jones, we've developed a method of (whatever) that can reduce your costs by as much as 20 percent."
- A reminder of a problem—a perfectly valid opener if the sales rep has the answer for it. "Mrs. Jones, many business managers like yourself tell me it's getting more and more difficult to control travel costs. Are you finding that to be so?"
- Something the sales rep shows the customer: a photo, a sample, an ad reprint.

Selling to Business and Industry

Most sales reps follow the general approach suggested by Roland M. Charles, Jr., major account executive of GTE Mobilnet, Inc.:

"First, I dress according to the prospect's business—that is, if I were calling on bankers, I'd wear a gray or blue pin-stripe suit, white shirt, and appropriate tie and shoes.

"Second, when I greet the prospect for the first time, I give him a firm handshake and a pleasant, 'Mr. Prospect, very nice to meet you.'

"Once seated in the prospect's office, I look around for clues as to his family or hobbies. If I see a mounted sailfish, I'll ask 'Did you catch it?' 'How much did it weigh?' and so forth. After a few minutes I get into my presentation."

Nick Debronsky of Unisys feels that the relaxer is very important, and usually bases it on sports trophies, photos of a sailboat, or other objects in the prospect's office. "At the same time," he says, "it's important to get your first impression of the prospect. Is he neat, sloppy, insecure, overbearing, or what?"

J. M. Garcia recalls an incident early in his selling career, when he was selling an advertising program for a bank in a small town in West Virginia. He had made an appointment with the owner of an auto body shop.

"My first relaxer step was to remove my coat, vest, and tie before making the call," he narrates. "The prospect was in his late 40s and had a large lump of chewing tobacco in his cheek.

"My second step was to identify myself and the bank and to explain that I was there to describe an advertising campaign. From his total lack of response I assumed that either (a) he did not trust me, (b) he thought I was there to foreclose on his shop, or (c) he couldn't speak because of the wad of tobacco in his mouth.

"My third step was the mental soft shoe. Noticing several photos of a fancy tow truck on the walls, I quickly changed the subject and began asking about them.

"His expression and attitude changed as rapidly as if I'd asked new grandparents to describe their grandchildren. He described the truck in great detail, took me outside to show it to me, and offered me the privilege of sitting in it. Obviously he was relaxed, the barriers were broken, and the rest of the call was an enormous success."

John Heitzenroder of Occidental Chemicals also finds pictures on the customer's wall a good relaxer.

"I like John Wayne movies," he says, "and one purchasing agent I called on had a 12-by-14 inch autographed photo of John Wayne hanging on his wall. It was quite clear to him that my interest in the photo was sincere, and this established a relaxed mood for our sales conversation.

"I made the sale, too, because our local distribution point enabled the PA to reduce his inventory by 75 percent. Instead of buying four 40,000-pound truckloads of the four chemicals he needed, he could get 10,000 pounds of each product in one of our trucks—and get faster delivery too."

Commenting upon objects in the prospect's office is not without its risks. One ardent fisherman caught a large muskie and had it mounted, only to find that his wife didn't want it around the house. So the fisherman gave it to his brother-in-law, who happened to be a purchasing agent. Two weeks later the purchasing agent asked him to take it back. Every salesman who came into his office insisted in talking fishing at great length, never suspecting that the PA had never fished in his life.

When John McCarthy, former sales training manager for General Electric, moved into an office in the GE building on Lexington Avenue in New York City, he found a large, ugly-looking crack in the plaster of his wall. To cover it, he went to a nearby Woolworth store and bought the largest painting he could find, which happened to be a view of the Eiffel tower.

Needless to say, every sales rep who called on him opened with "Oh, you're interested in Paris? Do you speak French? How often do you visit Paris?"

Patiently, John would explain that the picture was merely to cover up a crack in the wall.

"Paris is a great city," the sales reps would continue without even hearing him. "Vous parlez un peu le francais?"

Finally, John would walk over to the painting, demonstrate that it was nothing more than a cover for the crack, and finally get the sales rep down to business.

Both Jake Kulp of AMP and Bruce White of Maritz Motivation make the point that the sales rep himself or herself must be relaxed if the "relaxer" is to serve its purpose.

"An important point to remember during the first few minutes of a sales call in my industry is not to try too hard to impress the client," Jake says. "This type of overconcerned facade can easily be seen through by most people and will actually do more harm than good. If you are knowledgeable and sincere, the relaxer will serve its purpose and be effective. To gain my customer's interest, I often talk about other major programs within his company with which he may not be familiar.

"As to the opener, I find that some of my more successful openers concern relaying information about similar problems on other programs. This seems to convince the customer that I am no stranger to his worries and probably have a solution."

In a similar vein, Bruce White remarks that "*you* must seem to be at ease in order to put the prospect at ease. Relaxers will seem more natural if they are 'off-the-top-of-the-head' observations or comments, rather than a recited, rote patter.

"The exact spoken words are not so important as the tone of informality and relaxation—intent, not content. Family discussions are always appropriate to get the prospect talking.

"The opener can be a visual aid or a handout or often, in the sales-incentive industry, reference to a successful program for the prospect's company or even for a competitor."

If the prospect is pressed for time, get into the sales presentation without the luxury of a relaxer, says John Paul Jones of Monsanto. "If you do use a relaxer, don't let it go too long and use up time allotted to the presentation. Think of the prospect's time in terms of its money value to his company, and use it wisely. After the relaxer, if used, the opener or statement of purpose must be strong enough to bring the prospect's thoughts back to business."

"People buy from people they like," writes Janis Drew of the *Los Angeles Times*. "If you can achieve a friendly and relaxed atmosphere with an opening statement or two, you will have more chance of success when the time comes to ask for the business. People are more susceptible to suggestion when they can identify with you and feel a 'comfort zone' when you are present.

"Quite frankly, I modify my behavior to mirror the person with whom I am talking. If I'm calling on a shy or reserved person, I tone down my voice and gestures to emulate his more sensitive style. Conversely, if I'm calling on a gregarious personality, I'll make it a point to maintain a similar upbeat and outgoing style."

Further comments on this "mirroring" strategy from Ralph Eubanks of the Roerig Division of Pfizer can be found in the "Selling to Doctors and Hospitals" section of this chapter.

Janis's comments about people buying from people they like prompted one contributor to submit the oft-quoted remark that "first you sell yourself, then you sell your company, and finally you sell your proposition.''

Suggestions on relaxers from Gourdin Sirles of AT&T were:

1. The objective of relaxers and openers is to become ''non-threatening'' to the client, establish credibility, and lay groundwork for the rest of the visit.
2. Do your homework. Know as much about the customer, both professionally and personally, as possible.
3. Knowing and discussing industry issues and trends can help break the ice.
4. Establishing credibility is essential to sales success. Knowing where your customer's business is trying to go, and relating these goals to industry trends, will often relax the client and establish credibility.
5. Quickly learn what mood the client is in; don't create the impression that you're wasting his time.
6. If the client has a problem with an existing product or service of your company, fix that issue first.

Walter W. Patten, Jr., of McGraw-Hill finds that he can put the prospect at ease by thanking him for setting aside the time for their appointment. ''Then,'' he continues, ''I preview exactly what I plan to discuss before starting my presentation. This helps the prospect assimilate and recall the key points of the meeting.''

Selling for Resale

Our contributors in this selling category were unanimous in stressing the value of appropriate relaxer comments at the start of a call.

Larry Nonnamaker of Eastman Kodak Company sees his dealers anywhere from once every three months to two or three times a week, depending on volume and potential. Since he sees most of them so often, he finds it easy to learn their likes and dislikes, their hobbies and their families—information which he carefully records on customer records.

''Regardless of how often I see an individual,'' he says, ''I always use a relaxer at the beginning of my call. Since I know them so well, it's easy to pick an interesting topic, and this establishes the rapport our business thrives on.

"Being sincere while chatting about the relaxer is very important. If the customer regards you as not being sincerely interested in him personally, you'll have trouble later on convincing him that you are sincerely interested in his business. I try to be my natural self throughout the entire call, and the relaxer is a good way to begin that process."

Larry believes in going directly from the relaxer to an opening statement about his reason for the call. "Terry, I want to discuss with you your fourth-quarter promotion on Kodak film." He follows that up with a comment that makes it clear to the dealer that he expects an order on this call. "After we go through these promotions and set the ads, I'll need your order quantities to support this program."

"It's also important to read the individual right at the outset. If he seems uninterested in my opening statement, I'll come back with a more specific statement like 'These fourth-quarter promotions are crucial in reaching the goals set earlier this year by your management.' The opener should state your intentions and is important in setting the mood for the rest of the call."

Bob Chargin of McKesson feels that "you make a good impression by being well groomed, having a pleasant personality, and making an honest effort to help your clients. If you need a relaxer, compliment the customer on something about his place of business: the way the merchandise is displayed, the type of fixtures, or even the location."

Jonathan Vitarius of Nabisco Brands notes the desirability of "bridging" from the relaxer to the opener.

Poor:

Sales Rep: Hey, Joe, how about those Giants?
Customer: Yeah, that was a great game Sunday.
Sales Rep: Joe, we have a new product. . . .

Better:

Sales Rep: Hey, Joe, how about those Giants?
Customer: Yeah, that was a great game Sunday.
Sales Rep: Did you watch it on television?
Customer: Yeah.
Sales Rep: Then you saw that commercial for our new product, Blank. Here's why it will do well in your store. . . .

If the customer says he did not see the game on television, the bridge still works: "That's too bad, because if you'd been watching it, you would have seen the commercials for our new product . . ."

With most customers, he notes, you can use the same relaxer topic on call after call. If one topic doesn't work, try another one next time. If you don't seem to be able to rouse the customer's interest, ask other salespeople what turns this person on.

Pat Markley, also of Nabisco Brands, stresses the importance of treating each sales call as a brand-new leaf. "On a previous call, the store manager may have been in a terrible mood because of inventory problems or customer complaints or any number of things, and he may have vented his irritation on you. So you may feel dejected when you leave that store, but between that call and the next one, you need to erase that past experience and start the next call 'with a clean page.' "

Getting back to basics, Bill Clark of Cooper Tire reminds his sales reps that their personal appearance is important in creating a favorable first impression. "You want the dealer to look at you and think, 'That fellow looks like he's successful. His company must be doing something right. I'd better listen to what he has to say.' "

Bill uses several other types of attention getters: (1) photographs of other dealers' places of business, (2) a small gift such as a pen or pencil, or (3) an annual report that is a sort of storybook presentation about Cooper Tire. The sales rep says, "We'd like to know a little more about your company, and in case you don't know too much about ours, here's a little information about Cooper Tire."

Carl Unger of Zenith disagrees with the old cliché that one should never ask the customer, "How's business?"

"It's important to use a relaxer even with dealers you're seeing frequently," he says. "You can't just walk in there and start asking for the order. Often I ask them, 'How's it going?' Some people say you shouldn't ask that question, for fear the customer will tell you how bad business is, but if that's the case, I'm prepared to suggest ways he can improve it.

"I carry an ad kit right with me and lay out a lot of dealers' ads. If a dealer says business is slow, I say, 'Hey, how about running an ad like this?' If business is slow, he's not going to forget about it, so you might as well recognize that fact, and maybe the two of you can do something about it. I try to get all the dealer's problems handled first, and then go on with my own objective."

Cevin Melezoglu of American Greetings finds that managers of independent card and gift shops, and to some extent pharmacies, are always interested in learning about what's new in their industry. Since she sees five to eight different retail outlets a day, she has a fund of information about new products and new promotions.

"When I first walk into a store," she says, "instead of talking about American Greetings cards, I give them some useful information I've picked up in other stores. This makes them realize that I'm on their side, and then I'm ready to go into my initial benefit statement about greeting cards."

Dave Pitzer of Dr Pepper says that the art of a relaxed opening bit of chitchat is difficult to teach or train.

"If it's not natural," he notes, "the buyer will view this part of the call as a waste of his time. I always look at how the office is furnished to get some idea of the customer's likes and dislikes. Check for items like college degrees, awards, trophies, books, family photos.

"If you can find a common interest, you have found a great relaxer. I play racquetball myself. I called on a client in St. Louis for the first time last year and noticed a racquetball picture on his wall. After talking about racquetball for about ten minutes, we had a great meeting. Less than three months later I not only sold the account, but now have a racquetball partner when I'm in St. Louis."

Looking at sales calls from the standpoint of the retailer, Ed Lahue of Dial points out that the dealer sees ten or twelve sales reps every day and may find them boring unless the rep establishes a rapport by discussing the buyer's hobby or family, or the activities of his competitors. Since many companies are offering similar deals, this feeling of rapport with the sales rep is often a deciding factor.

When it comes to getting the dealer's attention with an opening remark, Ed finds that nine times out of ten, the dealer will be interested in learning about any new advertising or display money that's available.

Selling to the Consumer

The nature of the relaxer or opener depends on the type of call, points out John O. Todd of Northwestern Mutual. He identifies four distinctly different situations: (1) the cold call, (2) the referred-lead call, (3) the personal-friend call, and (4) the current-customer or client call. The following paragraphs are direct quotes from his contributions:

Cold calls. Probably necessary for the new salesman, and perhaps in some lines it remains a necessity. In my type of work, I long ago found it to be an unpleasant waste of time. It is my observation that the referred lead is easy to get, so I will leave discussion of the cold call to others in different forms of selling.

The referred-lead call. To procure a referred lead, one must do two things: (1) earn the right to ask, and (2) nominate possible people to help the willing nominator identify individuals who may qualify as prospects.

For example: Who is your boss? Who do you know who is doing very well financially? Do you have any brothers or sisters? Who are your toughest competitors? Are they friendly or nasty? Etc. etc. Make suggestions that will bring specific persons to the nominator's mind.

When I have been given the names, then I will want to ask further qualifying questions. The more I can know about someone before I call on him, the better chance I have of meeting that person under favorable circumstances. I say to the nominator:

"He (she) sounds like someone I would like to meet. Would you mind introducing me by writing an introduction on the back of my card? When I call upon him, I want you to know that what I will say to him will be about like this: 'Mr. Jones, I want you to know why Bill gave me this card of introduction to you. I asked him for it, because he said such nice things about you that I wanted to meet you. My business is life insurance, but I don't want you to feel any obligation at all just because Bill was willing to introduce us.' "

The personal-friend call. Here there will always be personal chitchat, but the problem is to get down to talking business so that one is not imposing upon a friend's time. Also, there is the need to remove any feeling that they are doing you a favor when or if you ask them to buy.

I like to clear the air of that in the very beginning. If this is my first business call on a friend, I will get to the subject somewhat in this manner:

"Jim, we've been good friends for a long time, and I have never talked life insurance to you before. I got to thinking about this the other day, and I thought of how distressed I would be if you were to be disabled, or even get hit by the proverbial taxicab and killed, and I then found out that Betty and your kids were worse off financially because I had not done my job.

"At the moment, I don't know much about your financial plans, and I have no reason to believe that you need or want more life or disability coverage, but if you don't, I presume it is for one of two reasons: either you can't afford it or, as you see it, you have no need for more."

Now the ball is in his court. I don't care which of these two reasons he gives me, because if he says he thinks he doesn't need any more, he is automatically saying that if he felt he needed more, he could afford it. And if he says he can't afford it, then he is saying that he would really like to have more, and all we have to do is to help him discover where he can find the money.

The current-customer or client call. This is the easiest call of all in which to start on a relaxed basis. One knows a great deal about the person, and there has almost always been an advance appointment made. Chitchat is appropriate so long as it is not allowed to waste time, and even though the client has become a good friend, all involved will recognize the need to get down to business.

"We find the concept of relaxers—what salespeople call 'petting the goldfish'—difficult to teach," says David Van Tosh of Encyclopaedia Britannica. "We use door approaches that require very little of that. We have an appointment, we are going there to provide information at their request.

"Years ago some salesmen used to stand facing the street, acting very casual, and when the prospect opened the door they would turn around and say 'Oh! [in a surprised tone] How are you?' When you think about it, that has to be the most ridiculous thing in the world. In the first place, in this crime-ridden age, the prospect wants to see who he's talking to. Second, if you have an appointment and they're expecting you, you don't need that cornball approach. They know you're there to try to sell them something, so let's be professional. Be facing them properly. If anything, stand where they can see you as clearly as possible. Stand at the side of the door that opens so they can see you as soon as it opens a crack.

"It's rigid company policy that the salesperson present a business card and introduce himself: 'I'm David Van Tosh from Britannica; here's my card.' That in itself is a relaxer (although I don't like that word). Once they're inside the first thing they have to do is to repeat the whole introductory process to the spouse who did not come to the door, so right away everybody knows who they are and why they're there.

"After that the salespeople can comment on anything they want—and they should, although I always felt it is better to listen than to talk. The prospect's favorite subject is 'I,' and it helps the salesperson a great deal to learn something about the family. But it's hard to teach. If you train salespeople to look around the room and ask 'Who's your decorator?' that works fine until the first time you try it in a shack, and then you get a faceful of knuckles.

"We don't have to ask questions to uncover a buying motive. People don't request information on something they don't want. Their interest is a 'given.' That's what makes selling Britannica a lot of fun.''

"First impressions are so important,'' says Denise Kaluzna of Tupperware Home Parties. "Look the part, dress accordingly, act professional. You must be confident, and that comes only by practicing. A *sincere* compliment and a few minutes of friendly conversation help build a relationship. Find something in common you can talk about.

"An opener to date a party might be 'Did you know most of our hostesses can receive $25 to $40 in free gifts just for having four to six people around the kitchen table for 45 minutes?' Let them know you won't push them into something they don't want right now. Maybe next month will be better for this customer, and we all need business next month, too.''

Gordon Wallace of Spitzer Dodge in Columbus, Ohio, doesn't believe in small talk to open the sale. "I want to keep their minds on the car,'' he says. "If they're thinking about the weather or golf or something, their minds are not on the car. If they make some comment about the weather, I always bring the conversation back to the automobile.

"At the beginning of the sale, I walk up to them, put out my hand and say, 'Hello, I'm Gordon,' and if it's a couple, the man will say, 'I'm George, and this is Mary.'

"The most important thing of all is to treat every customer with respect. I don't give them the fast shuffle, don't want them to think I'm a fast-talking, high-pressure salesman. I warm up to them. That's the most important part of the sale. You have to treat the customer like the cornerstone of the building. I don't care what you're selling, if you're snobbish, hateful, rude, high-pressure, anything like that, they're not going to buy from you. I try to treat each person like an egg.

"If they want to test-drive a car, I do little things like opening the car door for them, adjusting the seat, making sure the steering wheel is in the right position. A lot of salespeople don't do that—

they just let them get into the car and adjust the seat for them-selves.''

"Image is important in any business, but in the brokerage busi-ness it's essential," says Betty Cinq-Mars of Merrill Lynch. "I try to present a friendly but firm, crisp, and businesslike image to all my clients. So do my assistants, all beautiful and intelligent women. People like to do business with successful people, and we make sure that our clients see that in us.

"Our male clients are 'Mr.' to us, but we call women clients by their first names to avoid intimidating them.

"I also try to convey the message that I am a very busy person, because people often equate busy-ness with business success. It also prevents them from wasting their time as well as mine.

"Thus my opening remarks are brief and I go straight to the main issue. This may not be a good strategy in businesses where you have to proceed more slowly, but it is quite effective in a bro-kerage. I may start by complimenting the client on something or mentioning a mutual acquaintance, but it's never a big element in my approach.''

Judie McCoy, at the start of one of her "appointments" or dem-onstration sessions for Mary Kay Cosmetics, asks questions of each participant, letting her tell a little about herself, to put them at ease and establish rapport.

"If she's a career woman, I have to be a career woman. If she's a homemaker, I have to be a homemaker. If she's a single parent, I have to think like a single parent. 'Walk a mile in their shoes,' to be aware of their needs and where they're coming from.''

Hal Kessler of Terminix always gives his first name. On the telephone he never says "This is Mr. Kessler"—always "Hi, this is Hal Kessler from Terminix" or "This is Hal from Terminix." If a man on the phone says "This is Jack Jones," Hal calls him Jack. If a woman says "This is Mary Dugan," she's Mary, not Mrs. Dugan. "This lightens the conversation right off the bat," he says.

"It's very important to instill trust in the prospect," Hal says. "The first thing I do is shake the prospect's hand, very firmly. I look them straight in the eye. When people talk to me and don't look at me, I feel that they're either untruthful or insecure.

"And I'm always on time. Always. If I'm going to be late for any reason, I get to the phone booth and let the customer know it. Very important.

"At the start of the call I do a few things to soften things up. I pat the dog, play with the kids, tell the people I have three children. Sometimes they have children the same age as mine, and then we can discuss some of the problems we have with teenagers. Or if I see somebody has a bowling trophy or baseball pictures, I say that I do the same thing. I never discuss politics or religion.''

"Make 'em laugh!'' suggests Suzanne DeNoyior of Coldwell Banker Real Estate. "Many initial contacts with both buyers and sellers are made by phone, and if the rep can inject a humorous touch, it makes for a wonderful relaxer.

"I tell my people to look at themselves in the mirror while prospecting on the phone,'' she says. "If they keep a smile on their faces, the prospect will hear the smile in their voices.''

Suzanne recounted a tale which has been circulating for many years in the real estate business. A sales agent phoned an FSBO (For Sale By Owner) on a Sunday morning. The homeowner said, somewhat unpleasantly, that she wasn't cooperating with brokers.

A few weeks later, the rep drove past the house and saw that the "For Sale'' sign was still up. He knocked at the front door and introduced himself. The homeowner became very abusive, said she was sick and tired of being pestered by brokers, and slammed the door in his face.

The sales rep went around the house and knocked on the back door. Of course, the same woman answered. She was surprised to see him, but before she could say anything, the rep said, "I'm sorry to bother you. I hope you're not as cranky as the woman who answered the front door.''

The woman laughed, relaxed, and invited him in to inspect the house.

Jack Hallberg of Allstate tries to establish a personal relationship with his casualty or life insurance clients. "I'm not doing this just for today,'' he tells them. "I'm applying for a job as your insurance agent, not just for now but for the future. I want you to be able to deal with me the way you would with any other friend.''

Selling to Doctors and Hospitals

Ralph Eubanks of the Roerig Division of Pfizer is quite impressed with the techniques of establishing rapport based on "NLP''—neurolinguistic programming. "Each of us thinks we are normal,'' he explains. "We serve as our own reference standard and judge others based upon ourselves. Each of us likes people who are similar to ourselves.

"Our sales reps are trained to observe the doctor and to mirror the doctor's behavior in their own behavior. Let's say we call on a very introverted, quiet-spoken internist, a very analytical type of person. If I'm normally a very effervescent, outgoing, back-slapping type of sales rep, there'll be no rapport. We have to have the flexibility to be able to communicate in the mode the doctor prefers, which is his own.

"When a New Yorker goes down South, Southerners find it difficult to listen to what he's saying, because they're distracted by his fast speech. On the other hand, when a Southerner goes to New York, New Yorkers may get the impression that because his speech is slow, he's a little slow upstairs.

"I personally tend to speak rather loudly, and found that some soft-spoken doctors would practically cringe. They didn't hear my message, because I just wasn't their type of person.

"When you mirror the doctor's behavioral preference in speech volume, tone, and speed, it establishes a common bond, a rapport, and you become much more effective. You are conveying this message: 'I understand you. I accept you. I am like you.' It's difficult not to like yourself.

"The same thing applies to body language. It's a question of getting in tune and then leading the doctor. If the doctor is looking at your visual aid and leans back, you lean back. But you don't stay back. You come forward, and it leads him forward."

As an opener, Roerig sales reps usually use a general benefit statement, followed by qualifying questions to get the doctor talking about his or her problems, instead of the rep assuming that he knows what the problems are.

Peter Pappas of CIBA-Geigy believes in a bit of small talk to get the doctor away from his "patient world"—but just for a few moments, because of the time limits. "Recently," he says, "I complimented a doctor on the photographs in his waiting room, only to find that he was a 35mm photography addict and had taken them himself. Talk about hitting his hot button! I could hardly get him away from talking about his hobby."

The opener, again because of the very short time available for the sales presentation, is usually a carefully preplanned benefit statement such as, "Your desire to enable your angina patients to lead a better-quality life has led to the success of Transderm-Nitro—

a patch that protects the patient for 24 hours, thus reducing anginal attacks.''

This preplanned opening benefit statement leads smoothly into a presentation of the benefits to the patient (a better life style) and to the doctor (fewer night phone calls from patients).

6
Qualifying:
The Question As
a Sales Tool

Early in the interview, the sales rep usually wants to get the prospect talking about his problems, needs, or wants. There are two reasons for asking for this information.

One, it enables the sales rep to qualify the prospect by finding out if he needs the product or service, whether he can afford it, and if he has the authority to make the decision.

Two, even if the sales rep already has most of this information, it's good strategy to get the prospect to express it. One of the most powerful tactics in selling is to say, ''As you said earlier, Mr. Prospect . . .'' and then quote something the prospect has said. This reinforces the prospect's statement, and at the same time is a subtle form of flattery because it indicates that the sales rep considers the prospect's opinions important and is listening to every word.

Most people are willing, even eager, to discuss their business or household operations. The sales rep, however, ''buys'' the right to ask these qualifying questions by opening with a benefit statement: ''Mr. Green, other customers tell me that this process has reduced their costs by as much as 15 percent. To determine to what extent it might do the same for you, I need a bit of information about your procedures . . .''—and then the questions start.

A problem often faced in some forms of selling is the time-wasting prospect who really doesn't have the buying authority but conceals that fact. It would be undiplomatic to ask bluntly if the prospect has the authority to buy, but often one can get some clues with qualifying questions such as, "Tell me, Mr. Prospect, what procedures does your company follow in making this kind of a purchasing decision?"

Selling to Business and Industry

Reps selling to business and industry generally agree that the three aspects of qualifying the prospect are:

1. Finding out if the individual has the authority to buy or, if not, who does.
2. Getting information about the company's problems or needs.
3. Determining the dominating motive, or "hot button," of the individual.

"Prospects in our type of selling do not become clients after one presentation," says Greg Deming of American Express Travel Management Services. The strategy of the first presentation is to:

- Earn the right to ask questions.
- Agree on objectives of the call.
- Ask enough open-ended questions to determine:
  Organizational needs.
  Personal needs of your contact.
  Potential obstacles.
- Summarize needs from the organization's perspective, always testing that the needs are mutually understood.
- Ask and make statements regarding how the needs can be fulfilled.
- Reinforce the benefits of fulfilling the needs.
- Test for client reaction in terms of personal needs.
- State the benefits of moving to the next step in the cycle: the Needs Analysis. Outline what each of you needs to do to prepare for that next step, and set a date for the next contact.

"The key skill in this step is to translate the 'problems' cited by the client into organizational needs that your client agrees with. When your contact's level of awareness is equal to yours, you can begin to apply features and benefits to that need, but not before!"

"When calling on a new prospect," says Paul Lentz of Automatic Data Processing, "I like to start with the data processing manager to find out such key factors as age and type of software and hardware, number of states in which the company pays employees (the more, the better for tax filing), as well as current methods of data collection and distribution.

"In addition, I can determine if the manager will be an ally or adversary and what his or her attitude is toward outside processing. Many times decisions are made based more upon a prospect's attitude than on business judgment.

"My next step is usually to call on the key decision maker in finance (controller, treasurer, or the like). By this time I have some idea as to how I will present my services. For example, if the company has compatible hardware, I will want to stress our ability to use its existing equipment. If it pays employees in 30 states, I will stress the benefits of tax filing.

"Of course, if I get shot down at both these levels, I proceed to call on the human-resources, payroll, and tax departments. Even if you cannot develop any interest on the first call, try to get as much information as possible and leave the door open for future callbacks by asking permission to stay in touch. Very rarely will a prospect refuse you this courtesy, although once in a while you get the 'call me back in two years' response. People change, and corporate philosophies change. Six months from now you can call back with the background you require to tell your story effectively."

Says Roland M. Charles, Jr., of GTE Mobilnet, Inc.: "It is easy to make the mistake of thinking that the person you are talking to is the economic buyer—the one authorized to make the money decisions—when he or she is not. To avoid wasting time on an individual who is not the real decision maker, I simply ask, in a businesslike manner, 'Mr. Prospect, are you the economic buyer for your company?' If he is, I continue with my presentation; if not, I make an appointment with the company's economic buyer and with the individual who is doing the fact finding."

Gourdin Sirles points out that it's wise, if possible, to learn the decision-making process before making the call. "If that is not possible," he adds, "I think it's important to establish very quickly whether or not the contact has the authority to buy, and I directly ask, to avoid wasting time.''

"If this is an initial call and you have not had the prior opportunity to determine whether or not this person makes the buying decision,'' suggests Janis Drew of the *Los Angeles Times*, ''ask an intelligent question that discreetly reveals his involvement with the buy. Should you realize that the individual has no authority, of course you don't act rude and leave. Be brief, but ask for all the names on the account so that this initial call is not wasted.''

As to the fact-finding phase, John Paul Jones of Monsanto comments that ''handled properly, this is the most important part of the call. A strong opening with a statement of benefit will usually get the prospect to open up. At this point, the experienced sales rep will just sit and listen. Do not attempt to inject features, or to paraphrase the prospect's comments, as this may break the chain of information. At the end of this listening period, you will have most of the answers you need as to the prospect's need, fit, affordability, and decision-making process. If not, don't be afraid to ask.''

"Asking intelligent questions, listening, and paying close attention to the prospect's body language are all as important as giving your presentation,'' agrees Janis Drew. ''If the call is on a key decision maker, be sure to get as much solid information as you can. Probe for data that only this particular person might know. Information is the power source to fuel all your sales efforts. Get the client talking. You'd be surprised what you can learn when clients are relaxed and comfortable with you.''

"Your questions should be relevant and should follow a logical sequence so the client understands where you are trying to go,'' Gourdin Sirles adds. ''Use your 'third eye,' observe the client's environment and business situation.

"Use judgment and don't ask unnecessary questions, or questions with an obvious answer. I once had a salesman ask a client, while standing in the middle of a lumber yard, 'Where do you keep your supplies?' ''

He points out that ''the client must perceive the benefit of answering your questions or providing information. Using an example of what other clients have accomplished with your product or service can be a good lead into the questions.''

He adds that questions that are open-ended, starting with ''Why,'' ''How,'' or ''What,'' will elicit more information than closed-end, yes-or-no questions starting with ''Can you'' or ''Is it true that—.''

Jake Kulp of AMP differentiates between open-ended probes to obtain general information ("Tell me about your current problems") and closed-ended probes to obtain more specific information ("Do you have to shrink the size of your avionics box electronics?").

Bruce White of Maritz Motivation agrees that "some sales reps try to start digging up data too early, and don't adequately precondition the prospect so that the exchange of confidential information flows naturally. Remember that the client has to buy—usually in this order—the salesperson, the company, and the proposition."

The data he needs for preparing a proposal on a motivational program are so detailed that he arrives with a written list of questions prepared in advance, so that a busy marketing vice president can give the list to a subordinate to answer quickly.

An important function of the initial probing phase of the call is to identify the buyer's key benefit, says William O'Neill of Wausau Insurance Companies. "Remember," he cautions, "that the buyer's *key* benefit may not be what you, or your boss, or your company's marketing department, considers to be the most important benefit.

"Each buyer has his own 'hot button' that will motivate him to buy from you. It's my job to uncover that key benefit. Once I know what that key benefit is, I can ask, 'Mr. Buyer, if I can provide that benefit you're seeking, then do we have a deal?' If I've earned the right to ask that question, the buyer will respond positively."

Nick Debronsky of Unisys (Burroughs/Sperry) reminds us that many times the rep is dealing with a committee of anywhere from five to 25 individuals rather than a single decision maker. The rep must learn the identity of the really influential members of the committee, as well as make individual calls on every member to sell his proposition.

"I had a real wild experience one time," he recalls. "We made a presentation to a committee of 25 seated around a large table. Our major competitor had preceded us; we were the second and last to appear. After our presentation, the comptroller started passing out papers. When I asked what he was doing, he said, 'We're taking votes. Phone us tomorrow, and we'll let you know how you made out.' Fortunately for me we won, 25 to 0."

Selling for Resale

In a typical call on a retailer, Jonathan Vitarius of Nabisco Brands comments, the rep is thoroughly familiar with the store; determining the customer's needs is done largely in advance of the call. Probing questions are usually required only when a new outlet, a new product, or a new executive is involved.

Rich Ziegler of The Drackett Company agrees that "very little qualifying is necessary once we get to know the account, but for outlets that are new to the sales rep, or for buyers that are new to the business, we teach a skill that we refer to as 'the probing dialogue' to gather information on Drackett's six 'business criticals': distribution, shelving, merchandising, retail reorder, pricing, and new products."

Rich recalls phoning an out-of-town prospect who was in an unusual business: selling merchandise salvaged from fires, floods, train wrecks, or bankruptcies. When the prospect seemed to resent his questioning, Rich explained, "Sir, my intention is simply to find out a bit about your business." The prospect replied, "Son, the road to hell is paved with good intentions."

"It is difficult to believe how beneficial the use of questions can be until you have wasted a great deal of time because you didn't ask the right questions," says Larry Nonnamaker of Eastman Kodak. "Not only do you need to ask questions, but it is very important to concentrate on listening to the answers. Qualifying the dealer really is determining the dealer's needs through a series of questions, then meeting those needs with our products or services.

"Often you will take in a great product, and the dealer either doesn't want to buy it, or doesn't want to order the quantity you know will sell. The only way to uncover the reason for this behavior is to ask.

"I use different questioning methods depending upon how well I know the dealer. If I know the dealer well, I will ask very directly what concerns are preventing him from buying the product. Usually the dealer will give you a direct answer, which you are able to handle because of your pre-call planning. Occasionally you get pat answers that you know are not the real ones, but with a series of effective questions you can find out what the real concerns are.

"With new dealers I use a much less direct approach to find out who does the buying. It is important not to offend someone, as you never know who will be buying your product in the future. I also use less direct questions in determining their needs. If you are too direct, you may intimidate them and be unable to get the information you are looking for.

"I believe in using qualifying questions several times during the presentation, almost like a trial close, except that it is not concerned with the order. The more feedback you can obtain even before a trial close, the more likely your chances of addressing the appropriate needs and ultimately getting the order.

"If you can convince the dealer that you are sincerely interested in his best interest, you stand a much better chance of getting honest answers to your questions."

Determining who has buying authority is no problem for Ed Lahue of The Dial Corporation. "I can be quite blunt about it," he says, "because each store or chain has someone in charge of buying for that store."

When asking questions at the store level, Ed finds, it's easier to get answers if you preface the question with an interesting statement. "How are you doing with this item?" doesn't work as well as "Other stores in the area are doing well with this item—how are you doing with it?"

It is not a waste of time to get information from people who don't have the buying authority, comments David F. Clark of Simmons. "Although the individual may not make the final buying decision, he may be very active in the buying process," he says. These nonbuyers are often "influencers." Buyer Brown may be the final decision maker, but he does what Mrs. Brown tells him.

"The buyers of many retail operations," David explains, "will give out very little information about their true problems and wants, fearing that this will place them in an unfavorable negotiating position later on. A subordinate, or someone who will not be held responsible for the results of buying decisions, has little to lose in telling you about problems being experienced with current vendors.

"I was calling one day on the buyer of a small furniture store chain. After I finished my presentation, the buyer said everything looked very good and he felt we could be a good replacement for the line he was presently carrying. At that point he asked me, 'Why do you feel you can do a better job at the retail level than the current vendor?'

"I had previously spoken with several people on the actual sales floor. They were very pleased that I had taken the time to ask about any problems they had with their current product, and to get their opinions as to what products the store should handle to increase sales. They promised they would support me if I could get these products into the store.

"So I was able to tell the buyer I knew our products would sell because his own people wanted them and said they would support them.''

Dave Pitzer of Dr Pepper believes that the initial probing is the most important step in the sales call, because it provides information that will enable the rep to show the buyer that the product can help the buyer achieve his or her objectives or solve a certain problem.

''Fact finding also enables you to customize benefits to each individual account,'' he adds. ''For example, you find that a restaurant owner is interested in total customer satisfaction. When you inform him that Dr Pepper is the largest selling non-cola drink (a feature), you can then tailor the benefit: 'Mr. Buyer, the benefit to you is that you will satisfy a larger percentage of your customers by serving Dr Pepper.'

''I always try to ask questions during the fact finding that will benefit me later. For example, one of the features of Dr Pepper is that it sells proportionately more in the large sizes than all other soft drinks, the benefit being more ounces sold and more profit.

''During fact finding, I ask buyers if they are interested in selling more large-sized drinks. More than 95 percent will say yes. I save that information until I am explaining the features and benefits. I then say, 'One of the areas you told me you would like to improve on is the sale of large drinks. Let me show how Dr Pepper might assist.' ''

American Greetings has a formal qualifying procedure used for prospect accounts, reports Cevin Melezoglu. One part of the procedure is a form called ''Prospect Site Analysis/External Store Factors.'' This analysis rates various factors such as local competition, economic condition of the surrounding area, neighborhood population trends, adjacent buildings, customer traffic, and more. After rating all these factors, the rep comes up with an overall rating for the prospect as excellent, good, fair, or poor. The next step is an ''advance credit check.''

These two steps help the rep prioritize the list of potential prospects.

After this first phase of the qualifying process, the second phase is a detailed needs analysis. This is done by filling out data sheets to evaluate the account's potential and develop the sales presentation. The objective of these data sheets is to identify areas in which American Greetings is superior to competition and can help the retailer increase sales and profits.

The prospect data sheet asks questions regarding the present physical appearance of the greeting-card department, inventory control methods used, and merchandising techniques. This helps the sales rep consider how each of these areas could be improved, and that forms a basis for developing the proposal.

The competitive data sheets help the rep pinpoint American Greetings' advantages over the present supplier, as well as other suppliers' advantages over American Greetings. In planning the call, the rep considers how each topic will be handled.

"In the presentation," Cevin says, "we stress American Greetings' advantages rather than competitors' weaknesses to keep the presentation positive. If the prospect brings up competitive strengths, we emphasize American Greetings' offsetting benefits that will allow the dealer to make the change easily and profitably."

Selling to the Consumer

"Any teacher knows that a good student not only answers questions well but also asks good questions," comments Betty Cinq-Mars of Merrill Lynch. "It is important to ask pertinent questions in the short period of time you are with your clients. An astute client will sense the worth of a broker just by evaluating the questions the broker asks.

"Questions not only give me an idea of what the client wants but also help to clarify matters to the client. When I ask such questions as 'Do you want income or growth?' 'How much risk can you take?' or 'When will you need to take out the money?' they make the client evaluate his own investment objectives and give him a clearer idea of what he can and cannot expect to achieve.

"Since many people have unreasonable expectations of obtaining high yield without taking any risk, it is essential to clarify the picture. Without this clarification the client may never make an investment decision, always hoping something better will turn up."

"The first thing I do is try to qualify the customer," says Gordon Wallace of Spitzer Dodge in Columbus, Ohio. "I don't prejudge a customer. I've seen salespeople blow off some customer because the sales rep thought they wouldn't be able to make the payments or something, when actually it was a good potential prospect.

"The main qualifying question I ask is what size monthly payment they have in mind. The world is centered around payments—car payments, house payments, credit card payments. I close ten out of ten deals on car payments. If early in the deal I find out what payment range they want to be in, I show them a car that fits their budget. It can be an automatic with air and tilt and cruise and all that, and if it's in their budget, they'll buy it.

"If I don't know what their budget is, and if I show them a $15,000 car (around $400 a month) when they want to spend $200 a month, they won't tell me they can't afford it—they'll just say they want to think it over, and walk out.

"When people walk into the dealership and tell me they've been looking at another car, ten times out of ten I'll sell them a car because that other salesman has only set up the sale for me. Maybe he was rude, maybe he showed them a car that was too expensive. I ask them what they didn't like about the other car. If they say it was price, or color, or the salesman was a smart aleck, I know what I have to do to sell them my car.

"I don't want to do them an injustice by showing them a $15,000 automobile when they're looking for a $200 payment—an $8,000 automobile. Taking them down from a car they love to a car they really can afford is one of the hardest things I have to do. Sometimes you can trade them up from their payment range if you sell them on the advantages of the bigger car. I've seen people come in wanting a $200 monthly payment and leave with a $300 payment.

"One man came in to look at cars. He didn't buy, and I didn't get his name and address because I was out on the lot and didn't have pencil and paper with me. More than a year later he came back, asked for me, and bought a car from me. He told me he had asked for me because I treated him with respect."

In selling cosmetics, Judie McCoy of Mary Kay Cosmetics tries to get information about a woman's life style and, since she's in the image business, the type of image the woman wants to create: professional image, just going to pick up the children, doing volunteer work, or what? "Women don't buy jars," she says, "they buy feelings. The most important thing I can do is to get every woman to feel that she deserves to look her best, that she's worth it."

Qualifying questions are important in selling real estate, not only to make sure that the buyer is financially able to purchase the home he or she selects, but also to uncover the frequently complex motivations that affect the selection of a home.

"After having established a certain amount of confidence in our initial phone conversation," writes Suzanne DeNoyior of Coldwell Banker, "astute real estate agents remember that probing questions must flow into the conversation, and not be the conversation itself. Buyers are usually unwilling to divulge their personal financial status until they are well into the buying process. And this is especially true of the repeat second-time buyer. First-time buyers are easier in some respect, because they need more guidance in the qualifying and selecting stage.

"Because we have seen a tremendous inflationary market in real estate over the last ten years, we are also seeing a more educated buyer. Since homeowners are increasingly more willing to devote upward of 30 percent of their gross annual income on principal, interest, and taxes, they are more cautious about their purchase. They continue to employ licensed professional engineers to inspect properties in which they are interested in making a bid. So you see, the buyer probes as much as we do.

"I always tell new prospects that our first trip out is nothing more than a field trip. During this time I can assess their needs, their wants, and their dreams. I can carefully observe their body language, their decision making, and their sincerity while nonchalantly interjecting probing questions as to the feasibility of such a purchase.

"Do they have a home to sell before purchasing another? Do they have the required down payment? Are both husband and wife working, and can they use both incomes to qualify for financing? Do they have other nontaxable income that would help in obtaining a mortgage commitment?

"Since all buyers give us a price range in which to work, it is our job to ascertain if that price range is actually the most suitable for them. Show three houses on the initial appointment: one below the price range they have indicated, one at the price range, and another slightly higher. This creates a situation where probing questions are not an invasion of privacy."

When it comes to qualifying the potential buyer financially, the old rule is TNFG—Take Nothing For Granted. Suzanne recalls this story:

"A new agent who had been taught to probe and qualify all

customers attempted to do so with a new client who was a doctor. The client became very upset, insisting that he could afford anything he wanted to buy.

"So the agent found a waterview house in a very expensive area and successfully negotiated a deal. The homeowner questioned her about qualifying the client, and the agent reminded the homeowner that the potential buyer was a doctor and that banks never turned down professionals of that caliber.

"Two weeks before the anticipated closing date, the bank notified the homeowner that the doctor did not qualify for a mortgage."

TNFG.

In selling life insurance, reports John O. Todd of Northwestern Mutual, the qualifying questions are the first step in a carefully orchestrated series of questions leading inexorably to the close. The process is described in his book "Ceiling Unlimited," published by Lexington House in Lexington, Kentucky, and now in its fifth edition:

John first arouses the prospect's curiosity by giving him a couple of reasons for *not* being in the market for life insurance.

"Mr. Prospect, it would be presumptuous on my part if I came to you, knowing as little about you as I do, with the preconceived notion that you needed more life insurance. Indeed, life insurance may be the last thing on earth that you need or want."

He uses questions designed to produce answers which will close off avenues of escape that might later be used as objections. For example:

"Mr. Prospect, in order to feel that you have been a financial success, what percentage of your present income would you like to have as permanent income some day?"

Often the prospect will ask, "What do you mean by permanent income?" Mr. Todd answers that question with another:

"If for any reason you were to quit work tomorrow, what percentage of your present income would be permanent?" This indicates that income from personal earnings is temporary; income from capital is what is meant by "permanent income."

Suppose the prospect says that he might have as much as 10 percent.

"If the worse comes to the worst," John then asks, "could you or your family get by on as little as, say, 60 percent of your present income?"

Then John stops talking until the prospect either accepts the 60 percent figure or comes up with an estimate of his own.

"If," John continues, "you think you must have not less than 60 percent of your present income some day, and if only 10 percent of your present income would be permanent, is it fair to say that your problem is to accumulate—in the time that remains to you—an amount of capital that will produce 50 percent of your present income?"

This is not a purely rhetorical question, John explains. He will wait as long as necessary for the prospect to answer. "I want him to accept this as his problem, and until he does, there is no use going on. But when he does, the next question is really dynamite:

"Under your present plan, do you know how long it will take to do that?

"Suppose you don't have time. Would the need for income be greater or less?

"Mr. Prospect, if there were some plan available that was within your reach, and through which you could be absolutely sure that you would attain your own measurement of financial success whether you were given time or not, would you do what it takes?"

Selling to Doctors and Hospitals

The pharmaceutical sales rep usually knows a good deal about the prescribing habits of each doctor he calls on. This knowledge is based on his company's market research, on prescription records, and on previous calls.

"Therefore, my probing questions," says Peter Pappas of CIBA-Geigy, "are not so much about the product as about how it can fit into the doctor's regimen of drugs for a specific disease. If I can show him a benefit he is not getting from his present drug, he will adopt the product and prescribe it.

"Some doctors don't like to be questioned, either because they feel you're taking too much of their time or because they do not want to give out information about how they treat their patients. I make it a point on one of my visits to gather some information from the office manager, nurse, or receptionist about how I can better get to the physician."

Ralph Eubanks of Roerig cautions medical sales reps not to become so excited about a product that they bombard a doctor with solutions to a problem he or she doesn't have. Roerig reps are trained in the art of asking questions. Some aspects of this art:

Don't ask a question in a way that might embarrass the doctor. If the rep asks a question to which the doctor doesn't know the answer, rather than admit he or she doesn't know, the doctor is likely to say, ''Don't ask me any questions, just show me what your product will do.'' So the rep phrases the question in such a way that the doctor cannot appear wrong or ignorant. ''Doctor, in your opinion—''

Suppose the rep asks, ''Doctor, what pathogens are appearing mostly in ICUs (intensive care units) today?'' The doctor may conclude that the rep has some kind of information the doctor doesn't have, and is testing the doctor's knowledge.

But if the rep asks, ''Doctor, in your opinion, what are the most common pathogens—'' the doctor can give any answer he or she wishes without appearing ignorant or incorrect. ''We've found that this really opens doctors up,'' Ralph says.

Give a reason for asking the question. Doctors sometimes feel like sponges out of which the sales rep is trying to squeeze all possible information. To make the questioning process ''an interface rather than a face-off,'' tell the doctor why the question is being asked. ''The reason I ask, doctor, is that we're doing some research on this product . . .''

Another version of this technique is used when the doctor says, ''I can't give you more than a couple of minutes.'' The rep starts, ''Doctor, so that I can really save you time and get out of here in the two minutes you've granted me, would you mind sharing with me what you usually rely on when treating pneumonias in the hospital?''

''Now,'' Ralph says, ''they'll give you the information, because there's a reason for the question, whereas if the rep had simply asked 'What are you using for so-and-so?' the doctor would feel that it's none of the rep's business.''

In selling computer systems to physicians, J. M. Garcia used qualifying questions immediately after the relaxer or icebreaker. He summarizes the questions, and the reasons for asking them, in this way:

The Question	*Reason for Asking It*
"How many patients do you have?"	If there are not enough patients, the computer system will not pay for itself.
"What type of billing system are you using?"	If a manual or ledger system is being used, the computer system will be more efficient. If the computer system would not save time, a sales presentation would be a waste of time.
"Is there a significant volume of unpaid bills?"	If not, the automatic "dunning" system in the computer would not be of value.
"Do you have scheduling problems?"	The computer system can reduce time lags and provide backups for missed appointments, but this is of no value if the problems don't exist.

In selling GE imaging equipment to hospitals, the rep, after earning the right to collect information, will ask about the projected purchase date, whether the CON (Certificate of Need) has been obtained, who will participate in the decision-making process, and the number of times per day the equipment will be used (to determine the breakeven point). Such qualifying questions separate the curious shoppers from those who are serious about buying the equipment.

7

One More Time: Benefits, Not Features

Everyone knows that Robert Fulton invented the steamboat, but few realize that he also invented a submarine (though not the first to do so). While living in Paris in 1801, he actually operated it in the River Seine.

He succeeded in getting an interview with Napoleon, and told him something like this:

"Sire, I have invented a new kind of boat that operates under water. Last week I demonstrated it in the Seine. It plunged to a depth of 10 meters and went upstream for 1½ kilometers at a speed of 3 knots. It is operated by a hand-driven propeller (Fulton would have called it a 'screw') and has a porthole enabling one to see under water."

Napoleon's reaction: "Not interested."

But suppose the conversation had gone like this:

Fulton: Sire, your most important desire is to destroy the British army—is that not true?

Napoleon: Absolutely.

Fulton: And what is the one obstacle that prevents your invincible French soldiers from smashing the British army on its own soil?

Napoleon: The English Channel, of course—and the British navy.

Fulton: Suppose I could provide you with a method of moving your men across the channel in such a way that the British would be unable to see them until they reached the English coast—would that be of value to you?

Napoleon: Name your price!

The Golden Rule of Selling

The first version of Fulton's conversation with Napoleon is a classic example of an inept salesperson selling the features (speed, depth, method of propulsion) instead of the benefit ("This will enable you to conquer England"). A feature, as we've all been told so many times, is something that's built into the product or service, or that comes with it, such as a warranty or a service policy. A benefit is a desirable result the features produce for the user.

We don't buy products or services; we buy the benefits those products will provide to us, or to our companies, or to our families. All salespeople know this, but not one in a hundred applies it fully. We become so familiar with the features of our product or service that we fall into the boobytrap of talking features instead of benefits.

To illustrate the difference between feature-oriented selling and benefit-oriented selling, let's suppose that you walk into my store and ask for a hunting jacket. I happen to have a hunting jacket that is water-repellent, fleece-lined, and bright red.

Are those features or benefits? Features, of course. What benefits do they provide? Here they are:

Features	*Benefits*
Water-repellent	Keeps you dry.
Fleece-lined	Keeps you warm.
Bright red	Keeps you alive; you're not mistaken for a deer.

What are you looking for when you buy a hunting jacket: the left-hand list or the right-hand list? The right-hand list, obviously. If the jacket really keeps you warm, you don't care whether it's lined with fleece or peanut shells.

Using this hunting jacket as an example, let's look at three basic patterns of selling: (1) lousy, (2) so-so, and (3) professional.

A lousy sales strategy. You come into my store and ask for a hunting jacket. I say, "Here's one that's water-repellent, fleece-lined, and red—$169.95." The basic sales pattern: features only. Not very exciting.

You might be tempted to say, "If I tell him it's water-repellent, he'll realize it'll keep him dry." In other words, if I rattle off the features, I assume he'll see the benefits. No way. We can't afford to assume this. Remember the old cliché: the word ASSUME makes an ASS out of U and ME.

> **The primary role of the salesperson is to analyze the features of the product or service and translate them into benefits that fill the wants or needs of this individual prospect.**

A so-so sales strategy. "This hunting jacket is water-repellent, so it'll keep you dry. It's fleece-lined, so it'll keep you warm. And it's bright red, so you won't be mistaken for a deer and shot at."

Better. In fact, this is called the "features/benefits" method of selling, or sometimes the "features/results/benefits" method. Whole textbooks and training courses have been based on it. The only difficulty is that if the product or service is a bit complicated and has a number of features, the presentation could become quite boring. In selling a typewriter, for example:

"This feature is the automatic erase key. The result is that if you make a mistake, you can backspace to it and erase it automatically. The benefit is that erasures are clean, and you can finish typing the letter faster.

"This next feature is the shift key. The result of using this key is that the typewriter prints capital letters instead of lowercase letters. The benefit is that you can use capitals when they're called for, such as in a person's name or at the start of a sentence.

"This is the space bar. The result of using it is to separate the words. The benefit is . . ."—and by that time the prospect is asleep.

A professional sales strategy. You walk into my store and ask for a hunting jacket. I say, "Fine, I'm glad you came in. What do you hunt?" (Use qualifying questions to uncover the prospect's needs.)

If you hunt iguanas in the West Indies, I'm not going to show you a fleece-lined jacket. But if you hunt big game in Canada, I say, "Fine! I have just the jacket for you. This one will keep you dry in a downpour, because it's coated with a water-repellent chemical. What's more, it will keep you nice and warm in below-zero weather, because it has two inches of fleece lining. Also, you have a good chance of getting home to your wife and kiddies, because it's a bright red color and you won't be mistaken for a deer. It's a steal at $169.95."

What was the difference? Benefits first, then features. Benefits are what the prospect is looking for; features are mentioned only to dramatize the benefit, or to convince the prospect that the benefit will indeed be delivered.

Reorganizing the Story Around Benefits

It's possible to take any product or service and do a "features/benefits analysis" of it. List all the features, determine what results and benefits each one provides, then reorganize the story around the benefits. Here's an example, using a 35mm camera:

Feature	Result	Benefit
Electric eye	Correct exposure is set automatically	Better pictures Reduced film cost (less spoilage) Save cost of light meter Convenient
Reflex viewer	You see what the lens sees	Better pictures Reduced film cost (less spoilage)
f1.4 lens	Takes pictures in poor light	Better pictures Save flash-bulb costs Reduced film costs: use less expensive film less spoilage

Notice how the same features keep popping up in the right-hand column. Now reorganize the list around the benefits:

Benefits	Proof (Features and Results)
1. Better pictures	Electric eye automatically gives correct exposure
	Reflex viewer lets you see what the lens sees, gives better composition
	Fast lens produces good pictures in poor light
2. Cost savings	Less spoiled film because of electric eye, reflex viewer, fast lens
	Less expensive film because of f1.4 lens
	Save cost of light meter because of built-in electric eye
	Save flash-bulb costs because of fast lens
3. Convenience	Electric eye sets the aperture automatically

Please note that this is not the blueprint of a sales call. It's a dictionary of benefits. You stress the ones the customer wants, as disclosed by your qualifying questions.

The sales call consists in determining what benefits the prospect wants, offering those benefits, and using the features and results to convince the prospect he or she will get those benefits.

One more comment about benefits, and then we'll see how our pros apply the benefit-oriented style of selling.

A benefit need not be exclusive. Your competitors may have exactly the same features as you do, or very similar ones. But if you do the best job of converting those features into benefits of interest to the individual prospect, you have the best chance of getting the sale.

Selling to Business and Industry

Greg Deming, director of sales for American Express Travel Management Services in El Segundo, California, contributes a valuable insight into AE's philosophy of "client-centered selling." Portions of his sales manual for trainees are reproduced here as Figure 7-1; they first discuss client-centered selling, then indicate how it is applied in the needs analysis and in the formal presentation to the prospective client.

Figure 7-1. Excerpts from a training manual on client-centered selling.

Client-Centered Selling

Travel Management is a series of services which are bundled according to the needs of the prospect. Therefore, our method of selling is extremely client-centered. In order for you to explain how these services will satisfy a prospect's needs, it is critical to translate the features of our services into benefits for the prospect. Your success is entirely dependent upon your ability to identify and understand a prospect's needs and to communicate how the TRS benefits will satisfy those needs.

We have all been in situations where the prospect seems unwilling or unable to see the benefits of buying our service—benefits that appear so evident to you. This is because the client may not yet perceive the need, or may not see it in the same way you do. You can't apply benefits until the prospect perceives the need in the same way you do, in a way that permits the client to accept the benefit.

In order to be successful, the salesperson needs to take the time to understand two general needs: the organizational needs and the personal needs of the decision maker or decision influence.

Organizational Needs

A major corporation consists of many different departments or internal organizations. To make matters more complicated, more than one organization may be involved in the decision-making process.

In our environment of selling Travel Management Services, we often deal with Finance, Treasury, Accounting, Personnel, and Legal. The value of classifying each organization's need is that the salesperson is better equipped to establish a direction for planning the call, and to decide what questions need to be answered to precisely identify client needs. Each organization has particular needs, but they can be broadly classified as follows:

Finance: maintaining or improving monetary results, controlling costs.
Image: maintaining or improving prestige or credibility.
Performance: maintaining or improving productivity.

Organizational needs do not exist in a vacuum. They interrelate by function and usually influence each other. For example:

Finance need: The cost of travel within Ajax Corp. has risen 30% in the last year while revenue is up only 18%.

(Figure continues on pages 122–123.)

Performance: Travelers are given six different ways to pay for expenses, leaving auditing and accounting with no means of reconciling expense reports and actual expenses.
Image: Management is at a loss in determining how to control next year's outlays.

Though the same product feature may meet all three needs, the benefit to each organization should be explained differently.

Personal Needs

Each organization has key people who will make or influence the decisions of that organization. It is important that the salesperson understand, and relate to, the personal needs of each influence or decision maker. Each person has a little of all the needs mentioned below; the salesperson's task is to determine the dominant need for each individual.

Safety: Needs to avoid risk. Prefers guarantees.
Order: Dislikes "hip shooting." Needs structure.
Affiliation: Prefers team relationships. No desire to stand out.
Recognition: Motivated to be held in high regard. Doesn't need written guarantees, but must be confident of results.
Power: Usually desires extended control and influence over situations and sometimes over people.

By understanding both the organizational needs and the personal needs, the salesperson can plan each call to maximize the chance of moving forward in the sales cycle.

The Needs Analysis

The needs-analysis phase of the sales process is an in-depth interview, which may be with a decision maker, an influencer, or a facilitator. The objective of the call is to glean as much information as possible about organizational needs. No sales skill is more important in needs analysis than tactical probing. There are three types of probes:

Open-ended probes. These encourage the client to freely express information and help you identify a probe direction.
Closed-end probes. These direct the client toward a desired response.
Visualizing probes. These help the client see needs as you do.

The three phases of tactical probing, and the purpose of each, are:

Orienting: to earn the right to continue asking.
Analyzing: to gain specific information; to identify specific needs you know your product can satisfy.
Developing: to build the client's perception of needs; to introduce and gain acceptance of your product or service.

During the needs-analysis phase, the dialogue will tend to go from a general discussion of the client's business toward a specific definition of his or her needs. During the analysis phase, open-ended probes produce more focused responses; and finally, during the developing phase, visualizing probes help the client recognize the need for your services.

If the needs-analysis phase is done thoroughly, you now have a wealth of information vital to your next key event: a formal presentation or proposal.

The Formal Presentation/Proposal

This is commonly referred to as the "dog and pony show," and is probably the second most exhilarating experience for a salesperson (second only to cashing bonus checks). The formal presentation is also the risky event of the cycle. Poor attention to detail in the needs analysis and first presentation can make this presentation more guesswork and less logical recommendations. Shoddy workmanship in this event seldom results in a sale and never results in a second chance.

We attempt to use a consultative approach in presenting recommendations and closing. This presentation should, then, follow a format that specifically relates our recommendations to client needs. A good format to follow is:

- Reinforce the value of the information gathered by citing specific findings and examples.
- Agree upon the objectives of the meeting.
- Summarize and reinforce the agreed-upon needs.
- Give an overview of your proposal, then discuss each component as it relates to the prospect's needs.
- Request and respond to the prospect's reactions, questions, or concerns.
- Summarize and ask for commitment.
- Set a date for the next contact, and again summarize the key benefits to the organization.

Most contributors would agree with Nick Debronsky of Unisys (Burroughs/Sperry) that "this is the most important chapter in the book. None of us does a perfect job of selling benefits. I try to concentrate on what the computer will *do* for the prospect, rather than what it *is*. I've had clients buy an entire computer system and, after signing the contract, ask, 'By the way, which model of your computers did we buy?'"

"In the past," comments John Paul Jones of Monsanto, "most company in-house training programs focused on product knowledge (features). The attitude was, 'Look what we've invented; now go out and find a home for it.' Very little time was spent in probing for a need and fulfilling it with a benefit.

"During my early selling career, I used to carry a product data book filled with about 4 inches of features, and usually found that competition had been there with similar features. Later I found that the customer was only looking for a benefit or a solution to his problem, and by using this technique I became an extension of his business."

Bruce White of Maritz Motivation reports that, in order to ensure the success of a sales contest his company runs for a client, in addition to providing the incentives and the communication program, Maritz often has to train the client's sales force in feature/benefit selling. "It is always amazing to me to find out how many salespeople are in dire need of this kind of training," he says, "and how much more successful they are in the campaign as a result."

Jake Kulp of AMP adds his own definition of a benefit: "A benefit is a feature which has been selected and applied to the needs of a particular prospect in such a way that the prospect gains an advantage by using the product. Sales reps who do the best job of showing believable gains will outsell their competitors."

The aspect of personalizing the benefit to the individual prospect was also stressed by Bill O'Neill of Wausau Insurance Companies.

"Benefit selling is the absolute key to successful selling," he notes. "It is the focal point in getting the buyer to say yes. There's an old saying to the effect that 'nobody buys from a stranger.' When you demonstrate how your product will benefit him personally, your product or service now becomes relevant to him and you are no longer a stranger. Benefit selling can transform the relationship to a point where the buyer feels comfortable with you because you've demonstrated that you and your product can benefit him."

Benefit selling can also save time, points out Roland M. Charles, Jr., of GTE Mobilnet, Inc. "In selling state-of-the-art communications equipment and service to *Fortune* 1000 prospects exclusively, I find that they can be very demanding and time-consuming. Using the benefit/feature approach seems to reduce the decision-making time and more often than not allows me to walk out with the sale."

Commenting on the fact that a benefit need not be exclusive to be an effective sales point, Paul Lentz of Automatic Data Processing says: "Many sales reps familiar with their competitors' features and benefits will often fail to stress them on their own products because they have *assumed* that the prospect knows they are available from the other vendor. In fact, the competitor may have completely failed to mention a particular feature/benefit, so that this sales rep's mention of it gives his product a *perceived* competitive advantage."

John Heitzenroder of Occidental Chemical uses a benefit analysis method similar to the one described in the introduction to this chapter. If the prospect's goal is to get caustic delivered to his scattered plants at the lowest cost, the analysis would be:

Strength	*Benefit*	*Proof*
New product	Lower energy cost	Additional tons of production
Regional distribution points	Faster service	Eleven terminals
Technical service	Help in installing storage and handling equipment	Five tech service men
Branch office staff	Easier ordering	Automated order processing

There are times when a feature becomes a benefit. If the purchasing vice president says to one of his subordinates, "Next time you buy this alloy, be very sure that it's at least 40 percent copper," then to that subordinate, the 40 percent copper becomes a benefit. This principle is illustrated in the following comment from Janis Drew of the *Los Angeles Times*:

"It is imperative in selling space to clearly state the benefits to the advertiser. He has a need to reach a certain audience, and the benefit you provide is the medium to do this. A hypothetical example:

"You're a salesperson for the *Los Angeles Times Magazine* and have targeted E & J Gallo Wine as a prime account. You would go in with the following information:

> *Fact:*　Los Angeles is the No. 1 potential market for domestic wine. There were more cases of wine sold in Los Angeles in 1986 than in any other market in the United States.
> *Need:*　E & J Gallo Wine needs to reach this No. 1 market and penetrate it effectively and efficiently.
> *Benefits:*　(1) The *Los Angeles Times Magazine* delivers 32 percent of the Los Angeles market. (2) The *Los Angeles Times* audience is Gallo's audience.

"The demographic profile E & J Gallo has established as its primary target—affluent, educated, upscale adults who consume wine—is the audience we possess. The point is to illustrate to advertisers exactly what you can *do* for them, in straightforward language. Show them how you meet their marketing objectives."

A purist might say that reaching the Los Angeles audience is a result of the *Times* circulation, producing the end benefit of more sales and profits for Gallo. But to the advertiser whose need is defined as "a medium to reach the LA audience," the *Times* circulation is a benefit.

Sometimes the sales rep, to sell more of his product, has to sell the entire complicated system of which his product is only an element. Case in point: Steven Rand of Dun's Marketing Services often has to sell a direct-mail campaign to sell Dun's mailing lists.

"Prospects don't wake up in the morning and say, 'Today I'm going to buy a mailing list,' " he points out. "The list is only one component (although I believe the most important component) in putting together a direct-mail promotion, yet it has the least amount of sex appeal in the campaign. Everybody is all caught up in creating the mailing package, and typically little thought goes into the target audience. My job is to get prospects and clients who usually have limited direct-marketing expertise to reverse their thought process: Start with the target audience and create something that is of benefit for them so they will respond.

"I use two methods:

"One, I position myself as a direct-marketing expert, not a list salesman. I package myself as one who understands the direct-marketing techniques necessary to have their campaign reach more of the 'right' prospects and fewer of the 'wrong' people.

"Two, I use fear and insecurity. It's 'safe' to use Dun's Marketing (just as many buyers, uncertain about purchasing a computer, will buy IBM to be safe). Now that I've been with Dun's for 17 years, I can appear as one who has seen all the mistakes (and made a few myself) along the way and can help the client avoid the same pitfalls. I sell reassurance; the mailing list is just the by-product.

"The people I deal with are typically responsible for marketing, sales, advertising, data processing—or they're the owners of the business, who do it all. Frequently it's difficult to get these people to articulate their needs. On the surface they all want to achieve the same things: increasing sales while lowering sales costs, generating more leads at a lower cost per lead, getting a better return on the money they are spending, attaining their sales or new-product targets, and reaping the rewards of bonuses and promotions.

"You've got to get below the surface and find out what motivates them to buy from one supplier and not another, the benefits each is looking for, and you're on your way to identifying an approach that can lead to a sale and perhaps to a long-standing relationship.

"Develop a profile of the buyer. Will his selection of a supplier be a personal or a strictly business decision or a combination of both? What's his motivation? How does he perceive himself? How is he perceived in the organization? Is he the owner with an ego to be stroked or an entry-level marketing manager with a limited budget? Is he on a fast track or marking time to retirement? Has he reached his peak and been shuffled off to the sidelines? Is he looking for a success story to parlay into a new job opportunity elsewhere, or an old-timer comfortable in his position of responsibility and not looking to make waves?

"During your selling career, you'll meet them all. The quicker you identify the type, the better you'll be able to provide that buyer with the right set of benefits.

"For example, I've worked with a marketing professional who has been with four different office-equipment companies over the last 12 years. He was a product manager when I first met him, moved up to a marketing-manager slot at company No. 2, moved again to director of national accounts at No. 3, and finally arrived at VP marketing in a $500-million operation.

"All his moves have been within the same industry. He developed a reputation as a problem solver who turned around poor-performing operations. His goal when he started was to end up with exactly the type of job and responsibility he has now attained. Up front he let me know that, and I believed he could do it (with some help from me!).

"I started out with him as a mailing-list salesman, taking orders that averaged $500 per month, and have grown with him to where he now 'invests' more than $250,000 annually with me.

"I discovered that part of my charter with him at the beginning of each new job was to help him establish innovative marketing approaches. He believed his job was to make things happen, and that his best chances for getting approvals and budgets occurred within the first six months.

"I made sure I understood the marketing problems, and put the right resources of my company together to solve them quickly. This happened only because I understood the client's personal style and objective and worked with him to achieve his personal goals.

"I'm pleased that the company I work for recognized the value of the relationship and allowed me to cross 'territory lines' to capitalize on the relationship. I'm part of this individual's 'team for success,' which also includes a printer, a mailing and EDP service, a direct-mail copywriter, and a telemarketing consultant.

"By working with all of them, I've learned a lot about the entire process of direct-mail marketing that has been easily transferable to other accounts. I can't wait to see where this fellow ends up next!"

As mentioned in the Foreword, Gourdin Sirles of AT&T points out that because of the increasing cost of a sales call, much selling formerly done on a face-to-face basis is now handled by telemarketing, mass marketing, or direct-mail/direct-response methods. On the other hand, the fastest-growing businesses—financial services, information processing, and health care—involve products and services with a complexity not even thought of ten years ago.

"Marketing to these companies requires new ways of evaluating markets, segmenting marketing, selling, distribution, provisioning, and service," he says.

He offers the following suggestions for succeeding in this complex new world of selling:

1. Know your customer and related industry exceptionally well.
2. Know your products, at least on a conceptual basis, very well.
3. Know how your product can help your customer both strategically and tactically.
4. Understand which features and related benefits are important to your customer. Always express these in customer terms.
5. Demonstrate how the use of your product or service will produce bottom-line savings for the customer, or how it fills a need or want.
6. Know how your product is superior to, or different from, a competitive product. Always know your competitors and their strategies, and differentiate your products from theirs. If differentiation is not possible, then become the low-cost provider. The more complex the product, the easier differentiation becomes, particularly with service.
7. If possible, enlarge the scope of the sales situation so that more competitive, price-sensitive elements can be pulled through as part of the expanded solution to meet the customer's need.
8. Because of the complexity associated with purchasing decisions, more than ever customers need help in evaluating alternatives. The sales rep who does this best will be the most successful. Always focus on the customer, and then relate your product/service to his unique needs.
9. The less help a customer needs, the less chance that face-to-face selling will succeed.
10. Build customer trust and confidence. Take a longer-term view. Always follow up and meet commitments.

Selling for Resale

Contributors came up with several variations of the "features/results/benefits" grid. Gary Rucker of Whirlpool, for example, uses a "features/functions/benefits" analysis as in this example on a feature of a dishwasher:

Feature	*Function*	*Benefit*
Power-clean module	Separates out food solids, which go down the drain	Food is not deposited on plates during rinse cycle; "you don't find a green pea in your coffee cup"

Rich Ziegler says Drackett sales reps use a "feature/advantage/ benefit" matrix, an "advantage" being defined as "what a product feature does," while a "feature" is "a prominent or conspicuous quality or characteristic of a product or its promotion program."

In their training programs, he reports, the features-only type of selling is known as the "spaghetti theory"—throw enough spaghetti at a buyer's wall and some of it is bound to stick. Rattling off a string of features or benefits without interacting with the buyer is called the "spray and pray" method of selling.

Rich disagrees with the "benefits-because-of-features" sales presentation; in the fast presentations he has made on the retail floor, the best flow seemed to be "features/product-advantages/ buyer-benefits."

Still another version was offered by Cevin Melezoglu of American Greetings. The company's sales reps use the formula: "feature . . . feature function (general benefit) . . . benefit (personalized benefit)." This method takes the feature function one step further by providing specific benefits to match the needs of this specific buyer.

Suppose, for example, the hunting jacket is being bought by Mr. Jones, who is going to hunt elk in Northern Canada and who has six children. The pattern:

Feature	*Feature Function (General Benefit)*	*Benefit (Personalized Benefit)*
Water-repellent	Keeps you dry	It often rains in Northern Canada this time of year, Mr. Jones, and this jacket will enable you to hunt in the rain with less discomfort.

Fleece-lined	Keeps you warm	Or the temperature may drop well below freezing in Northern Canada, Mr. Jones, but this jacket will allow you to hunt in comfort.
Bright red	You will not be mistaken for an elk	You'll go home safely to those six children of yours.

Most of the reps selling to retailers stressed the difference between benefits to the consumer and benefits to the retailer. For example, says Ed Lahue of The Dial Corporation, a feature of Dial soap is that it comes in four different colors. The benefit to the consumer is that he or she can select a color that fits the decor of the bathroom; this leads to more retail sales, which is the benefit to the buyer.

"We pound benefit selling into the heads of our recruits," Ed goes on, "because basically, a buyer wants to know what you can do for him. The battle for space in a retail store is very competitive, particularly in the bar-soap category, in which you have four major companies competing for a small amount of shelf space. If the sales rep is talking user benefits, the retailer is thinking, 'What's my margin? How much space will I need to display the product? How can I tie it in with other items?'

"A poor way to sell would be to say, 'Mr. Buyer, I think you need more space for Dial soap.' The answer is, 'I think I have enough.'

"The better way is to say, 'Mr. Buyer, we have an out-of-stock problem on your Dial soap. You're losing sales because you can't pack out enough items onto the available shelf space to keep it in stock until your next order comes along. Let's pick up those lost sales by allocating a few more facings to Dial.' "

Carl Unger, who sells Zenith, is thoroughly familiar with the user benefits of Zenith TV sets, because he helps train new retail salespeople by working with them on the selling floor. The consumer benefits he stresses are:

1. "You're getting millions and millions of dollars worth of entertainment right in your living room at little cost except the cost of the set."
2. "It's easy to use because of the remote control" (now found on 85 percent of Zenith color TV sets).

3. "This set uses no more electricity than an 85-watt light bulb because it uses energy-efficient transistors."
4. "The beautiful cabinetry makes it an attractive piece of furniture."
5. "If you're thinking of it as a gift, this is a gift that keeps on giving."

To the dealer, the benefits are profitable sales because (1) it's a recognized name, known for quality, (2) it turns over quickly on the floor, and (3) there are many repeat sales. The dealers are of course interested in the user benefits, because they sell the sets to customers.

Concentrating on features is one of the most common mistakes new reps make, in the opinion of Dave Pitzer of Dr Pepper. His company uses the "So what?" test in training.

"If the rep makes a statement and the buyer could say 'So what?' the rep has not stated a benefit. When he answers the 'So what?' question, he is talking benefits.

For example: "75 percent of Dr Pepper is consumed by 13- to 39-year-olds." So what?

"A higher percentage of Dr Pepper's total consumption comes from your key customers, as compared to all other flavors." So what? "So that means Dr Pepper will satisfy more of your key customers, which means more repeat business, which results in more profits." Oh!

A feature of Cooper Tire's operation is its speedy order handling and delivery system. "That's a feature, obviously," says Bill Clark, "so we have to make it a benefit by reminding the dealer how important it is to him to be able to get what he wants, when he wants it."

Like other tire manufacturers, Cooper stresses quality—a feature which converts into the dealer benefit of less time wasted handling adjustments, and a benefit to the trucking customers of less shutdown time. And since Cooper's product may appear similar to everybody else's tires, Bill tries to find some feature in which they are different, and then stresses the benefits of that feature.

"Our billing procedures are simple and understandable, whereas some of the others are very complicated. The dealer benefits of our simpler bills are fewer errors, and better handling of cash flow."

Because the benefits to the user are what produce the benefits to the dealer, observes Larry Nonnamaker of Eastman Kodak, it's often important to bridge the gap and make a two-tiered presentation.

For example, to a consumer, the automatic film advance means he will not miss that once-in-a-lifetime shot because he was winding the film. To the dealer, this means that the customer will use (and purchase) more film and photofinishing services.

Larry points out that in selling the dealer on a complicated program that includes product, merchandising, advertising, and promotion, it's important to convert all those features into benefits to the dealer.

"The fact that the price point is $19.95 means very little to the dealer except that it may be competitive," he says. "But when you couple that with the fact that he can make a 25-percent gross margin, he suddenly becomes a lot more interested."

Another example would be the fast f1.4 lens, which enables the user to get better photos in dim light. This becomes a dealer benefit because his developing service will find more printable pictures per roll developed.

A final note on selling for resale: "The answer to benefit selling is simple," says Bob Chargin of McKesson Drug. "The best benefit any salesperson can sell is the salesperson's ability to service the customer. Even the finest manufacturer produces an occasional lemon. It's up to the sales rep to see that the problems are dealt with.

"It's relatively easy, however, to give your company an image advantage. Go through the store and find a department where you can help it increase sales. To illustrate, we may carry a better line of cosmetics or home health-care products than the competitor. Soon the store owner begins relying on you for profit-making recommendations."

Selling to the Consumer

In selling real estate, the features of a house are easily observed, but the experienced salesperson never assumes that prospects will make the transition from feature to benefit. That is the No. 1 job of the successful agent.

"During our trip to see the house, it is important to engage in small talk," says Suzanne DeNoyior of Coldwell Banker. "This small talk is initiated and guided by the agent. It is meant to find out as much as one can in the shortest amount of time. It is meant to probe for the needs, wants, and desires of the prospect.

"Suppose in the conversation the woman indicates she is concerned about the safety of her children while playing in the neighborhood. This is a clue to the agent to point out the safety features of the quiet street, the cul-de-sac, the large fenced yard, and so on. This conversation is translated into a mental note that safety is a real priority to this woman.

"Or, if I find the male buyer likes gardening work, the features of a large yard, a spacious garage for storage of tools, or a neglected property may turn into a benefit to this particular buyer when all these features would have the opposite effect on someone who hates outdoor chores.

"Ending benefit statements with a question is a cardinal rule in any type of sales. 'Mrs. Jones, the southern exposure of this den is wonderful for plant lovers, don't you think?' (We are probing here to see whether plants are important or not.) 'My goodness, this dining room will be wonderful for a large family dinner next Thanksgiving, won't it, Mrs. Smith?' (Does she have a large family or not? Very important to some buyers.)

"These probing questions often have a two-fold benefit, because the present homeowner often speaks up and creates a rapport that often turns into a sale. Carefully observing the body language here lets an agent know if it's time to make a quick exit or if there is an opportunity to dawdle so the features can be translated into benefits."

Two examples of benefit selling cited by Denise Kaluzna of Tupperware Home Parties:

"Did you know, Mary, that by using our Ultra 21® Ovenware you save yourself the time it takes to wash out two additional storage containers? Without Ultra 21, you have your first pan, your container for leftovers, and the pan you rewarmed the leftovers in. That's three times at the sink. With Ultra 21, you bake it, take it, serve it, and save it, all in *one container*. Aren't there other places you'd rather be than at the sink?

"By using our Modular Mates® storage system, you'll never have to worry about bugs getting into the containers. And there won't be crumbs falling through the bottom of the boxes. That means less time wiping out cabinets and more free time for you."

In recruiting the dealers who line up the hostesses and perform the demonstrations at their parties, Denise has very concrete benefits to offer. "You can make more money in two hours than many people earn in two days," she says. "And besides, we get paid for doing what other people can be fired for doing—laughing, having fun, and even eating on the job."

"The life insurance salesperson," says John O. Todd of Northwestern Mutual, "can't offer benefits that the prospect can see, touch, or feel. The rep is, in fact, covering a risk that people don't really like to talk about. Therefore, the life insurance salesperson must simply compel the prospect to acknowledge that the risk is real before talking benefits.

"Our task is to help people understand their objectives," he writes in his book *Ceiling Unlimited*. "Once these objectives are understood, then finding the solution becomes utterly simple and purely academic. It is virtually axiomatic that when they understand their objectives, their minds naturally reach out to find a solution.

"Never forget this quote from Ben Franklin: 'A man is best convinced by reasons he himself discovers.' This is a basic principle of salesmanship too frequently overlooked. So, to influence people to take steps which will cure their financial ills, we do our best work when we are the mirrors through which they themselves discover the cure."

It's just the opposite in selling Mary Kay Cosmetics, says Judie McCoy, because she is selling benefits the prospect can see and feel. She gives hands-on lessons to groups of two to six women in how to use the Mary Kay products in skin care and makeup.

"The benefits are primarily the appearance, the feeling on the face, and the emotional thrill of knowing you look better than you did before. They would naturally expect me to tell them how much better they look, so I stand back and get them telling one another 'It looks great!' I just play it very low key and let them sell to one another."

"In selling pest control services," says Hal Kessler of Terminix, "the first thing we do is to inspect the house. We make a graph of the house, marking on it where the problem is, what the problem is. We explain how we're going to resolve the problem, what it's going to cost them, and why the service has to be continued for a certain length of time.

"If they have a pest problem, they know they need our services, because the pests we treat for are very often wood-destroying and actually do structural damage to their house. Termites eat a house, carpenter ants eat a house, rats and mice do a lot of damage to a house. Our service costs less than it would cost the homeowner to repair the damage.

"We have one competitive advantage in that we use odorless chemicals. Many other exterminators use chemicals that have a rather heavy odor.

"We also give the customer sanitation reports showing what chemical was used, how it was applied, and so on. We also give them suggestions on what they can do themselves to help solve the problem, such as closing up the holes where rats and mice can come in or, in the case of restaurants, cleaning up the grease deposits where roaches can breed.

"The sanitation report is also helpful to a restaurant in that when the state comes in to inspect, they can show them these papers that indicate what Terminix is doing regularly for them."

Gordon Wallace waxes practically lyrical when asked about the benefits of Chrysler autos.

"I talk about front-wheel drive," he says. "Safety. Gets you through the snow. Better starting and stopping. Five years from now, everything will be front-wheel drive.

"I talk about the seven-year, 70,000-mile warranty that Chrysler offers. Ford and Chevy give only a six-year, 60,000-mile warranty.

"I talk about the 50,000-mile rust protection package.

"I mention the lower price of the Chrysler car vs. a similar car of another make, like an Omni vs. a Chevette or a Ford Escort. Our sticker price is better. We work on about an 8-percent markup, whereas Ford and Chevy and others work off a 22-percent markup.

"I also tell them how Dodge has developed a variety of styling. Our different models look different. With Ford and Chevy, two models that differ in price by as much as $8,000 will look almost alike."

Selling to Doctors and Hospitals

Because of the short time available in most pharmaceutical presentations to doctors, says Peter Pappas of CIBA-Geigy, one doesn't have the luxury of verbalizing a whole list of features and benefits but must stress one or two that might influence the doctor. Although the physician isn't actually the buyer, he or she will prescribe the drug that appears best for the patients because of such benefits as greater effectiveness, fewer side effects, wider spectrum, less frequent dosages.

An example: "Doctor, the Transderm Nitro patch is taken once a day, and its continuous delivery of medication (nitroglycerin) protects the patient from anginal attacks for an entire 24 hours. The patient prefers this to taking oral medication every four to six hours. But for you, doctor, because the protection is longer-lasting than that of most oral medications, that means fewer telephone calls from your patients at night—and, more important, the patient should feel better because he is having fewer attacks."

Translating technical features into benefits is perhaps more important in selling to doctors than in other forms of selling, suggests Ralph Eubanks of Roerig, simply because physicians have a lot of "cognitive clutter" on their minds and won't exert the mental energy to convert product features into patient or doctor benefits.

"Because we're dealing with very intellectual, high-ego people," he explains, "there's a tendency for a rep to think, 'It's stupid for me to translate this feature into a benefit.' Actually, it's very important, because otherwise the doctor will often just tune you out.

"Some reps might have a tendency to say, 'This drug for diabetes has a long half-life' and let it go at that. (A half-life is the time it takes half the drug to be eliminated from the system. The longer the half-life, the less frequently the drug has to be administered.)

"Instead, the rep should say something like, 'Because this drug for diabetes has a long half-life, your patient needs to take it only once a day, and that's a lot more convenient. That also means that compliance is going to be better; you don't have to worry about your patient skipping that noonday, or that second or third tablet you have to prescribe with some products.

"Another example: We have an intravenous antibiotic with a half-life of two hours, so it has to be administered only once every two hours. But we translate that into benefits by saying to the doctor, 'Doctor, the real value of this is that your patients are not going to be immobilized all day with IVs hanging on them; they're going to be able to get up and move around. And then you save the cost of the additional IV solutions required with some other preparations.

"You still have to convert the technical features to benefits."

J. M. Garcia of General Electric says that in all his years in business, he has seen no product so loaded with features and benefits as GE's ultrasound unit, which produces images of the inside of the human body by means of ultrasound waves. The ultrasound sales reps drive the equipment around in vans to give demonstrations in hospitals.

"This is a demo-driven market," J. M. comments. "Our reps are great at demonstrating the features and features of the product. That's not a typo: I mean features and features. But you can't really blame them, because that's how we train them: to sell features. Demonstrating an ultrasound unit can be feature-driven!

"After all, it's like purchasing a stereo unit, an automobile, or a riding tractor. All those items have a lot of gadgets that are fun to operate. And the keys to success in these gadget-demonstration-driven products are:

1. Always, always, always give the customer a hands-on experience with the product.
2. Never, never, never go through a laundry list of features during the demo.
3. Have the prospect experience only those features that you and the prospect have mutually agreed will satisfy his needs.
4. Always be sure that the benefits are stated prior to, and after, the hands-on experience.

"Several years ago, I wanted a new stereo unit. The salesperson showed me one with a 'graphic equalizer.' When I asked why, he explained that by adjusting the graphic equalizer I could literally bring in or take out entire sections or tones of the orchestra. He proceeded to demonstrate, then switched to a radio channel and asked me to try it. I wrote out a check immediately. That hands-on experience was exactly what was needed to make the sale.

"Remember: feature/benefit, or hands-on-experience/benefit. If it's not feasible to experience the product hands-on, then have the prospect visualize it."

8
"Reading" the Customer: Sensitivity and Body Language

Amateur sales reps—and even some experienced ones who should know better—are so busy talking, or thinking about what they are going to say next, that they don't "tune in" on the prospect's reactions.

Yet it's obviously important to be able to get a feeling for what's going on inside the prospect's head. If the prospect is already sold on the proposition, the sales rep can close right now and not waste time in needless yakking. If the prospect is skeptical, the salesperson should make sure the prospect is convinced of one point before going on to the next one.

How can a sales rep become more sensitive to the prospect's feelings?

Some years back, the big fad was "sensitivity training" or "encounter groups," in which business executives spent five days telling each other exactly what they thought of one another, no holds barred. Despite this harrowing experience, honest tests showed that participants' sensitivity didn't increase a bit.

Some companies train their sales force in "body language"—using the prospect's posture or gestures as a clue to the prospect's mental attitude.

A number of psychologists and sales consultants have developed methods of classifying prospects into (usually) four basic types. For instance, Drake-Beam Associates classifies all prospects as Conceptualizers, Thinkers, Affiliators, or Activators. Buzzotta, Lefton and Sherberg classifies both salespeople and customers as Dominant/Hostile, Dominant/Warm, Submissive/Hostile, and Submissive/Warm. Dr. Robert Blake divides the entire human race on the basis of concern for people and concern for results.

Some psychologists doubt the validity of these pigeonholes, pointing out that every individual is unique and likes to be treated that way rather than as a standardized component of a group. However, these courses are useful at least in encouraging sales reps to think about their prospects' personalities and reactions.

Here's what our pros had to say on this subject:

Selling to Business and Industry

Contributors were unanimous in stressing the importance of heeding the customer's reactions and motivations, but divided on the value of special courses in body language and related subjects.

All would agree with Janis Drew of the *Los Angeles Times*: "A sales effort is an *exchange* of communication. You are not a guest lecturer. No matter how good your product is and how well prepared you are, you will not succeed if you are insensitive to the vibrations your client is sending."

Having empathy, which allows the rep to read the prospect, is an important component of good selling, she continues. "For example, if you determine that an individual is highly intelligent and well informed, elevate your sales story to its highest level. Use your vocabulary and don't be afraid to move rapidly to the close. But if the person appears slow or dull, be careful to stress each point before moving on to the next. If someone is preoccupied and you can't pull him out of it, be sensitive to this rigidity and arrange for a later appointment."

"The ability to read a potential customer's body language is essential to successful selling," says Roland M. Charles, Jr., of GTE Mobilnet, Inc. "Body language can alert successful salespersons to any doubts or suspicions that must be removed before the sale can be closed."

"Although a person can say anything he wants in reaction to

your statement," points out Mike Ciarcia of Turner Construction, "the physical reactions like facial expressions and body language are the *real* indicators of the person's real reactions."

"When I first go into a person's office," says Nick Debronsky of Unisys, "I look for objects that will give me some clue as to his personality. Does he have pictures of his family or his sailboat, are there a lot of certificates and rewards, is his office neat or sloppy?

"I look for dominant, demanding persons, because these usually are the decision makers. The ultraconservative person is reluctant to change and takes forever to sell."

Charlotte Jacobs of Pitney Bowes said that a course in sensitivity and body language given in her office was useful but largely common sense.

"I have found that no matter what a customer's signs and body language may be portraying," she says, "what has been important to me is just to let the customer talk about himself or his business or whatever he wants to talk about. That seems to take the tension out of the initial stage of the interview.

"If the sales rep is nervous and talks too much, especially on the first call, that puts the customer's defenses up. If the rep will just sit back and let the customer talk about what he wants to talk about, all of a sudden his arms start to uncross and his body relaxes.

"I'm conscious of body language primarily at the start of a first interview, because that's when the prospect's guard is up. Once he's asked to see a proposal, it's quite a different situation. You know the customer, you are exchanging information, and body language is less important"

"In order to get a feeling of what the prospect wants," advises John Heitzenroder of Occidental Chemical, "let him talk without interrupting. I've found that most salespeople are better talkers than listeners. Listen carefully, try to uncover the buyer's need, and be flexible in trying to satisfy that need."

"Reading a prospect is less an art than a science," in the opinion of Jake Kulp of AMP. "The sales rep directs closed-end or open-ended questions toward the prospect. If the response is negative, more time needs to be spent on the subject; if the response is positive, we can assume agreement and go on to the next topic."

"Until recently," confesses John Paul Jones of Monsanto, "I gave little attention to this subject. My job was to sell, his was to listen and buy. As for a prospect's inner feelings, they should not enter into a business decision—but they do.

"After attending an advanced selling course, I attempted to group my customers into the four Buzzotta quadrants (see the beginning of this chapter) and found it fit well. After that I gave more thought to personalities and responses."

"Reading customer reactions is very important," says Nick Debronsky of Unisys. "Often a number of people are involved in a major computer decision, and it's important to sense the underlying reactions of each one. If one of them is wedded to another supplier and resents your interference, it's important to know this and tactfully get him on your side. If you make an enemy of him, he can make things tough for you."

A couple of unusual thoughts from Bruce White of Maritz Motivation:

"While 'style awareness' training is ten years old, it is still in vogue and helping sales personnel to read prospects better. Everything from the prospect's office decor to his 'power yellow' necktie are clues to his personality and style. Blending with the style, rather than conflicting with it, improves the opportunity for a sale.

"The drama training I had in college helps me get inside the shoes of a prospect, trying to think and act in a way that complements the prospect's style. All salespeople act out their presentations, and need training that focuses on poise, movement, eye contact, speaking and listening skills. I think the 'drama coach' approach is required for most sales forces.

"An old sales manager gave me a tip on selling to women. When they touch their hair, it is a subconscious buying sign, a signal that they are receptive to the sales presentation or the salesperson. I've seen it work several times—and not just in business situations!"

As usual, Gourdin Sirles of AT&T offered a thoughtful summary of the topic:

1. Everyone likes to feel 'special.' Make your customers feel that way, and you have a better chance to succeed.
2. If the customer has a problem with a previous order, shipment, or service, deal with this before trying to sell something new.
3. Listen to the client, hear what is really being said, determine the client's concerns and needs. Have empathy for the client.
4. Always focus on helping the client, not on yourself. If the client tends to avoid decisions, help make the decision; if the

client is dominant, be supportive and provide direction. ''Go with the flow.''

Selling for Resale

Dave Pitzer of Dr Pepper was one of those who were skeptical about the value of special courses on reading the customer.

''I've been through the course on Style Awareness created by Personnel Predictions and Research, Inc., which classifies people into Analytical, Driving, Amiable, and Expressive. I've taken the Gwaltry/Spalding course on the Management Tree. I've also been exposed to training in body language.

''In all cases, the information was interesting, but I seriously question its application to everyday selling. To receive any value, I believe it would take years to perfect these skills. I would rather concentrate on the basics of selling than introduce another variable to worry about. If you are trying to read the body language or analyze styles, you might not be listening to what the buyer is saying. Most reps have trouble listening, anyway; why add another obstacle to hearing the buyer?''

David Clark of Simmons agrees. ''Although I believe it is necessary to take these body-language clues into consideration, I also believe it is possible to rely on these clues too heavily and possibly miss or misinterpret what the buyer is really saying.

''The key seems to be listening. If we listen actively to what the prospect is saying, many of the objections can be handled satisfactorily. It is important for both parties to understand what each wants and is trying to achieve in the negotiating process. I have seen situations in which both parties wanted the same thing, but since neither was listening to or trying to understand the other, the negotiation reached a standstill and both parties lost.''

''I, for one, don't believe in psychological classifications,'' says Bob Chargin of McKesson Drug. ''People are people, and no two are the same. A prospect could fit into one category Monday and a totally different one Tuesday. What's more, salespeople don't have time to categorize prospects. If they did, you can imagine what would happen to the sales call if they put a prospect in the wrong category and treated him accordingly.

''There may be something to body language. But the most important thing a sales rep can do is pay attention to the prospect.

Watch his facial expressions and listen to what he says. Forget sales pitches. Try having a conversation. Then you won't be worried about what you're going to say next.''

Jon Vitarius of Nabisco Brands points out that ''a lot of guess-work goes into your anticipation of how the customer is going to react to your benefits. Therefore, it's important to get a 'feel' for how well your sales call is working. If your initial approach was wrong, you may have to 'change benefits in midstream.' ''

A. R. Flores of Alberto Culver notes that reading the prospect is sometimes easy but at other times requires probing. ''The obvious or easy signs that the prospect is ready to buy are a strong interest in your product, indicated by a succession of questions, or strong responsive body language that indicates interest and even excite-ment over the concept you are proposing.

''But sometimes the buyer is less demonstrative, either on pur-pose (as a negotiating tool) or because he is not convinced of the need for your product. Here it is essential to use probing questions to determine his level of interest. This can be determined by asking questions which reveal his knowledge of the facts being presented. When the level of feedback is strong, the rep can feel certain that the buyer has a high level of interest in the product and is ready for a trial close.''

Cevin Melezoglu of American Greetings is not only a believer in body language; she offers a few specific suggestions:

- When the customer reaches for a brochure or an order copy, that's a buying sign.
- When the buyer cups his hand over his mouth, that signals that he is holding something back.
- Crossing arms indicates the buyer's concern or possibly a question I failed to answer.
- The buyer's disposition is independent of the sales rep, so don't take it personally.
- Being sensitive involves probing to bring unexpressed doubts to the surface. ''Mr. Jones, I sense that something is on your mind. Is it something you'd like to talk to me about?''

''Rather than put buyers into pigeonholes,'' advises Ed Lahue of The Dial Corporation, ''treat each buyer as a different individual, whether he's behind his desk or in the aisle. The biggest criticism I hear about my competitors is their canned sales presentations. That's the worst thing you can do, because each buyer is unique, and you have to fit your presentation into his personality and the situation in his particular chain or store."

"The salesperson needs to know what truly motivates the buyer," adds Rich Ziegler of The Drackett Company. "Is it strictly a desire for profit, or a desire to excel, or a desire to imitate? When you have determined what really motivates the buyer, you can organize your proposal around that motive."

Because most of his calls are on established accounts, Larry Nonnamaker of Eastman Kodak gets to know his customers well, and reading them becomes easier with time.

"But even with people you do not know," he adds, "you can usually read them by watching for signs. I look for nervous signals first: squirming in the chair, fiddling with a pen, going through desk drawers.

"If you can tell that the prospect is uneasy about something you have said, question the prospect further to uncover the real needs before painting yourself into a corner with a premature trial close.

"I also look for buying signs: nodding of the head, looking at the inventory sheet, agreement with the value of a benefit I mention. At that point, regardless of where I am in the presentation, I write the order. Once I have the commitment to buy, then I can discuss quantities, advertising, and merchandising."

Selling to the Consumer

Betty Cinq-Mars of Merrill Lynch finds that her sensitivity to her clients' emotions is one of her strongest weapons in understanding and selling to clients.

"I am a very, very sensitive person," she says. "I easily recognize the emotions of my clients. Even in a phone conversation, the client's tone of voice, the pauses, the clues of excitement or anger don't have to be terribly pronounced for me to know what they mean.

"I flow with it. I use it to my advantage. If a client is angry, I have learned to take his side. I pretend that I am in the same position he is and try to feel compassion for his problem, no matter how ridiculous it may seem.

"At the end of the sale, the flow of conversation tells me how forcefully I can close. I can sense who wants to be pushed into a decision and who needs time to consider it. If I am meeting with a couple in the conference room and sense that they need time to talk things over, I make an excuse for leaving the room, and when I come back in five or ten minutes, they'll buy 60 percent of the time.''

Judie McCoy of Mary Kay Cosmetics is another believer in neurolinguistic programming because it helps develop a rapport.

"Even when working with a group of six women," she says, "I determine the system in which each one is strongest—audio, visual, or kinesthetic—and communicate with each individual, one on one, in her system. Each has her own needs and her own objectives, and I have to deal with each one separately."

David Van Tosh of Encyclopaedia Britannica, on the other hand, viewed a videotape on neurolinguistic programming and decided, "If I had to teach it to the sales force I'd have two thousand babbling idiots. I tried it out on my wife that evening and she asked me what the heck I was trying to do."

"Being sensitive to the needs and fears of the potential home buyer or seller," says Suzanne DeNoyior of Coldwell Banker, "is the key to winning the confidence of many a prospect. It is possible to change a dominant/hostile prospect into a submissive/warm prospect, but it takes practice and sometimes an extreme amount of finesse.

"First off, the sales agent must intrinsically believe that the prospect *needs* us, *needs* our services, our experience, and our expertise.

"Second, the agent must stop a moment: stop, look, and listen to the prospect's individual needs. Everyone we work with is unique, yet many of their concerns are common to human nature.

"Whether they verbalize their fears or not, every home buyer or seller wonders, 'Am I doing the right thing? Will I make the necessary profit from my sale to go on to another house? Will the timing work to my advantage?' "

Says this successful manager, "Empathy and understanding are needed here. Be a friend. Empathize. Dispel fears *before* they are voiced. As Franklin Roosevelt once said, 'We have nothing to fear but fear itself.'

"Sellers and buyers have the same trepidations, yet they do not always have the same needs. An example of poor forecasting of customer needs concerns a house that had been difficult to sell primarily because of the poor housekeeping habits of its occupants.

After showing the house to a potential buyer, an agent apologized for its condition and said that an industrial cleanup crew would make it livable in short order. The couple did not react to this statement and made an offer that was accepted.

"After the new owners had settled in, the agent dropped by to say hello and was dumbfounded to discover the house even dirtier than it had been before."

The lesson here, claims Suzanne, is "Never assume anything where life styles are concerned."

Denise Kaluzna of Tupperware Home Parties stresses the importance of listening to your customers or dealers, being sensitive to their feelings, and thereby getting a better understanding of their needs.

"I had just recruited a dealer and all systems were go," she relates, "when she called to tell me she had changed her mind. I took a deep breath and asked, 'Did I do something to offend you?'

" 'Yes,' she said. 'When I first talked with you, you said I could set my own hours, but later when you were helping me set my schedule, you have me busy every other night.' I said (sigh of relief), 'Is that all? We have guidelines but no rules. If one party a week is all you want to do, that's fine with me.'

"She has been with Tupperware seven months now and is my top dealer, holding two or three parties a week."

John O. Todd of Northwestern Mutual agrees with the importance of body language, or what is sometimes called the "chemistry" of the buyer–seller relationship.

"One of the nice things about my business," he says, "is the fact that I can choose the people with whom I would like to do business. No one can tell me that I must go back and see someone with whom I feel no empathy."

He finds that when prospects are unresponsive, a good strategy is to get them talking about some other subject. "Tell me about your son—how old is he? Where is he in school?"

In later "clinical training" after the rep has completed the three days of initial training and gained some experience in the field, Encyclopaedia Britannica stresses the importance of observing body language. "For example," says Tom DeLaMater, "if the people are 'touchers' and touch you, they become more relaxed when you touch them."

9
Using Visual Aids

There are basically three types of visual aids:

1. Demonstrators of the entire product or some aspect of it (including films of the product in action).
2. Proof materials such as installation photos, testimonial letters, brochures, or ad reprints.
3. "Sight sellers," "pitch books," or "sales organizers," which present an organized story in visual form (the fewer the printed words, the easier it is for the seller to use these tools).

Visual aids can add impact to the sales story in several ways:

They can clarify or explain.
They can prove or convince.
They can dramatize.
They help the prospect remember.

Two pointers on using demonstrators: (1) get the prospect into the act, and (2) remember that you can demonstrate only features, not benefits. Be sure to capitalize on each feature you demonstrate by relating it to a resulting benefit.

Tips on using the sales-organizer type of visual:

- Practice with it before using it on a prospect. Otherwise your spoken story won't be in synch with the printed pages.

- Don't ask for permission to use it—lead up to it by making a challenging benefit statement and offering to show how it is produced.
- Get agreement, or at least some reaction, from the prospect at the end of each page or two-page spread.
- Close whenever you spot an opportunity. If the prospect seems ready to buy, don't worry about the rest of the pages he'll never see.

Selling to Business and Industry

"Visual aids can be very useful to the successful salesperson in keeping the prospect's attention at its peak and enabling the prospect to conceptualize his use of your product or service," notes Roland M. Charles, Jr., of GTE Mobilnet, Inc. "A visual aid can provide a tangible aspect to an intangible product or service."

Except for that general comment, every contributor in this category of industry selling mentioned a different type of visual aid!

Jake Kulp of AMP spends much of his time selling new product designs to engineers. This requires prints, sketches, and drawings. "I use them so often, it would be difficult to speak without them."

"Meetings attended by many people and involving many action items benefit from an itemized list of responsibilities and drop-dead dates so that all can come to agreement and be held accountable," he adds. "Blackboards work well in this function, and most conference rooms have them."

"Only in the past few years have we made extensive use of visuals," writes John Paul Jones of Monsanto. "Prior to the 1970s, they were almost nonexistent in my business of selling to the converter or manufacturer.

"Recently I have used the 'sight seller' or 'pitch book' type of visuals, as I feel they help organize the presentation with a more rhythmic flow of events or features. I have used them very effectively in introducing two new plastic products. Both were designed to minimize some of the deficiencies encountered in competitive products. After establishing a need for the product, I felt that an orderly presentation of features, rather than talking from memory, would prompt more participation and leave no unanswered questions.

"I do not attempt to use visual aids until the need and benefit have been established. When this is done, a visual with few printed words will usually get the customer involved and bring to the surface any additional questions. Excess verbiage in the visual aid only clouds the thought process, as I have already given that information to the prospect in his terms.

"I never use films, possibly because eye contact is lost and the prospect's sensitivity and body language are nonexistent. Testimonials and ad reprints are rarely used due to the competitive nature of my type of selling."

In making a presentation to a group, Charlotte Jacobs of Pitney Bowes likes to use a homemade easel chart covering the main points. This, she feels, makes her appear more organized and keeps the discussion on track.

A tip from Charlotte: When writing on an easel pad or blackboard during the presentation, never turn your back on the group.

In selling the services of the Turner Construction Company, Mike Ciarcia naturally uses visuals that summarize his message. The visuals consist of words, in black, on a four-color background. He uses a "story book" collection of these charts in 11" × 17" format when talking with an individual, enlargements of them when speaking with groups, and 8½" × 11" reductions as leave-with documents.

"The biggest reason for visuals," Mike says, "is to organize myself and to show the client where I'm going. Well-done visuals convince people that you're professional and organized in your approach.

"One tip: Keep words to a minimum and keep them very generic. This enables you to use the same visual a number of times—but more important, it gives you the opportunity to customize and adjust your presentation to each prospect.

"For example, my visual has only the word 'Schedule' instead of 'Most Accurate Scheduling System.' While making my presentation, I get the client's reaction to the word 'schedule' and then zero in on his concerns. It's possible that he's more interested in 'the most understandable schedule' than 'the most accurate schedule.'

"By using visuals that summarize our services, I get 'next step' closes all the time: 'Here's what we do next.' We also use a lot of technical visuals of things like site layouts, schedules, logistics, and other items necessary to the proper planning of a construction project. We're usually presenting this information to technical people, and they're always impressed with well-done visuals.

"I'm convinced that when we're selected to handle a project, it was the result of a good presentation, and that happens only when we have good visuals."

Janis Drew of the *Los Angeles Times* tends to use visuals only in presentations to groups, feeling that they often interfere with eye contact in presentations to one or two individuals. Visual aids tend to stay in the memory longer and more vividly, she believes, but should be used creatively to attain a goal that could not be achieved in other ways.

"My best use of a visual aid," she recalls, "was in selling *Omni* magazine to Apple Computer. The graphics and art of the magazine are one of its main features. The 'spirit' of the magazine could best be depicted by a slide presentation built around the works of famous artists published in the magazine.

"It worked well with the Chiat Day advertising agency, because their emphasis was on the creative execution of their ad campaigns for Apple, and the editorial environment was very important. In another session, of course, I presented the figures to justify their purchase."

In selling a computer system, says Nick Debronsky of Unisys, the best possible visual is a demonstration of the computer program itself.

"To do that," he explains, "we invite the prospect into one of the Productive Centers we have around the country, where we have not only the PCs but also consoles networking with our mainframe computers.

"It's very important that the sales rep know the product well and, in our industry, the software. The sales rep should be able to demonstrate the program, possibly with some backup by a technical man. If somebody like a systems analyst handles the demonstration, he's likely to get so technical that he completely loses the customer.

"Let the sales rep do the demonstrating, and by all means let the prospect get his hands on the program, but by all means KISS—keep it simple, sucker!"

Bruce White of Maritz Motivation reminds us that when we hear *and* see something, we remember 50 percent more of it than when we merely hear it. "In a service industry, though," he notes,

Figure 9-1. **Bruce White's visual aid summary.**

	Advantages	*Disadvantages*
Slide-plus-tape or video-tape	1. Tells your story *without interruption* to any number in the same way. 2. It quickly and efficiently glamourizes awards such as travel and merchandise gifts. 3. It uses readily available resources (TV, tape player, projector, screen).	1. Production, as well as the hardware, can be expensive. 2. The sales rep cannot involve the prospect in two-way communication. 3. An elaborate setup may be necessary; this type of aid is unavailable during a chance sales opportunity, such as a conversation on an airplane.
Flip charts	1. They let you hold the prospect's attention (whereas a handout discourages eye contact and causes the prospect to focus attention elsewhere). 2. They allow instant word/graphic review and cognizance (some vocabulary may be unfamiliar to the prospect without the visual). 3. They are flexible: it's easy to go back, add written comments, remove pages, and so on.	1. It requires practice to make words easy to read, to flip pages smoothly, and to become sufficiently familiar with the visual to be able to use the "key phrase technique" so as not to appear to be reading the text. 2. The presenter needs considerable stand-up presentation skills, poise, and speaking ability to include the entire audience. 3. A flip chart is only as good as the distance from which it can be seen.

	Advantages	Disadvantages
Handouts	1. They involve the audience (touch and feel). 2. They can be thorough and detailed. 3. They are available for review and reference. 4. They offer the "sizzle" of color, graphics, and utility (in the case of dimensional items or premiums).	1. They can fall into the hands of competition. 2. They do not carry the sales rep's enthusiasm and sense of urgency. 3. If the book is handed to a prospect, he'll start flipping through it looking for the price and get lost. The sales rep must avoid this by handing out the book *after* the presentation.

"the product is not as easily visualized as is a tangible, manufactured product. More imagination is necessary in conceiving a visual that will capture the attention and interest of the prospect." He summarizes the pros and cons of various types of visual aids in Figure 9-1.

"In one concept presentation," Bruce recalls, "I did not review my slides prior to the meeting and found that they had been reversed for a rear-screen presentation with a combination of writing and speaking. This lost some effectiveness, but at least I knew my presentation well enough to be able to deliver the message without the slide."

Bruce also uses dimensional conceptualizers, which are, in effect, three-dimensional, tangible "demonstrators" of an intangible concept. For example, Maritz uses a metal pyramid (Figure 9-2) to visualize Maslow's hierarchy of needs and a workable postage scale (Figure 9-3) to show the comparative "weight" of cash versus intangible prizes such as honors, recognition, and awards.

"These items," Bruce reports, "remain behind as a gift and continue to tell the sales rep's story after his physical presence is gone. They are perfect for desk tops or credenzas, and because they are frequently sought after by other prospects, they are excellent door openers."

Figure 9-2. The Maslow pyramid, one of the "dimensional conceptualizers" used by the Maritz Motivation Company.

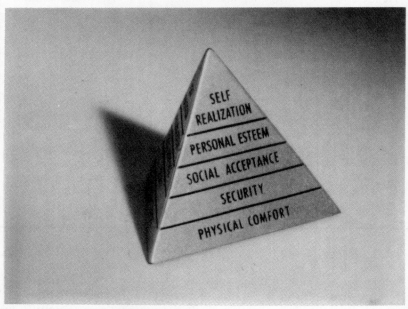

Courtesy Maritz Motivation Company

John Heitzenroder of Occidental Chemical says that although his company occasionally uses a slide presentation, "the most effective 'visual aid' we have is to bring the prospect to the plant that produces the material they are going to buy from us.

"Our friends are usually greeted at the door by the plant manager, the production superintendent, the laboratory supervisor, and a process engineer.

"We meet in the conference room and use a flow diagram showing the production process, followed by a walking plant tour to observe the process.

"We then visit the lab to review quality control procedures and convince the customer or prospect that our employee 'signs his work with quality.' We next review the sampling, loading, and invoicing procedures and actually see the loading of tank trucks and tank cars. When prospects see that our delivery equipment is actually on a scale while being loaded, they are assured that the invoices will be accurate and that they will get what they pay for.

Figure 9-3. *Another of Maritz's dimensional conceptualizers.*

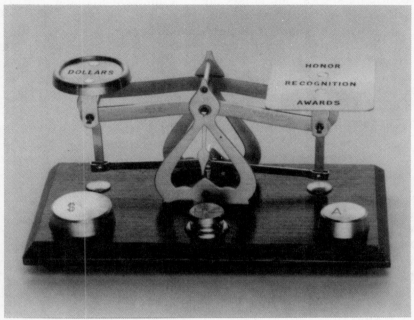

Courtesy Maritz Motivation Company

"The plant support has been invaluable. We have contracted a lot of business through sales/plant team effort."

Bill O'Neill of Wausau Insurance Companies suggests that this chapter should have been called "Using *All* Aids."

"Because an insurance policy is only a piece of paper and a promise to perform in the future, it is imperative that I demonstrate that we will indeed perform as advertised. One of the best ways to do this is to bring in support and service people from headquarters to make a presentation to a group of influencers at the customer's office.

"I start with a short film (we have a whole library on various subjects) and then have each of the support people give a very *short* presentation on who they are, what they do, and how they service the policyholder's needs.

"This approach serves two purposes: First, it helps close the sale; second, because they have been involved in the sale, the support people make sure to provide the best possible service to the policyholder during the life of the contract. The prospect feels good because he knows I am backed up by professional people who actually confirm what I have been promising.

"A word of caution: Be sure, when using other people, that you, the sales rep, maintain control over the whole process. Explain to each participant exactly what is expected of him or her, how much time to take, and what areas to emphasize. Be sure they are well versed in their respective fields. If some of them may get 'stage fright' in front of a buyer, rehearse them. It is the job of the account rep to coordinate the entire presentation."

Although the proposal itself is not thought of as a visual selling aid, it can be, Bill says.

"I have a pet peeve. So many times I have seen a fellow account rep work hard to find a prospect, develop the prospect, sell the account to underwriting, sell it to the loss control department, get it by the credit department, sell it to the claims department, only to fall short because he got lazy in putting together his final written proposal—a tragic and unprofessional mistake.

"I sit down and handwrite my presentation, taking the time to make it comprehensive, coherent, and eye-appealing. I use every graph, chart, cover letter, coverage page, and premium comparison I can get my hands on.

"After all my efforts, I owe it to myself and my prospect not to skimp on the final product. And of course, while I'm doing this, I'm learning and rehearsing the in-person presentation I'll make on my final call.

"I don't rely on computerized proposals, because they are impersonal. I can't learn my presentation by ripping a sheet off the printer. It has to be handwritten by me.

"I've heard all the stories about how some people give quotes on the back of an envelope or a piece of scrap paper and are successful. Maybe so, but I wouldn't want to go up against a truly well-written, professional proposal with a piece of scrap paper in my hand."

Selling for Resale

"Visual aids are a tremendous sales tool," says Bob Chargin of McKesson Drug. "I use a company portfolio that is divided by departments: drugs, cosmetics, sundries, and so on. Naturally, it is constantly changing. I've found that the better the layout of the printed material, the better it's received. Color is far more effective than black and white.

"I'm also fortunate to have samples of various products. Samples are a tremendous sales aid. Often they will sell themselves. A word of caution: Never prejudge an item or a sample. I have, in the past, felt that some items would turn out to be dogs, only to find that they were great money-makers for my customers as well as for me. Prospects, by the way, are a lot like samples: Don't prejudge them. If you do and you're wrong, you could lose a potentially good customer."

Of all the reps selling to retailers, Larry Nonnamaker of Eastman Kodak was the one least sold on visual aids.

"I am not a big believer in them," he writes. "I have used them, and they certainly have a place in some types of selling. I don't believe visuals aids will make you an effective salesperson; they can be used only to supplement an already effective presentation.

"Some reps overuse visual aids because they lack confidence in their own selling ability. Excessive use of visual aids becomes boring and makes the sales presentation look canned. In our business, we need to tailor our programs to the individual dealers, and we certainly cannot convey the impression of a 'customized' call while showing a canned presentation that the prospect feels has been seen by everyone else in the city.

"I sometimes use a photo of a product that is not yet available to show dealers the high-tech look and the professional packaging, but I prefer to use the product itself if available. I want the dealer to feel the quality, test the features, and sell himself on the benefits to the user. The dealer may have used a camera in the past, and may comment on the fact that if his camera had had the DX coding feature (camera automatically adjusts to the film speed), he would not have shot rolls of film at the wrong speed—a benefit.

"It is important while using visual aids that you control the prospect's attention. While the dealer has the camera in hand, you need to keep his attention and make sure he hears what you are saying."

Others were more enthusiastic.

"Visual aids are used on approximately 90 percent of our trade calls," reports Dave Pitzer of Dr Pepper. "They are usually in the form of a sales organizer, which contains information about the brand as well as promotions, point-of-sale displays, and quality assurance.

"For larger accounts we use slide presentations or overhead-projector presentations.

"The tips on using visual aids that I emphasize most are these:

"1. The key to using any visual aid is to summarize each page or slide in your own words. Do not insult the customer's intelligence by reading it to him verbatim.

"2. Memorize the information. If he knows the information completely, the rep can present the selling message in his own words. An analogy can be drawn with actors: If actors know their lines and don't depend on cue cards, their performance is better.

"3. If the visual cites information from a source, sell the reliability of the source, or the information will be less believable.

"4. If possible, always localize the presentation by backing up national statistics with local information. In my business, we use national brand share-of-market information developed by SIP (Share of Intake Panel) for our brand story. We also have access to regional SIP information. However, I stress the results in each major market, as well as those of individual operators. By taking the information one step further, we can show the restaurant operator what is happening nationally and regionally and, most important, what's happening in his own backyard."

Ed Lahue of The Dial Corporation says, "Visual aids are important in selling displays. Without the visual, it's hard to explain how the three-tiered display of Dial soap will build sales. The photo also gives the dealer an idea of how much space it will take. My boss is always telling me that visual aids are 80 percent of the sale.

"Couponing and trade promotions are much more convincing when shown visually. For example, if we're going to have a free-standing newspaper insert on Dial soap, we show the dealer the actual coupon that's going to be inserted in the newspaper."

Ed echoes one of Larry Nonnamaker's tips on visuals: "Don't let them do the selling. Use them to reinforce what you are saying, but don't use them as a crutch."

A. R. Flores of Alberto Culver stresses the importance of maintaining control of the visual aid. "Frequently a buyer will attempt to physically take possession of a visual aid and flip or turn the pages himself. This must be avoided at all costs."

His second key point is the one made by Dave Pitzer: "Don't read every word on the page. Use the visual as an outline or guide to your presentation. Highlight the key points on each page, but avoid reading every printed word. This will make your presentation stronger, smoother, and infinitely more effective."

"Even if you are using a sales organizer," says Rich Ziegler of The Drackett Company, "have the product with you so the buyer can clearly see what you're selling. For example, we recently introduced a new wet mop. Our reps would go into the buyer's office with a bucket of water to demonstrate how dramatically the wet mop would absorb it.

"Keep your sales organizer clean and free of out-of-date materials. It's easy to neglect it and leave old material in it. Then it gets bulky and heavy, and the salesperson is inclined not to use it."

David Clark of Simmons finds visual aids very useful in showing a new product or merchandising plan to a dealer. "The Chinese say that a picture is worth a thousand words. I say that it can help clarify complicated points and add interest to dull ones.

"I have seen some professionally prepared presentations where the rep read from a script with little or no emotion or belief in what he was actually saying. The rep needs to practice with the visual so that he can add his credibility and excitement to the planned presentation. He can slant the story to the individual prospect, indicating to the prospect that the rep has taken the time and effort to try to understand his particular needs, and feels that his business is worth the extra effort."

"Face it," says Jon Vitarius of Nabisco Brands, "we live in a very visual society. Visual aids, bold, colorful, bigger than life, are the most effective selling tool at Nabisco Brands. The visual aids help introduce the product to someone who is not familiar with it, and give the entire story instead of a small segment.

"For example, each sales period we receive a sales brochure full of pictures of our products on end displays. Most customers visualize the entire end display in their store and often say, 'Give me one of those, it looks good,' instead of buying a single product."

His Nabisco Brands cohort, Pat Markley, points out that when one has only a couple of minutes with the customer, the visual aid can make the point more quickly than a time-consuming oral description. The elaborate full-color brochures also imply that the company must believe that the product has a future if it was willing to spend this much time, effort, and money in presenting it.

"Once," she recalls, "we had a contest for store managers in which the prize was a nice, wood-crafted chime clock with one of the Nabisco Brands logos on it. I was finding it difficult to sell the contest until one day I duplicated pictures of the clock and showed them to customers, saying 'This is what you can win.' From then on everyone was in the contest."

Cevin Melezoglu of American Greetings feels that samples are the best visual aid for her, enabling the buyer to see and feel the quality of the product. She also uses a "Selling Proposal Kit" prepared by AG's training department, which incorporates various methods of convincing the dealer of the profit advantage of American Greetings and has blank lines where the rep can tailor the presentation to the specific prospect.

"Another great visual aid I've used," she says, "is a simulated photo or artist's rendering of what the prospect's greeting-card department will look like with our fixtures and merchandise. This is created by using miniature store fixtures and props, and matches the store's floor plan, carpet color, windows, and adjacent departments. It literally brings our merchandise right into the dealer's store."

Selling to the Consumer

Encyclopaedia Britannica USA has for many years used a visual presentation that reps call the "read-off" but which is referred to as the "preview" when talking with a prospect. It is a pictorial presentation of the encyclopedia and its benefits to the family.

A rep leads into the presentation by saying, "I've been instructed to give you a preview of our new edition—it's mostly pictorial." From then on, says David Van Tosh, the only guidelines are to properly pace the presentation and make sure all the key points are covered.

"There is so much preselling," he explains, "that the product itself is recognized as the best in the world. We've been in business since 1768, and you don't last that long without being the best. So we usually have a very, very interested prospect and a magical thing happens: Our salespeople become friends of the family whether they make the sale or not."

Whether "dating" (setting up demonstration parties) or recruiting dealers, Denise Kaluzna of Tupperware Home Parties always hands out literature with her name and phone number stamped on it. "I've received many phone calls from prospects because someone got hold of my material," she reports.

The Tupperware catalog is another form of visual. Customers often phone to order from it. Denise, who is interested in converting users to dealers, says, "I'd feel guilty if I didn't tell them what they'd receive for just having four to six people over for 45 minutes. I really feel people would have demonstrations over and over if they felt that enough people would show up and that they'd be successful, so I do my best to convince them it will be successful."

"There can be no success in real estate without the use of a presentation book," reports Suzanne DeNoyior of Coldwell Banker. "Sales agents prepare a tailor-made 'brag' portfolio that visually shows the marketing process involved in selling a home. Used in conjunction with a verbal presentation, this visual aid is the bible of our business. As an agent grows in success, so too does the presentation portfolio. It is chock-full of the company's philosophical message, testimonials from satisfied clients, photos of our staff at work, and certificates of recognition the agent has won.

"The portfolio is a story of the company *and* the individual. It represents a cue card for a step-by-step story of our firm's services, our triumphs in the competitive market of real estate sales.

"Individually and collectively, the presentation book is meant to dispel the three greatest fears of the potential home seller: price, time, and convenience realization. If a home is priced and marketed correctly, it will sell quickly, at the fairest market value, with the least amount of inconvenience.

"A mini-presentation book is always left behind for the client to read. This helps to ensure continued name recognition and message retention."

One of Suzanne's agents was recently called to make a presentation. When she arrived, she was faced with an audience of six people from three generations in one family. Not knowing if the elderly couple (whose home would be entered on the market) were the actual and dominant decision makers, the agent proceeded at an unusually rapid pace in delivering her message, being careful to make eye contact with each member around the table.

The agent ended with a smile as she closed the book. A short silence was broken by the couple's daughter, who returned the smile and said, "My goodness, you certainly do *love* your job, don't you?"

"Yes I do!" the agent replied. "I feel as though I adopt a new family each time I take a listing. I get to know the house so well that I actually miss it and the people in it when the house is vacated.''

The agreement was signed on the spot.

In showing a small group of women how to apply Mary Kay cosmetics, Judie McCoy uses a flipchart that goes step by step through the procedures she is explaining and the women are applying.

''They see it in the book, they hear me explaining it, and they do it themselves,'' she says. ''They're learning in three ways: seeing, hearing, feeling.''

Jack Hallberg of Allstate Insurance says that computer printouts projecting the results of various interest-sensitive types of investment have become an essential part of today's life insurance salesmanship.

John O. Todd of Northwestern Mutual finds that the simplest visual aid of all is a legal-size yellow tablet on which he draws simple diagrams enabling prospects to understand how the proposed financial plan will help them attain their objectives.

For example, he might say, ''Mr. Prospect, let's let a straight line represent the life of a man.'' He draws:

A   B ———————————————————— C   D

''At A a person is born, and until B he is totally dependent while growing up. At B he starts earning a living. At C the earning and accumulation period ends when he retires, and at D comes the end of life. Isn't that a simple but correct way to see what happens to all of us human beings?''

The answer can only be an agreement. Knowing that a monologue is never as effective in selling as a dialogue, John designs visuals that lead into questions most likely to receive a positive answer.

''Ah, yes,'' he continues. ''But no one has a lease on life, so we all know that D can move over in front of C, anywhere from B to C, don't we? (Agreement) So from B to C each of us must accumulate enough capital to provide money at work to replace man or woman at work. Is that a fair statement of your plan in life?''

He also carries with him his looseleaf ''Technique Book,'' a series of one-page visuals on such subjects as ''Disability,'' ''Inevitable Gain,'' and ''Man's Life.'' Titles for corporate prospects include

"Deferred Compensation," "Supplementary Pensions," "Competition," and so on. The pages are tabbed so that he can quickly flip to the illustration for any point he wishes to cover.

An example is the "Inevitable Gain" graph (Figure 9-4) of a permanent life insurance policy. The numbers are in thousands of dollars.

The graph compares the total return on a life insurance policy (upper dotted line) and a noninsurance investment (dashed line). At age 45 the individual buys a $225,000 permanent policy, paying a premium of $10,000 a year for only eight years and letting the dividends buy additional insurance. At his death, his beneficiaries receive the growing proceeds of the policy, indicated by the dotted line: $235,000 at the end of the first year, $487,000 at age 65, $1,365,000 at age 85. There is no income tax on the dividends as they accumulate.

On the other hand, if this individual invested $10,000 a year for eight years in securities that paid 8% after taxes, compounding the value of his investment by reinvesting the dividends, the total would be that shown by the dashed line.

"This graph almost speaks for itself," John explains. "It demonstrates not only the fact that everyone knows about life insurance—that is, that if the insured dies early, the gain on life insurance is enormous—but also that no matter how long the insured lives, the payoff is always a tremendous gain over the premiums that have been paid."

He uses an overhead projector for presentations to groups such as executive committees or boards of directors. Advantages of the overhead are:

1. The transparencies are easily made in the office.
2. It is unnecessary to dim the lights and put the audience in the dark.
3. The speaker can face the audience and observe people's reactions.
4. By using drop-ons and lift-offs, the speaker can force the audience to concentrate on the point being made.
5. The speaker can bring all eyes back to himself or herself instantly by turning off the projector.

Whenever a standardized presentation has to be repeated many times—as in explaining a benefit plan to groups of employees—his

Figure 9-4. *"Inevitable Gain" chart.*

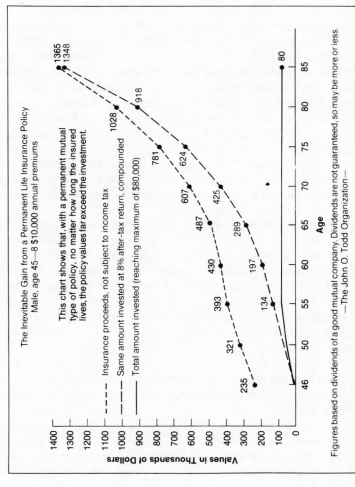

The Inevitable Gain from a Permanent Life Insurance Policy
Male, age 45—8 $10,000 annual premiums

This chart shows that, with a permanent mutual
type of policy, no matter how long the insured
lives, the policy values far exceed the investment.

- - - - Insurance proceeds, not subject to income tax

— — — Same amount invested at 8% after-tax return, compounded

———— Total amount invested (reaching maximum of $80,000)

Values in Thousands of Dollars

Age

1365
1348
1028
918
781
624
607
487
425
430
393
321
289
235
197
134
80

Figures based on dividends of a good mutual company. Dividends are not guaranteed, so may be more or less.
—The John O. Todd Organization—

Courtesy of John O. Todd. Used by permission.

company makes videotape presentations. "This is a particularly valuable visual aid when you want to be sure that a correct and uniform presentation is made," he says. "Obviously, this would be far too expensive except for something that can be used over and over again."

In selling extermination contracts, Hal Kessler of Terminix makes a graph of the house, on which he marks down the problem areas.

"We also have two very good brochures," he says, "one for commercial accounts, the other for residential accounts. It illustrates what we're going to do, where we're going to do it, shows pictures of the various insects—it's excellent and extremely helpful.

"The company's policy is for us to sit the customer down at a table and go through the brochure, explaining step by step what we're going to do. Personally, I find that a little canned. After a while, handling every call the same way, you'd wind up with a very boring job. The way I do it, I usually have the people accompany me while I'm inspecting. If I find a problem, they're right there to see it.

"If I do use the brochure, it's just a matter of going through it line by line with a pencil, underlying what I'm saying to them. But I prefer just to talk with them and be friendly with them."

In selling automobiles, the demo ride is the equivalent of the demo in other sales fields, says Gordon Wallace of Spitzer Dodge. "That's when I try to sell them on the difference between the two cars. How it starts. How it stops. How it shifts."

Betty Cinq-Mars of Merrill Lynch simply doesn't believe in visual aids. "Conversation is the only real tool in my business," she says. "To barrage clients with reports is futile. In fact, when I find a person who studies reports as a pretense for not making a decision, I confront him immediately with: 'So you're a reader and like to read reports?' The truth is that he's not ready to make a decision.

"My visual aid is to paint a word picture that lets the client visualize the investment process from start to finish. I review the mechanics of opening an account and walk them descriptively to the end product and (hopefully) what it will do for them.

" 'Let's say,' I will tell them, 'that you decided to accept the proposal I made to you today. Here's what would happen. I would ask you a series of questions to open your account. I would then implement your decision to buy X and sell Y. You would then have five business days to settle. That means, Harry, that you would put a check in the mail to cover the difference. You would then get a statement each month listing your assets. I would send you updates every 13 weeks. We are both responsible for watching your investments.'

"And so on. He sees the process. He comes closer to making a decision.''

Selling to Doctors and Hospitals

In selling Diacon computer systems to doctors and dentists, J. M. Garcia used a visual in a tent-type binder. One page would list some information requirement in the doctor's office, and the following page would show a computer printout, with relevant lines highlighted, to show how that information was made available.

Peter Pappas, who sells pharmaceuticals to doctors, calls the standard sales visual a "detail piece" which sets up some medical problem and then illustrates, by graphs and charts of studies, the solution for it.

"The detail piece is so complete that it's often not practical to go through the entire visual in the limited time available on most calls," Peter says, "so I tend to use it only to make a point such as product effectiveness, or something that might attract the physician's attention ('hot button').

"Beginning reps start by going through the entire sales piece the way they were taught in the training department. But in the real world, they quickly learn the artificiality of using the entire visual in a time crunch. That's a no-no. You don't score points with a doctor by dragging him through a visual from page 1 to page 6. So use the visual only to make points."

Reprints of articles from medical journals and studies are also widely used, but again only to make a specific point rather than to summarize the entire article.

10
Overcoming Objections

The most difficult prospect to sell is "the great stone face"—the person who sits there like an expressionless Buddha. The sales rep does not know whether the prospect is hostile, skeptical, interested, or even sold.

So thank heavens for objections! If a prospect isn't convinced, isn't it considerate of her to tell the sales rep what road blocks will have to be overcome to make the sale?

Rarely does the sales rep encounter a brand-new and totally unexpected sales resistance. Ninety-nine percent of them are old familiar objections heard every day. This means that the seller can experiment with various methods of handling common objections to find the one that works best for him or her in most cases.

An objection merely shows that the prospect hasn't been sold on the benefits. If she wants the benefits badly enough, she won't even consider the negative factors. So the basic strategy in overcoming an objection is to handle it as quickly as possible and get back to the benefits.

This chapter covers the basic strategies in handling any sales resistance; the next two chapters deal specifically with the two most common and troublesome objections: "We're satisfied now" and "Your price is too high."

Basic Approaches to Objections

Here, then, are some basic attitudes toward sales resistance.

Listen to the objection, completely. Many sales reps are so eager to handle an objection that they don't even wait for the prospect to complete his or her statement before jumping in with an answer. This is rude. It subconsciously says to the buyer, "You stupid jerk, your thought processes are so crude and obvious that I know what you're going to say even before you say it."

Even if you have heard the same objection ten times so far today, remember that to the prospect, this is the first time he has uttered it. It's his brain child, so please don't step on it!

Evaluate the objection. While you're listening, ask yourself, "How important is this objection, really, and why is the prospect bringing it up at this point?" Some objections amount to no more than a bit of dust the prospect is throwing in your face; they can be handled briefly or sometimes even ignored. On the other hand, if the objection is serious and important to the prospect, the prospect may not really hear the rest of your story until you have handled the objection to his or her satisfaction.

"Get in step." The objective of the sales call is to build agreement, not disagreement, between you and the prospect. Therefore, no good sales rep would ever say something like "No, Mr. Jones, you're wrong about that." Instead, the rep, without agreeing with the objection, agrees that the buyer is wise in bringing it up. "Yes, Mrs. Smith, some people do have that impression, but as a matter of fact—" This step is sometimes called "acknowledging the objection."

Qualify a very general objection. If the prospect makes some very general statement like "I don't like your company" or "I don't believe in that type of product," you can't possibly handle it without uncovering the more specific reasons behind the general statement. "I'm sorry to hear that, Mr. Brown. Would you mind telling me why you feel that way?"

Some Specific Handlers

Whatever the objection, one or two of the following "handlers" will usually be appropriate:

Acknowledge the objection and keep going. If you have evaluated the objection as a minor smokescreen, you simply agree with it and continue your presentation. It's not as "high pressure" in real life as it seems in cold print. "Your company is farther away than our present supplier." "That's true. Now, a second advantage of using our product . . ."

Offset the objection with benefits. Some objections are quite valid. There's rarely a product or service that perfectly meets the needs of every potential buyer. So you simply say, "Yes, that is one disadvantage. But on the other hand you get this . . . and this . . . and this . . ."—and you recap the benefits that far outweigh the minor disadvantage.

Convert the objection to a reason to buy. "I don't want to buy this product because . . ." Sales rep: "It's interesting that you would say that, Mr. Prospect. That's exactly why it will be so valuable to you . . ." This technique is sometimes described as "When he hands you a lemon, hand it back in the form of lemonade."

Use the third-party method. This is a way of detouring around the objection without meeting it head on. The prospect voices an objection. You reply, "It's interesting that you'd bring that up, Mr. Jones. Are you familiar with the Smith company?" You name a third party he or she knows and respects. "Well, when I first approached them, they said the same thing." And you quote the third party as voicing the prospect's objection even more forcefully than the prospect did. "But after considering it very carefully, they decided to go ahead with my proposal, and they're delighted that they did. Why not phone them and ask them about it?" Notice that there really is a Smith company that bought your product; that much of the story is true, although you may have "romanced" their objection a bit. Even the Federal Trade Commission accepts what it calls "legitimate puffery."

Beat the prospect to the punch. If you keep running into the same objection on most of your calls, and if the objection is important, plant the answer to the objection early in your presentation, before the prospect brings it up. Once anyone has voiced an opinion, he or she tends to defend that position if it's challenged. Therefore, it's easier to convince the prospect of your answer before the prospect raises it.

Postpone your answer. Although this is not possible in short presentations such as those made in a retail store or in a doctor's office, it can be a good strategy when making a detailed, carefully prepared presentation, especially to a group. If you're in the midst of a complex sales presentation and the prospect interrupts with an objection that is completely off the track, you can say, "That's an important consideration, Mr. Prospect, and I'm coming to it in just a minute. Meanwhile . . ." and you get back to your planned presentation.

Selling to Business and Industry

"It's important to view the prospect as an individual with very personal wants and needs, not simply as a corporate hurdle to a successful sale," notes Bruce White of Maritz Motivation Company. "Objections may be voiced for a variety of reasons, and if one of them happens to be a personal dislike for the sales rep or the rep's company (based on past experience, for example), you will never be successful in cushioning the objection with 'Yes, I understand that, Mr. Prospect, but have you considered . . .'

"If, for instance, the prospect is receiving personal benefits from an existing supplier, anything from free lunches and other goodies to under-the-table payoffs (and we all know these situations exist frequently), there's a slim chance of making a sale by answering objections which are mere subterfuges.

"Certain sales situations demand more involved selling efforts and better rapport with the prospect. Sometimes you can appeal to the prospect's desire to be a hero in his corporation, by showing dramatic results in the prospect's company through the use of your products or services. . . . Case histories sell!

"Some prospects will abandon their objections when they feel that their peers have already 'bought in' to the presentation. The third-party technique is extremely useful when the referral is from within the prospect's own company, especially the top management group. That's why selling from the top down is often so effective.

"Remember, no prospect likes to feel that he is being 'sold.' He likes to feel that he is making a good, informed buying decision that represents an intelligent choice. Most prospects change their own mindsets; the sales rep merely facilitates the change. Hence the word 'change agent' has come into vogue to replace 'salesperson.'

"If the prospect has made up his mind against you or your product, no amount of feature/benefit selling will be effective. You will need to get behind the personal feelings, whims, likes and dislikes of the prospect and create a situation in which the prospect convinces himself that it is in his best personal interests to reconsider."

Charlotte Jacobs of Pitney Bowes mentally categorizes objections on the spot as either easy or difficult. If it's easy, she usually provides a "proof source"—what others would call a "third party." If a prospect says, "I don't think those ink colors you use in your postage meters would look good on the envelope," the answer might be, "Mr. Jones in your Legal Department uses the purple ink and tells me it looks fine."

"If the objection is more difficult—if the prospect does have a point or raises some question I can't answer," she goes on, "I re-state the objection. This does two things: (1) I make sure that I really understand the objection, because the prospect will correct me if I misinterpret him, and (2) it gives me time to think about some way to minimize the objection.

"If the objection is a valid one, I try to minimize it. The prospect may say, 'The counter on your copiers only goes up to 99.' That's valid, so I minimize it by asking 'How often do you print more than 99 copies of the same document at one time?' and then go on to the positive aspects of the equipment."

Roland M. Charles, Jr., of GTE Mobilnet, Inc., says he uses two versions of the third-party handler. "If I have a satisfied customer in the same industry as the prospect," he explains, "I first recap the reservations that first customer had before buying, and then have the present prospect contact a strategic individual—Purchasing Manager, Vice President, President—in the customer company and basically let that individual sell my product for me. This lends credence to what I have already told the prospect and credibility to myself as a professional salesman.

"Second, I use 'third-party' information from trade journals, newspapers, and other periodicals to convince the prospect that my product is as good as I say."

Nick Debronsky of Unisys points out that an objection can stem from a personal experience that may go back many years.

"For example," he recounts, "in dealing with an important prospect, he just did not like my company. It took me two or three months before I could confront him with this problem. Finally he leveled with me and told me about an incident years before in which somebody from my company had done something to him he didn't like. By finding out what's in back of that kind of hostility and by making amends the best way you can, you can often get the prospect into a more positive attitude."

Greg Deming of American Express Travel Management Services

takes a negotiating attitude toward an objection, which he prefers to call a "concern."

"Your job," he tells his reps, "is to determine what obstacle or objection is causing the prospect's hesitation to award you the business. Your key skills are tactical probing and negotiating. Negotiating solutions requires:

- Reinforcing areas of agreement, and active listening to concerns.
- Probing to clarify concerns.
- Summarizing what's important to the client and what's important to you.
- Suggesting an approach that would leave important needs intact, then probing for reaction and ideas.
- Asking for a commitment to a revised proposal.
- Summarizing agreement, reinforcing the client's decision, and specifying action steps."

John Heitzenroder of Occidental Chemical also finds that some objections can be answered on the spot while others require gathering additional facts and benefits to present on a future call.

John Paul Jones of Monsanto disagrees with the strategy of either postponing an objection or acknowledging it and continuing. "As long as the prospect has something on his mind to the extent of expressing it verbally," he says, "if you ignore it, you will lose him and he'll tune out the rest of your presentation. I believe you must stop when the prospect speaks, even if it is an objection, and try to clear his mind before proceeding. A benefit brought up at this point may only go part way in recapturing his attention."

Bill Clark of Cooper Tire, rather than looking puzzled when a dealer brings up an objection, sometimes indicates that he had expected to hear it. "We hear that objection frequently," he says, "and here's our solution to that problem . . ." and he answers the objection.

If a prospect has not brought up an objection, Bill sometimes tries to draw out an objection as a lead-in to the close. At the end of the presentation, if there have been no objections, he will say, "We occasionally get an objection to some part of this program because it is not fully understood. Can you see any reason why our line wouldn't fit into your marketing plan?"

If the dealer has no reason—close! If he does have an objection, answer it and close!

"We have a tendency to talk too much when we should be listening," comments Mike Ciarcia of Turner Construction. "I imagine myself holding a pencil in my mouth; this makes me sit quietly. If a buyer has some negative feeling, he has to get it off his chest before he can react positively. Neglecting the process of overcoming objections is building on thin ice.

"The four steps in effectively dealing with an objection are:

1. Listen to it.
2. Acknowledge it.
3. Explore or question for clarity.
4. Respond to it."

Bill O'Neill of Wausau Insurance Companies believes it's good strategy to agree with the prospect when he or she brings up a valid objection.

"Right now the costs of commercial insurance are skyrocketing," he explains. "If a prospect brings it up and you disagree, he'd think you were conning him. So I agree, and that defuses the objection to some extent. Then I explain why these increases have occurred and what he can do to minimize his premiums. I also point out that premiums were artificially low for many years, so that over the long run, the average cost has been reasonable.

"Agreeing with legitimate objections, while not comfortable for the sales rep, is an honest way of dealing with them. No product is perfect. The important thing is that the weight of the positive facts I have presented minimizes any objection the buyer may have.

"I recall one buyer who asked me to give him three reasons why he should want to buy his insurance from me. I gave him five possible reasons, and he bought!"

Selling for Resale

"It is when the objections begin that the true salesperson inside all of us springs into action," says Larry Nonnamaker of Eastman Kodak. "If every buyer said yes immediately, selling would be boring and our companies wouldn't need us anyway. Anyone can write down an order, but the true salesperson can overcome most objections and increase the size of the order.

"I look on an objection as an opportunity to show the buyer why our product is right for him, and why its benefits outweigh those of our competitors—although of course I never throw dirt at the competitor's product."

Some of his suggestions on overcoming objections:

1. Anticipate what objections are likely to arise and prepare for them in advance. Have several possible answers in mind, and use the one that best fits the specific situation.
2. Listen hard to the dealer; observe the body language.
3. If you are unsure about what the true objection is, ask questions to find out.
4. Never overcome an objection by promising something you can't deliver.
5. Be careful in using the third-party method if that party is one of the dealer's competitors.
6. Often an objection can be turned into a reason to buy. "For example, the dealer may complain that the gross profit on our film is lower than that on a competitor's. But when I point out that our film turns 14 times a year compared to the other's six, he sees that ours generates more profit for him."

American Greetings has developed an interesting slant on the subject of objections.

"When handling an objection," says Cevin Melezoglu, "it is important never to get defensive or argumentative with the buyer. In our sales training programs, we have completely deleted the term 'objection' and in its place inserted the words 'question' or 'concern.' At first when we implemented this change, it seemed silly, since a rose by another name would smell as sweet, and calling an 'objection' a 'question' or 'concern' does not change the fact that the buyer is resisting the sale. However, it helps the rep handle the 'question' or 'concern' in a more helpful and positive manner. Instead of assuming that the buyer is opposing the proposal, the rep assumes that the buyer is simply unaware of the full range of benefits, or that the rep has not clearly answered all the buyer's questions.

"I have found that actually listing the most common 'concerns' on index cards with possible responses to them on the back of each card to be of great help. This way I have a growing reference list of possible road blocks to the sale and methods of handling them. I keep these index cards in the car and frequently refer to them and update my responses.

"In qualifying a very general objection, I find it helpful to ask probing questions to discover the buyer's true concern. I start out asking very open, probing questions such as, 'Mr. Smith, you said you were not happy with our service program. Could you tell me what aspects of our service you are disappointed with?' Following a series of open probes to discover the true concern, I narrow the focus to the specific issue by using closed probes. An example would be, 'Mr. Smith, if your delivery time is too long, what delivery time would be acceptable to you?' This commits the buyer to specific concerns so that if I can overcome them, he/she will feel obligated to buy. If there are concerns that cannot be overcome, I restate the outweighing benefits."

The Drackett Company, Rich Ziegler reports, divides objections into two categories:

1. *Resistance*, which is nonspecific and does not respond to logic—such as "I'm not interested" or "I don't like your company." The strategy here is to remain neutral, make no attempt to convince, and instead draw out the customer with open-ended questions.

2. *Opposition*, which is specific and can be handled logically— such as "It doesn't meet our price point" or "I have an inventory coming up." Here the strategy is to show empathy (see the buyer's point of view), provide information, and seek agreement with an open-ended question.

Dave Pitzer of Dr Pepper comments, "Good salespeople are born, but it takes proper training to become a handler of objections!" He believes in reducing the buyer's opportunities for objections by anticipating them and building in the answers during the presentation. (Larry Nonnamaker of Eastman Kodak was a bit leery about this method, feeling that it might suggest to the dealer an objection that otherwise might not have occurred to him.)

"It is my personal belief that the *process* of handling objections is as important as handling the objection itself," Dave continues. "Since most objections are familiar, the sales rep should know various responses to them. The process we utilize involves four steps:

1. *Determine* if the objection is real or false. Simply restate the objection and ask if there are any other concerns. If there are

more concerns, restate them and ask for more. When you
have them all, ask for the most important. Work with that
one first; it's probably the real one.
2. *Refine* the objection. 'Dr Pepper costs too much' doesn't tell
us much until we refine it to determine how much is too much.
3. *Convert* the objection into a question. 'What you are really
asking is, what do you get for the extra 10¢ per gallon?' or
'If I can show you how Dr Pepper will actually be less expensive than your current product, would you be interested?'
4. *Handle the objection.* Since the rep has heard it before, he
should have the answers.

"We recently compiled a list of responses to 30 of the most
common objections heard in our day-to-day activity," Dave continues. "Our training department is formalizing the information and
developing an Objection Handbook. The intent is to memorize two
or three responses for each objection so that when an objection
arises, the rep can concentrate on listening to the buyer rather than
thinking about how to handle the objection."

Dave submits this example of the four-step process (note that
steps are indicated in brackets):

Customer: It sounds good, Larry, but we don't have time right
now to run any kind of product trials.

[1. Determine]

Sales Rep: I see, Chuck. You're concerned about time. Is there
anything else?

Customer: Well, Larry, business is really tight right now, and
you're asking us to increase our costs. We really can't afford that.

Sales Rep: I see, so you have a concern about time and a concern about increased costs. Any other concerns?

Customer: No.

Sales Rep: Which of these two is your biggest concern?

Customer: Larry, the key is we can't afford to increase our
costs now or anytime, for that matter.

[2. Refine]

Sales Rep: Can you tell me more about cost concerns?

Customer: Well, I recognize that you have quality products

. . . at premium prices . . . and you're $2 more per tank than what I'm using. I just can't afford to pay $2 more.

[3. Convert]

Sales Rep: Well, if I could show you that the $2 we are talking about would help you achieve your annual objectives you mentioned, would you consider buying it?

Customer: If you could show me that, I'd consider it.

Ed Lahue of The Dial Corporation says that some retailers, who see perhaps 30 or 40 sales reps a week, get a bit bored with the process and often open the conversation by "throwing a little dust" in the sales rep's face. This becomes a sort of game for some buyers, but is easily countered by an attention-getting opening statement.

The suggestion about building agreement rather than disagreement applies especially in the case of the younger sales rep calling on the older buyer, Ed points out. "You never want to come through as the young sprout telling the old veteran that he has been wrong in what he's been doing for years," Ed says. "Rather than getting into a win-lose situation, you convert it into a win-win situation by getting him thinking about some of the benefits of your product."

Both Ed Lahue and Rich Ziegler, who sell household products, agree that in the fast-paced on-the-floor presentation it is unwise to postpone an answer to an objection. If you do, they say, the buyer may not hear the rest of your story.

It is often possible to convert an objection into a reason to buy, Ed says. "For example, if the dealer says bar soap takes up too much space, a possible answer is 'That's exactly why you'll want to use this three-tier display, because it takes up only the space of four floor tiles and will generate a lot of profit for you.'" Citing success stories of other stores—the third-party method—is also effective for him.

"The phrase 'sales resistance' sometimes implies an emotional resistance to all forms of selling," says Bob Chargin of McKesson. "This isn't an inborn trait; it's a negative reaction from frequent encounters with con artists who try to get people to buy products they don't need. Funny thing is that these hucksters call themselves 'salesmen' and look upon everybody else as 'order takers,' but I don't know of one of these self-proclaimed salesmen who has ever kept the same job for more than a year.

"As to specific sales objections, the simple way to handle them is to find out what the objection really is and then point out the benefit. Be fair to your customers, give them a reason to trust you, understand their needs, and you'll be surprised how few objections you'll get.''

Selling to the Consumer

"I love objections," says Judie McCoy of Mary Kay Cosmetics. "I feel that if you don't have objections, you don't have a sale. I've done a lot of appointments (facial demonstrations) where everything was cool, everybody said, 'Oh, this is nice,' no objections at all—only nobody bought anything, because they weren't thinking about buying. When people are really considering a purchase, they'll ask questions and raise objections. Every objection is really a buying signal.''

Judie uses the popular "feel-felt-found" method of overcoming an objection. "I know how you feel, Suzie. My next-door neighbor felt the same way, but she found that—'' Actually, it's a version of the third-party method.

She also feels that you don't get to the real, basic objection until the prospective buyer has raised two or three other objections. "If a person says, 'I really can't afford it,' I'll overcome that objection and then ask, 'If we have established that there is a way to get the product, is there any other reason why you would not be willing to purchase the product today?' And she'll give me a second objection, and I'll handle that. People use masking objections, and often you don't get to the true one until you get to No. 3 or No. 4.''

She overcomes the "can't afford it" objection by planting an answer early in her presentation. "I'm not here for a one-time sale. When you purchase Mary Kay products, you're also getting me; we're going to work together for a long time. My objective is to find out what you want in my product line, and we can work together so I can show you how you can get it.''

If the "can't afford it" objection comes up again at the close, her response is, "Remember, earlier, I said there are many ways we can work together so you can get it. We women are all good at creative financing,'' and she suggests various ways of obtaining the product (discussed in the chapter on closing).

"If there were never any objections, there would be no need for salespeople,'' observes John O. Todd of Northwestern Mutual.

"I know that every prospect I call on for the first time has had many opportunities to buy insurance during the past year. If he wanted it, and could afford it, he would have bought it. Therefore, I know in advance that he has objections."

John's strategy, as mentioned in Chapter 6 on qualifying, is to pair up two objections in such a way that if the prospect agrees to one of them, he has automatically eliminated the other.

"Mr. Prospect," he says, "I have no reason to believe you need or want more life insurance, but if so, I assume it would be either because you can't afford it or because you feel you have no need for additional insurance."

The prospect is boxed. If he says he can't afford it, that means he'll buy it if the agent can show him some way of affording it. If he says he doesn't need it, that means he'll buy it if the agent can show him a need.

Another insurance man, Jack Hallberg of Allstate, says that "in any type of selling, overcoming sales resistances comes with experience. When you encounter one you can't overcome, you reflect upon it afterwards and decide how you'll handle it next time you hear it."

"Never take rejection personally," advises Denise Kaluzna of Tupperware Home Parties, "because every no you hear gets you closer to a yes. You need a memorized way to overcome each objection. Listen to the customer's objection, assure her that you understand, then come back with a different close.

"For example, when I ask a woman to become a dealer, she might say, 'I have small children; I can't get away.' I reply, 'I understand that with small children you must be busy. But tell me, how many hours a week do you think a part-time job would require?' Usually she'll estimate 20 hours. So I respond, 'In Tupperware, three to six hours is a part-time job, and you will earn full-time money on a party average of, say, $200. That's $50 profit to you by spending three hours a week, one party a week—or $100 for six hours and two parties a week.'

"If a woman says 'My husband wouldn't let me,' I may try to talk with the husband, or I may simply ask her, 'Does he know how much money you'll make for a couple of hours' work?' Or I might say, 'I never yet met a girl who couldn't overcome her husband's objection when she really wanted to do something.' "

"The secret of handling objections is to understand what the real objection is," says Betty Cinq-Mars of Merrill Lynch.

"In the first place, I try hard to anticipate objections by asking lots of questions. 'Do you have money to invest at this time?' 'Are you actively seeking an investment?' If the client answers yes to those questions and still doesn't accept my suggestion, I ask him plainly what is wrong with it. I will not accept an answer like 'I don't know; it just doesn't sound good.' I make him tell me what would sound good and try again. If I don't succeed, then I go back to those first two questions. I don't want to play games. I don't want my time wasted.

"I always accept rational or emotionally understandable objections. 'I don't have any money.' 'I am strongly tied to my other broker, and I can't be disloyal to him/her.' I don't give up. I simply agree with them and say that in time I will earn their trust and they will ask me to manage part if not all of their investments. I NEVER give up."

Similar determination is shown by Gordon Wallace of Spitzer Dodge, who says: "I just don't take no for an answer, because I know they didn't walk into an auto dealership to buy an ice cream cone or get a haircut. You've got to keep it in your head, 'Hey, these people are here to buy a car.' It's my job to sell them one.

"If they say, 'We're not going to buy a car today,' I reply, 'You didn't come in here to eat lunch.' I said that just today to one couple looking at an Omni. They went to a dealer across the street, then came back and bought the Omni.

"You get objections like they don't like the color, they don't like the way the car rides, they want to look around—that's when you need to overcome all objections by saying 'What does it take? What if I can do thus and so for you; do we have a deal?'

"The most important thing is that they have to like you. They have to feel trust and confidence in you."

There are two objections which Hal Kessler of Terminix encounters frequently.

1. "Why do I have to have this done every month? Why can't you do it once and for all, or every other month?"

Answer: "We're fighting not only the live insects but the eggs as well. The strongest chemical the law allows us to use has a 30-day residual. There is no chemical that will penetrate the egg capsule, and the eggs can take from two to 10 months to hatch. If treatment is not performed every 30 days, eggs will hatch and further infestation will occur. That's why service must be performed monthly."

2. (From the husband) "Why should I pay you $30 a month to get rid of a few mice? I can do it myself."

Answer: "What business are you in, Mr. Prospect?"

"I'm a roofer."

"Mr. Prospect, if I have problems with my roof, I don't fix it myself; I call in a professional roofer. If you have problems with mice, you don't do it yourself—you call in a professional exterminator."

If you make this kind of statement in a light, good-natured way, Hal says, people agree with it and even get a little chuckle out of it.

Suzanne DeNoyior of Coldwell Banker explains that under state and local laws, a real estate agent can't solicit a homeowner who is already under a contractual listing agreement with another broker.

"We must gain our foothold before the potential seller puts the house on the market," she says, "and that's when they're in a shopping mood. Human nature is such that everybody wants to pay the least for the most.

"The first step in overcoming objections is to assume, ahead of time, that we will meet resistance. No product is perfect. There's bound to be a flaw somewhere. But with every negative thrown our way, we can reach into our duffle bag of positives.

"Buyer resistance is often an invitation to be proven wrong. It's a mind game. Objections are hidden queries. They are 'teach me' pleas.

" 'Tell me, Miss Jones, why should I consider your services over that of your competitor's?' or

" 'Everyone tells me that XYZ Company sells houses quicker than any other broker, and XYZ Company is willing to list at a lower commission than you are.'

"Overcoming these objections is easy when you are ready for them. Statistical data are the most legitimate tool. Compare your competition's track record with your own. Point out that you and your company have a proven sales record. Present testimonials.

"This is where Coldwell Banker has an edge. We are the largest real estate firm in the country, and we are part of the Sears Financial Network. As such, we offer buyers and sellers discount coupons on products and services sold by Sears, as well as other incentives and savings geared to the market.

"Then ask the prospect why he would object to your commission if you bring in a sales contract that is beneficial to him. If his price and terms are met, your commission does not affect him."

Selling to Doctors and Hospitals

Roerig's pharmaceutical sales reps use the "get in step" tactic, which they call the "agreement frame." "We don't agree with the content of the doctor's objection," Ralph Eubanks explains, "but we agree with his right to express it. We'd say, 'I can see that this would certainly be an important consideration . . .'

"We don't use the 'yes, but' technique, because that little word 'but' backfires; it negates what you've said before. We prefer the 'yes, and' technique. 'This is true, doctor, and what is also true . . .'" We've eliminated the 'but.'

"We believe in answering an objection right away. If you don't, it dams up the doctor's receiving channels. He'll be so preoccupied with the objection that it acts as a barrier to hearing you."

Peter Pappas of CIBA-Geigy recalls a former district manager who compared an objection with a head-on collision of two autos.

"Once they collide," he said, "the site is a big mess, with metal and glass all over. As a result of the accident, cars going in both directions cannot move until a wrecker clears up the accident site. The same applies to a customer's objection. Until you clear it up, there's no getting by it, no advancement toward the sale."

"I consider the objection important enough," Peter says, "that I stop talking to hear the objection out. If I have something in my hands, I put it down to give my complete attention to the physician, indicating by my body language that I consider his concern of the utmost importance.

"In discussing a drug with a physician, he'll often have a question or even an objection about how the drug works, what body systems are affected, how it will affect older people, and so on. I usually can address his concerns by using material that I have with me.

"If not, I'll mail him a reprint answering his questions, and then go over it with him next time I stop in his office. Physicians are quite appreciative of the fact that you've gone out of your way to get them the information, and this can only be converted into prescriptions written for my product."

11

Handling the "We're Satisfied" Objection

An old-time pre-World War II sales trainer named Burton Bigelow built his whole sales philosophy around the phrase "empty his bucket."

"If the customer is satisfied with his present position," he would explain, "his bucket of satisfaction is filled up to the brim, and you can't possibly pour in any desire for your product until you first empty some of that satisfaction out of his bucket."

In brief, the sales rep politely points out a weakness, disadvantage, or danger in the customer's present arrangements—without knocking competition, of course.

Often the key to getting a part of the satisfied customer's business is to convince the customer of the advantage of having a second source of supply. Possible benefits include:

1. A second source of information about industry and market conditions.
2. A fallback source of supply in case of a stoppage of the customer's major supplier.
3. A means of getting better service from the major supplier—"keeping him on his toes" with the threat of competition.

4. A yardstick against which to measure the performance of the present supplier. A bank representative calling on a potential corporate depositor was told, "We're satisfied with our present bank. They give us good service." The banker merely asked, "How do you know?"—and kept his mouth shut while the prospect's mental gears churned.

Selling to Business and Industry

In selling print advertising for the *Los Angeles Times*, Janis Drew encounters two versions of the "I'm satisfied" objection:

One, the client is using only broadcast media, with no print budget and no "creative" (the art and layout for the ads) available. "You're not going to sell this person . . . now," Janis says. "But marketing strategies and media allocations can change at any time, so keep planting a top-of-the-mind awareness of your medium with the agency and the advertiser should this occur."

Two, the client is using a competing print medium. Here Janis would go head to head against the competition with a solid presentation of both the editorial and marketing advantages of her publication.

"For example, if you were the sales representative on *Esquire* magazine and Hitachi Consumer Electronics was buying *Gentleman's Quarterly* magazine instead, you would do the following:

1. Make an initial call and ask exactly what benefits *GQ* had endorsed: circulation, readership, audience and product demographics, merchandising, ability to penetrate the Hitachi target market, and editorial compatibility with the product.
2. Go back to your office and prepare, with your research department, a specific head-to-head presentation on how *Esquire* compares with *GQ* in the above criteria. Obviously, the comparison will show that your performance is better than the competition's.
3. Give a formal presentation, stressing the differences between *Esquire* and *GQ*, highlighting specifically the areas just mentioned. It's your job to position your magazine relative to the competition. Summarize it in writing so the agency and client can study the data later.

"I once had a professor in graduate school say something I never forgot," Janis recalls. "After turning in an English essay test,

I expressed my doubts as to whether the information I presented was accurate. He said: 'There is no *one* way to answer. Set a premise and prove it. If you can support it, it's right.'

"I feel the same way about the selling and buying of advertising. There's more than one media plan that is effective and will work. If you have learned why the client bought the competition instead of you, go back and show him another truth: yours."

Janis also notes that perseverance is the best overall method of winning a satisfied customer away from competition, and John Heitzenroder of Occidental Chemical agrees. "I call on somebody else's satisfied customers every day. I continue to probe to get the customer to talk freely about his supplier, price, shipping points, and so on. Once I am sure of the customer's needs, I offer the appropriate benefits. I'll continue summarizing benefits and asking for an order for *months* until I become a second supplier."

The "we're satisfied" objection is one that John Paul Jones of Monsanto has heard almost every day for the last 20 years.

"Monsanto did not get into the field of producing and selling 'engineering thermoplastics' until several of our competitors had 'filled the bucket' with excellent products, wound tightly to engineering specifications that precluded the use of alternates. Most of our key prospects were so brainwashed, they tuned out the offerings of a newcomer.

"To break this chain, I was forced to offer my products and services as an alternative source, settling for a minor share to prove my worth. I never attempted to go for the 'bomb and the quick score'—just a step at a time."

Overcoming the "we're satisfied" objection often calls for dramatic effort *and* expense, says Bruce White of Maritz Motivation Company.

"In the incentive business, a long-time incumbent motivational agency may be very difficult to unseat. Selling the prospect on an alternative source of supply is tough because of the duplication of effort required in working with two sources.

"It's always easy to gain entry by suggesting that most businesses are open to new ideas and techniques. Talk experience and case histories, especially in the prospect's industry. Suggest a research effort such as a field study (funded by you, of course) to prove sincerity and uncover opportunities for motivational campaigns.

"Sometimes asking for a 'test' will prove successful, providing, of course, that the sales rep is confident his product or service will be victorious in the test. This would involve a side-by-side comparison with the competition, or possibly a 'trial' effort in a small way with one office or one branch. Most prospects are open to a something-for-nothing approach.

Nick Debronsky faces a particularly tough version of the "we're satisfied" objection in trying to sell his Unisys computers (formerly Burroughs and Sperry) to companies that now have one or more of his major competitor's computers. In making a complicated decision, some buyers tend to prefer the largest manufacturer in the field as a security blanket. If something goes wrong, the buyer can always say, "I went to the largest supplier."

"In trying to replace one of Mr. Big's computers," says Nick, "the rep has to be very persistent and very patient, but there's usually a back door somewhere that can be found: something the present system can't do as well as yours can, some problems with the software, something that's not working as well as it might. If you really understand the user's problem and go in there with a solution to it, he'll buy your package no matter what kind of computer he has now.

"For example, a large manufacturer in California had three of our major competitor's computers, but they weren't controlling the assembly line satisfactorily. I talked with the manufacturing control manager, and he got me an appointment with the vice president, manufacturing. At our first meeting he said, 'Talk fast. You have two hours. After that, IBM's coming in, and I'm going to sign a contract for a new computer system.'

"We literally turned that into a 15-month campaign, and they finally bought three Sperry systems. The whole point is: It wasn't the computer they bought, it was our solution to their manufacturing problems."

Charlotte Jacobs of Pitney Bowes says that when people say they're satisfied with their present suppliers or arrangements, that merely means that they don't want to talk with the rep. If a company says it is buying all its office equipment on a nationwide contract, she asks, "Will you allow me to compete for the business when the contract is about to expire?" Practically all prospects realize they would be doing their company an injustice by failing to consider competitive proposals.

In asking permission to submit a proposal, Bill O'Neill of Wausau Insurance Companies reminds the prospect, "Getting a quote from me at no cost or risk to yourself may simply confirm the fact that right now you're getting the best possible coverage at the most reasonable cost. That's worth finding out, don't you agree?''

Roland M. Charles, Jr., selling GTE Mobilnet, Inc., cellular communications, represents a "wire line company" (public utility), and often sells against a privately owned "non-wire line company." When potential clients say they are satisfied with their present service, Roland always asks, "How do you know?"

"This," he says, "puts the ball back in their court and gives me a chance to pinpoint specific differences in order to get a portion of their business, if not all of it."

Selling for Resale

Some contributors felt that if a retailer is thoroughly satisfied with its present sources, the rep can best spend time with more receptive prospects.

"There is no way, in my line of sales, to overcome the 'we're satisfied' objection," says Bob Chargin of McKesson Drug. "If a customer is satisfied, then his sales rep is doing a good job. What is important is to call on that 'satisfied' customer occasionally, not to bug him, but just to let him know you'd still like his business. When you find he's no longer so satisfied, you can make your move."

Dave Pitzer of Dr Pepper knows well what it is to sell against entrenched competition. "In the soft-drink business," he explains, "the cola companies are the King and Queen. Every food service outlet will sell some type of cola, so Dr Pepper's objective is to be the best second national supplier.

"It is very common for a restaurant chain to begin getting a better deal from a cola company immediately following a presentation by Dr Pepper. The cola companies want 100 percent of the volume, not 80 percent.

"But very often the 'we're satisfied' is a false objection used just to get rid of sales reps. In these situations, it is important to use communications skills to get the buyer to open up. General questions like 'Could you expand on that?' or 'Tell me more' will often get the buyer away from the 'satisfied' and on to something else. Often I've used the question, 'Tell me what you like most about your present supplier.' ''

The same thought was expressed by Cevin Melezoglu of American Greetings. "One way I handle the 'we're satisfied' objection," she reports, "is to ask the buyer, 'What about the current supplier leads you to be so satisfied?' Once the buyer lists the factors, I present information emphasizing American Greetings' advantages on these points.

"By using this method, I am able to shift the emphasis away from the customer's current satisfaction to a yardstick against which to measure the performance of his present supplier against American Greetings."

"I do not believe that anyone is ever truly satisfied with what he or she has," says Larry Nonnamaker of Eastman Kodak. "Everyone wants more sales, more profits, more personal satisfaction.

"With that in mind, if someone says he's satisfied, I first ask myself why? Is the buyer too busy to talk? Is he hostile? Did he have some bad experience with our company? Does he have an office full of our competitor's souvenir pens?

"Based on what I see or feel, I will then begin probing carefully. If you probe too quickly, he may not respond honestly or give you the time you need. I try to establish some kind of relationship so that on this call or the next I can get the information I need to develop my selling plans.

"In our marketplaces, things move too fast, there are too many technological advances and new products for anyone to be satisfied for very long. I believe this is one of the easiest objections to overcome."

When a dealer tells Carl Unger of Zenith that he's satisfied with the lines he now has, Carl's response is, "Gee, that sounds great. I'm glad your suppliers are taking such good care of you. However, have you ever considered that Zenith makes several products that are in great demand and that your present suppliers don't make?" He mentions the high sales volume other Zenith dealers are enjoying in these products and then asks, "If you have about 20 percent of your local market now, why not add these Zenith products and capture 40 percent of it?"

Ed Lahue of The Dial Corporation is most likely to encounter the "we're satisfied" objection when he suggests that a retailer reset (rearrange) the entire bar soap section. If it's an old store, especially in a rural area, the retailer will probably respond that his present arrangement has worked well for years.

The answer, of course, is that products and consumers' tastes are changing rapidly. "To get you the best profit from that shelf space, Mr. Dealer, we'll get rid of some of those old items which are no longer selling so well and replace them with newer, faster selling merchandise."

Selling to the Consumer

When a woman says, "I have all the Tupperware I need," Denise Kaluzna's response is, "Do you own any of the new Ultra 21® Ovenware? How are you enjoying it? Did you know that Tupperware releases about 20 new products a year? When was the last time you saw a catalog?"

"The 'I'm satisfied' objection is easy," says Betty Cinq-Mars of Merrill Lynch. "I make the client say more by saying 'Great! How well did your broker perform for you last year?' or 'How is your pension fund doing?' They often tell me, 'I don't know.' Then I say, 'Hmm. Are you certain you should be satisfied? Should we maybe talk again next week after you have looked up the numbers?'

"This doesn't work all the time, but it works sometimes. I at least give them a run for their money. My feeling is that every call counts—what was the point of making it if I'm going to give up that easily when a prospect says he or she is satisfied?"

When a prospect tells John O. Todd of Northwestern Mutual that he is satisfied with the $100,000 worth of life insurance he now has, John uses questions such as these.

"How did you decide $100,000 was the right amount?"
"Is it term or permanent?"
"What company is it with?"
"Tell me about your family."

This gets the prospect talking, and John can end the conversation by saying, "I would be very glad to look over your whole financial program with you. Then I will take the information back to my office to give it some study on my own time. Included in the information I would want to know is whether you are still insurable, which we can discover if I just send one of our paramedics around to take your blood pressure and fill out a few questions. Would you rather have this done in the morning or the afternoon, some day next week?"

He finds that this will usually "empty the bucket" of satisfaction and get him on the way to a sale.

Judie McCoy of Mary Kay Cosmetics usually encounters the "I'm satisfied" objection when telephoning a woman to invite her to an "appointment" or demonstration. If the woman says, "I only use Brand X, and I'm quite satisfied with it," Judie's response is, "Terrific! I know several women who used to use that product. That's all the more reason why I'd like to get your opinion on our product." Asking someone to give an opinion is almost irresistible.

If, at the end of the demonstration, one of the prospects says she still has a supply of her present brand left, Judie's response is, "That's terrific. How does your face feel now?" The prospect usually replies, "I really like this." Judie: "Wouldn't you agree it's something like getting a prescription from your doctor? If he prescribes something that works better for you, you'd start using that even if the first one wasn't used up, wouldn't you?"

When Hal Kessler of Terminix International phones a commercial account such as a restaurant and finds that it feels it has no pest problem or is happy with its present exterminator, he may or may not try to overcome the obstacle.

"If he is very happy with his present arrangements," Hal says, "I feel it would be a very tough sale with a slim chance of closing. Time is precious. I can invest my time more profitably elsewhere.

"But if I feel I might have a chance, I may say, 'Mr. Jones, let me come down and give you a free inspection and explain the advantages and the costs of having your building serviced by Terminix. You may find that you like the way we do things compared with the way they're being done now.'

"Or, if I feel the possibility of a sale doesn't justify the free inspection, I'll say, 'Well, Mr. Jones, do me a favor. If you should have any extermination problems in the future, please be kind enough to give me a call. Meantime I'll send you out a letter and a brochure explaining what we do, and if you have a problem in the future, please give me a call.' "

Selling to Doctors and Hospitals

J. M. Garcia, when selling Diacon computer equipment to doctors and dentists, had two ways of replying to prospects who said they were satisfied with their manual methods.

One would be to ask, "Are you really satisfied with spending a day and a half getting your bills out when you could do it in two hours? Are you really satisfied with taking two hours to set up the day's files when it could be done with the touch of a button?"

Another method would be to say, "I know how you feel, Doctor. I was satisfied with my Volkswagon until I got a BMW.Then my expectations about transportation changed radically."

When a physician tells a Roerig rep that he or she is satisfied with the medicine currently used, the reply is, "Dr. Jones, I certainly appreciate the fact that when you're using something that is giving you what you want, you see no reason to change. May I ask you this: If I can show you three real advantages of our product, would you be willing to reconsider?" Usually the doctor will reply, "Okay, let's hear what you have to say."

"Notice," says Ralph Eubanks, "that we ask him only to 'reevaluate' or 'reconsider.' It would be a little pushy to ask, 'Would you be willing to prescribe it?' As to the three advantages, you can usually find three differences in your product—subtle ones, but they can be massaged. You can often think of advantages to one segment of his practice: elderly people or children or hypertensives. I don't believe in asking for too much; once you have part of his business, you can expand it. If the rep asks, 'Will you put all your pneumonia patients on our antibiotic?' the doctor is not going to agree. It's too complex a disease—he has to run tests on each patient to identify the pathogen."

Peter Pappas of CIBA-Geigy encountered the "I'm satisfied" objection head-on when his company introduced a potassium supplement in tablet form about 11 years ago. Doctors were almost universally prescribing a liquid version, since an older tablet version had proved unsafe because it occasionally perforated the stomach lining. When CIBA-Geigy reps introduced their new Slow-K® tablet, the doctors' responses were that tablets were dangerous and that the liquid worked fine and cost less than the new tablets.

The CIBA-Geigy rep first had to convince the doctor of the safety of the new tablet, and then continue to reinforce the negatives of the competition. This was accomplished by positive selling: "As you know, doctor, the liquid version has a strong and very unpleasant metallic taste. When you ask patients to take it before breakfast, on an empty stomach, it can destroy their appetite for hours. As a result, they're tempted to skip the medicine, and that makes their condition worse.

"Our tablet contains the same salt as the liquid—potassium chloride—and it's easy and pleasant to take. Your patients will find that well worth the few pennies of difference, and you'll have less trouble with compliance."

"It wasn't easy, but slowly doctors began switching their patients to the tablet. In the last ten years, Slow-K® has sold 10 billion tablets and captured 50 percent of the market—not too shabby a record in penetrating a market that was 'satisfied.' "

12

Handling the Price Objection

Unless the sales rep has the least expensive product or service in town, a frequently heard objection is "Your price is too high" or "That costs too much."

The sales rep is justified in politely asking the prospect, "In what way?" or "How do you mean?" because the price objection is really three different kinds of objections masquerading under one name. The best method of overcoming a price objection is determined by the nature of the objection. It may mean any of the following:

"I want it, but I simply can't afford it." In this case, the sales rep tries to help the customer buy the product by (1) arranging for a financing or lease plan, (2) arranging a trade-in or sale of the customer's existing equipment, or (3) selling a less expensive model, or a smaller quantity, or part of the proposed activity.

"I can get the identical product elsewhere at a lower price." If this is really the case—bearing in mind that the prospect will sometimes use this ploy to try to beat down the salesperson's price—the sales rep must be prepared to offer additional advantages of doing business with his or her company. This might be better maintenance or service, the availability of related products or services, or assistance with the customer's manufacturing or marketing plans.

"I can buy a less expensive product (service) that will serve my needs

just as well.'' The strategy here is to point out the benefits of the unique features of the sales rep's product or company. This is not limited to the product itself; it can include such things as service, warranties, credit terms, or marketing assistance.

Selling to Business and Industry

Price is rarely a problem to Nick Debronsky of Unisys. "If I have a solution to their problem," he says, "who cares what the price is? In most sales of big computers, price isn't a major consideration."

Bruce White of Maritz Motivation submitted a summary of the strategies in countering a price objection, as they apply not only to the intangible motivational programs he sells but to tangible products as well.

"There's a big difference between *actual* and *perceived* value," he writes. "Most objections to price probably should be countered with the query 'As compared to what?' Obviously, this is flippant and cannot be literally said in most cases, but the viewpoint of the buyer can be biased in many ways. His perspective is developed over time by many stimuli: observations, experiences, competitive claims, and so forth. He may, in fact, not know the current value of the seller's product or service.

"The sales rep needs to determine the prospect's level of understanding and sophistication regarding the product being offered, and to be prepared to respond in a way that supports *value*, not cost. The tools the sales rep uses are product differentiation, product support, product value, and product application.

"Product differentiation. Point out unique features and benefits. Convince the prospect that no like product or service exists.

"Product support. People, after all, make the difference in manufacturing, delivering, and servicing the product. Sell your people. Team up on prospective customers.

"Product value. Over and above the price tag, there are extrinsic and intrinsic values. Depending upon the nature of the product or service, these might include:

Resale value
Frequency of service
Warranty
Availability

Loan value or guaranteed buy-back
Packaging
Reputation of company or product

"The list goes on—and so should the sales rep!

"*Product application.* Sophisticated methods of *applying* the product or service will often win the sale when price alone will not. Creativity is the key to opening the customer's mind to avenues previously unexplored.

"In the sales-incentive business, for example, certain types of structures have favorable tax treatment for the sponsoring organization and for the award winners. If those areas are not thoroughly explored, the sales campaign can backfire when 1099 or W-2 forms are issued.

"Assuring the customer that this concern is being addressed can create credibility and lead to the sale. One would think that all suppliers would understand and practice this in dealing with prospective customers, but the tax issue is complicated and is often simply avoided by salespeople.

"Sometimes the price objection is not real—just the prospect's way of looking for a 'deal.' The sales rep needs to be sensitive to this prospect's need to 'win.' Have a backup offer ready, one that varies the look of the proposal or does some unique discounting or rebating based on volume. You can often get more business or close faster with a different pricing proposal.

"We've often been able to compete favorably against low-priced competition by offering program-promotion allowances pegged to awards volume. As merchandise and travel awards increase, an accrual fund develops based on a percentage of billing. The fund can be used to buy additional program services such as promotional materials.

"Whenever the prospect asks the supplier to 'sharpen his pencil' (read: lower the price), the supplier needs to take some type of action. Refusing to change a bid rarely results in a sale. If the prospect is under no time constraints, this phase of whittling down the supplier's price can go on indefinitely, so be prepared to link the 'new deal' with a 'limited time offer' or some other cutoff technique.

"The 'new deal' could be one or more of the following:

Actually reducing the price.
Changing the product or service delivered.
Changing the terms.

"For example, if a travel program cost is 'too high,' we'll often resubmit a bid that:

Reduces gross margins.

Changes the hotel or itinerary features, such as cocktail parties or entertainment.

Removes or changes elements that are fixed but hidden, such as the number of accompanying travel staff, insurance, or gratuities.

"Obviously, it is preferable to reduce price without reducing profitability, although competitive pressures can often cause shrinking margins."

Janis Drew of the *Los Angeles Times* describes a different kind of price objection:

"When selling space to national advertisers," she notes, "a 'price' objection usually takes the form of 'we don't have the budget to go deeper.' For example, a computer manufacturer may be buying a selection of the 'business books' (*Fortune, Forbes, Inc., Wall Street Journal*) and the 'newsweeklies' (*Time, Newsweek, U.S. News and World Report*), but you're selling a general-interest publication such as *Life* magazine. The advertiser tells you he doesn't have the funds to go outside the tier of business and newsweekly publications.

"You have to demonstrate what customers they're missing by eliminating your readership. To increase market share, the advertiser needs to extend his traditional audience, which is often already saturated, and go beyond the 'core' target audience. If it makes sense, he can't afford *not* to advertise.

"Also, if your advertiser has a limited budget, always show him how your medium can extend his investment so he's not just buying space. Involve him in merchandising and research products that will benefit his distribution at no additional cost. Be creative.

"I firmly believe that people will pay for what they've been made to believe has a value. It's a level of expectation that is met."

"He who lives by price dies by price," quotes Bill O'Neill of Wausau Insurance Companies. "I try never to discuss price or make any promises about cutting premiums, because that leaves me with just one arrow in my quiver. If I can't deliver on my promise of lower premiums, then I won't get—and don't deserve—the sale.

"Rather, I discuss value, getting more for the buyer's premium dollar than he is currently getting. If you get an account by price, that account will leave you for price. If you get an account because of superior service and effort and value, that account will stay with you regardless of price.

"Buyers are smart. They know the benefit of a value-oriented service or product in the long run.

"Believe it or not, I recall a fellow account rep who did not get a good account because the premium was so low as to be incredible. It was a legitimate premium—just too low. A year later, that same account rep went back to that same buyer with the same insurance program, but due to changed industry conditions the premium was now 30 percent higher—and he got the account!"

Price objections are the most difficult obstacles encountered in selling commodity chemicals, reports John Heitzenroder of Occidental Chemical. "Price has been king for the last few years, because raw-material costs affect the profitability of the manufactured products. The sales rep must see the buyer's point of view, but at the same time point out the advantages of product quality, service, and technical support. The buyer will let the supplier make a reasonable product today in order to have the security of buying from a long-term viable supplier."

Often it's possible to overcome a price objection by giving the prospect the "whole picture" of the product application, says Charlotte Jacobs of Pitney Bowes. "When somebody tells me, 'I can get similar equipment for $2,000 less,' I point out that we have the best service department in the industry, and that over the years that may be worth many times over the saving on the less expensive equipment. Or sometimes the competitive equipment requires paper or labels that are much more expensive than ours. The price objection forces me to be creative and to look for the one little niche in the total picture that will grab the prospect's attention."

When John Paul Jones of Monsanto hears the "Your price is too high" objection, he often counters with "In what way?" or "How do you mean?" If the sales rep knows the buyer, he can delay the close, uncover the real reason behind the price objection, and come up with an alternative solution.

"When faced with the buyer who says he can get the identical article elsewhere at a lower price," he adds, "I see nothing wrong with asking him to document this lower offer. It then becomes a choice between meeting the competitive price (if service and assistance are really equal) or bringing out new benefits to make your product attractive at a higher price."

Jake Kulp of AMP points out that a product may be overengineered or overdesigned in the sense that it can perform more functions than the customer needs. In that case, the customer will not pay a premium price for product attributes he does not need.

"On the other hand," Jake adds, "while the up-front cost of using a less expensive product may look attractive to a buyer, other costs of using it may be much higher due to our superior quality. More and more of the major companies are trying to assign a dollar value to high quality and service."

Roland M. Charles, Jr., of GTE Mobilnet, Inc., finds that the rep can usually overcome a price objection if he can cite unique benefits of his product, or show that it will help the customer increase his productivity. "As the old saying goes," he adds, "you get what you pay for."

Selling for Resale

A price objection raised by a wholesaler or retailer may mean one of several things: (1) both the wholesale and the retail price are so high that customers won't buy; (2) the wholesale price should be lower because the going retail price doesn't leave enough margin; or (3) "I need a lower wholesale price to compete against other brands with lower retail prices than yours."

"It's important to clarify the price objection," points out Dave Pitzer of Dr Pepper. "In my business, confusion over the real net price stems from the multitude of allowances or discounts that all our competitors offer. Since Dr Pepper is net-priced, it is sometimes difficult to make price comparisons. I've had buyers tell me Dr Pepper was more expensive than what they were using, only to learn that it was actually less expensive.

"If your product really is more expensive than competition, there had better be reasons why, and the salesperson is responsible for communicating these reasons to the buyer. If you are successful in communicating the added benefits, you will most likely get the sale.

"Dr Pepper is occasionally higher in price than the brand we are competing with. The major points of difference we discuss include:

"*National brand awareness.* Typically, the brand we are competing against is what we call a 'flavor,' such as orange or root beer. Neither product has national brand awareness.

"*Incremental marketing support.* The cola companies support their cokes and diet cokes but do not place support behind their flavors. Therefore, when restaurant operators add Dr Pepper to their fountain machine, they continue to receive the marketing support of their cola suppliers, *plus* they now receive support from Dr Pepper as well. This incremental support reduces the actual price."

When retailers tell Pat Markley of Nabisco Brands that they can buy identical cookies for less, Pat reminds them of the value of the Nabisco Brands name (which speeds turnover) and of the better service Nabisco Brands gives its retailers. A large retail outlet may see a Nabisco Brands rep as often as four times a week.

If the retailer mentions a less expensive competitive product, Pat points out that many of these imitation brands are here today, gone tomorrow. If a customer buys one of the off brands, likes it, and comes back to buy again, only to find it is no longer available, the retailer gains nothing but ill will.

Her cohort at Nabisco Brands, Jonathan Vitarius, says the price objection can be raised by either the retailer or the consumer. If the dealer complains about low gross margin, Jon reminds him of the sales volume in Nabisco Brands and points out that the turnover rate more than makes up for a lower margin percentage. If a customer complains about costs, his answer is, "It costs money to produce a high-quality product. Did you know that the figs in our Fig Newtons are imported from India to assure the highest-quality figs? How many other fig bars go to that expense?"

Bill Clark of Cooper Tire uses a third-party method of overcoming a price objection. If the dealer asks about prices prematurely while Bill is presenting his program, he says, "Price is the thunder of our program, and I'm not going to let you steal our thunder— we'll get to prices in a minute," and goes on with his presentation.

If the dealer mentions a lower-priced competitor after hearing Cooper's price, Bill says, "Smith and Jones and Green (all successful Cooper dealers) get the same competitive offers you do, but they've found it more profitable to handle our line." It's reassuring to the prospect, Bill feels, to know that other very successful dealers have decided to go with Cooper.

If the competitor is a much larger tire manufacturer, Bill counters with the benefits of doing business "with a small company in a large industry": (1) More personal contact—"We call on you eyeball-to-eyeball instead of handling you by phone." (2) Cooper handles order filling and shipping more efficiently than some larger companies. (3) "When you send a truck to our distribution center to pick up tires, it's in and out in an hour, compared with half a day at some large distribution centers." (4) Cooper quality is as good as anyone's. (5) Cooper doesn't try to control the dealer's promotions. Some major tire manufacturers insist that their name dominate the dealer ads. "We let you advertise your company; we don't force you to advertise our tires."

Sometimes a retailer will say, "My competitor down the street is advertising tires at $30. How can I pay you $28 for your tires and compete with him?" Or a wholesaler will complain, "My competitor is selling a tire for $25 comparable to the one you want me to pay $24 for. I can perhaps get a dollar more for your tire, but not $5 more."

Bill can sometimes offer an additional discount if the customer buys a larger quantity, but when that's not possible, the answer is: "Price is the last thing consumers think about when they buy tires. They may talk price, but what they really want is quality and reliability."

When a dealer asks Ed Lahue of The Dial Corporation for a better price, the answer is that Dial will give the dealer extra allowances for advertising or display. If he knows there is an advertising allowance of $1 a case, Ed will say to a dealer, "Mr. Buyer, if you can issue me a purchase order for a full truckload today, I'll call the office and get you that dollar a case."

"Of all the objections, the one I hear most is price," says Bob Chargin of McKesson Drug. "We are all price-conscious. When I'm not selling, I'm a consumer, and I like to get the most for my money. I've learned, however, that price isn't everything. I know there are discounters who can beat my price, so what I have to sell is our financing, our design department, or my own services.

"An example: Although the bulk of my job is to sell products for resale, there are times when I sell other products like fixtures or carpeting to the pharmacies. A few years back, one of my accounts, the cornerstone pharmacy in a rural shopping center, decided to recarpet. He had gotten a lower price from a discounter. The recarpeting was a sticky job, because all the fixtures and goods had to be moved outside overnight. Since the weather was inclement, the druggist decided to rent some movable storage containers at a cost of more than $500.

"When I discovered this, I asked him to hold off for a short while. I made a special trip to the area and surveyed the shopping center. I found a small enclosed mall area that closed at 11 P.M. I phoned the owner of the center and explained our problem. He was more than happy to let us use the area overnight. The pharmacist was overjoyed. That $500 in savings made his new carpet a real bargain that the discounter couldn't match.

"Also, there are times when I might suggest that a customer buy a much larger quantity than usual during a promotion. Price objections evaporate when I explain the overall savings and higher profit margin."

In Carl Unger's case, it is often a question of showing a dealer how to overcome a price objection. For example, one dealer complained that a customer told him a competitor offered a brand-name VCR for $60 less than his already low retail price.

"What did you do about it?" Carl asked.

"I told him to go back and buy it from that dealer."

Carl almost exploded. "There is no reason that sale shouldn't have been yours," he said.

"Did you tell him about the excellent service you give on VCRs—that you had been to the Zenith school, had purchased special tools, and were highly experienced in servicing VCRs?

"Did you tell him that you have been providing good service to your customers right here in this town for 16 years?

"Did you mention that your price includes a special additional tape-head warranty for another year that could save your customer $150?

"You have all these things going for you that your competitor doesn't have, and a fine product as well. If I were that retail customer and you had told me all these things, I would have bought from you."

And the dealer had to agree.

There will always be a low-price leader in every category of service or product, notes A. R. Flores of Alberto Culver. "If your product or service is higher-priced, it is important that you establish the superior qualities and benefits of your product over your competitor's. Know the quality of your product in comparison to your competitor's. 'The pleasure of the cheap price will be forgotten long before the disappointment of the low quality.' "

In the greeting-card business, says Cevin Melezoglu of American Greetings, the bare gross-margin figures can be misleading, because other policies of the manufacturer can either increase or decrease the true cost to the dealer.

"We use a new formula called Direct Product Profitability, or DPP for short," she reports. "It is a more accurate measure of the profitability of a product than merely the gross margin.

"For example, the dealer's costs are reduced (and true gross margin is increased) if the supplier gives him discounts for prompt payments, provides promotional allowances, or passes on the savings realized if the dealer uses his own trucks to pick up the product.

"On the other hand, his true gross margin is reduced by costs incurred in transportation, warehousing, display fixtures, and the labor involved in receiving and merchandising.

"When American Greetings uses the DPP formula to overcome the price objection, our products become much more desirable. Other companies charge retailers freight costs, refuse credits for unsold seasonal merchandise, offer no discounts for early payments, and have no allowance for outdated cards. When these factors are mentioned, the American Greetings profit advantage becomes apparent."

"Because we work in a highly competitive business environment," notes Rich Ziegler of The Drackett Company, "price and quality usually go hand in hand. In order to whittle away at price, it's necessary to whittle away at some value: content, packaging, delivery, service, variety, options, and so forth. Salespeople have to know where those values are and how they translate into prices."

Rich urges sales reps to learn the added values of their products so thoroughly that they're actually enthusiastic in explaining to a prospect why their product is worth the additional cost.

A dealer benefits by buying from a company that has a consistent pricing structure, says Larry Nonnamaker of Eastman Kodak.

"There are many brands of 35mm cameras on the market, covering a very wide price range. Sometimes a dealer will think he has made a great buy in getting a volume discount from a competitor that Eastman Kodak will not meet. What the dealer doesn't realize is that the other supplier may be giving an even larger volume discount to some other dealer, putting this first dealer at a competitive disadvantage.

"In addition to its consistent pricing, there are other benefits in handling Kodak products that often outweigh a competitor's lower price—such things as our product quality, national advertising, dealer advertising allowances, the well-known brand name, and our policy of repairing or replacing defective products."

Selling to the Consumer

The reliability of the sales rep's company is a frequent way of overcoming lower-priced competition. For example, when a prospect tells Hal Kessler of Terminix that he can contract cheaper exterminating services elsewhere, Hal's answer is, "You can always go to Joe's Corner Pest Control (a fictitious name, never a real competitor), but will he be around in two years if you need him? Terminix has been in business for 50 years, and it'll be here 50 years more."

"Also," adds Hal, "when a prospect says he's been talking to a lower bidder, we inform the prospect that we don't sell price, we sell quality. For example, we offer extra service at no extra charge if for any reason it should be needed between the regular monthly treatments."

"When prospects try to haggle over the price of a car," says Gordon Wallace of Spitzer Dodge, "I simply tell them, 'If you think you're going to get a discount on this car, you're wasting your time and mine.' Then I sell them on the dealership, our years in business, our outstanding service department, the way we take care of customers. Of course, I've already sold them on the benefits of the car."

"Should my client use a discount broker?" asks Betty Cinq-Mars of Merrill Lynch. "Few of my clients would. I service them to a fault. Paying full-house commissions gives a client the right to count on me for advice and updates. They know it. This is not a big problem for me in Kalamazoo."

The type of price competition encountered by Suzanne DeNoyior of Coldwell Banker is the homeowner who wants to pay less and get more: the prospect who questions the commission percentage.

"This is a big bugaboo in real estate selling," she says. "Homeowners want and deserve the best service, the most advertising, the greatest exposure, but many want it at a reduced rate. This is where I have a real problem, because one homeowner should not receive a discount when another homeowner is paying the usual commission percentage. We cannot reduce our commitment to service, and therefore cannot reduce our commission percentage. Every homeowner is treated equally in our marketing techniques and cannot be shortchanged.

"Commission rates vary from locale to locale. They are not regulated by law, and there are no strict industry guidelines. There will always be 'discount brokers'—those who take a listing for several percentage points below the average of their competitors. The homemaker is always cheated of advertising, of service, of multiple-listing exposure. In any service industry, a discount can be taken from only one source: service.

"I have always been ready for the price objection, because I honestly believe that I am worth every dollar I earn. I would rather not work with a homeowner who asks me to compromise my professional values. When put on the line where commission is concerned, I look the homeowner in the eye and ask how he would react if his boss asked him to take a cut in salary. I point out that as an independent contractor, I work strictly on commissions with NO fringe benefits. Believe it or not, some homeowners and buyers think we work on a salaried basis."

In selling life insurance, price usually is not as important as other types of objections, reports John O. Todd of Northwestern Mutual. A mutual insurance company uses its earned dividends to reduce the costs to its policy holders. Although it is common practice to illustrate possible future results by assuming that future dividends will be at the present rate, these dividends are not guaranteed, and 20-year projections are considered as illustrations only.

"Years ago, after my first three years as a broker, I studied the past and current performances of many companies. Year after year, Northwestern Mutual stood at the top. It was about the only company I was unable to sell as a broker, so on the premise that if you can't beat them you'd better join them, that is what I did in 1931. In the years since then, neither my policyholders nor I have been let down.

"So when it comes to price, I nearly always can show that I represent the best price. But there is more to it than that. To most buyers of life insurance, the product is only partly the company—there is also the agent. I can point out the kind of services I provide and gain confidence as a result of my record."

Jack Hallberg of Allstate Insurance sells both casualty and life insurance, and usually runs into a price objection only when selling casualty.

"In the casualty lines, there are times when I'm not the cheapest company on the street in a particular type of insurance. In that case, I have to give the customer a reason for paying a little more—my own availability as an agent, the quality of our claim service, my company's financial ability to handle claims. In casualty insurance, that's all he's buying—our ability to deliver in case he ever needs us."

On the life insurance side, Jack's previous experience was helpful. "In my former retail work selling appliances for People's Gas," he recalls, "we didn't have any competitively priced lines. We sold the best. We were always higher than the competition. So I learned to sell quality. When I came to Allstate, which usually has a competitive price, it was like picking cherries off a tree.

"Sales reps get too hung up on price. When I give a talk to young agents, I always tell them, 'Think of the way you buy things. Do you always buy the cheapest suit? The cheapest car? Usually not. People rarely buy solely on the basis of the lower price. The decision is based on a number of factors.' "

Jack feels that selling life insurance today is easier than in any of the 18 years he has been in the business. One reason is the ability to sell "interest-sensitive" products like Universal Insurance, which offer big tax advantages that were retained in the 1987 tax overhaul. As the policy accumulates cash value, the interest on that cash is tax-deferred until withdrawn. Explains Jack:

"In the old days, I could say to an individual 30 or 40 years old, 'You can take out a $100,000 life insurance policy, and if you die, your estate gets the $100,000, and if you live to the age of 65, you get your money back.' But now I can say, 'Depending upon how much money you put into your Universal Life policy, you'll get back four or five times your investment if interest rates stay about where they are now.'

"Again, I find that what helps me is the ability to make a friend. I say to a prospect, 'I have two kids who have gone through college, and one of them is in grad school now. I have a son who's a freshman at Notre Dame and another just starting high school. If these kids are going to get through school, with tuitions what they are today, I need your help.'

"People like to help people. There are lots of people who, when they pay their auto insurance premiums, are thinking, 'Well, I'm giving Jack a hand in getting those kids through school.' "

"When prospects object to the price of the Encyclopaedia Britannica," says David Van Tosh, "we try to show them that they can handle it. It's the old dictum: There's always a sale made—either you sell them on the idea that they can afford it, or they sell you on the idea that they can't.

"The set includes 32 volumes, each about 9 by 12 inches, a total of more than 31,000 pages, top quality paper, beautiful color plates. The prospect has been in a bookstore before and knows how much a book like that would cost."

If a guest at a Tupperware party says she'd like to own the merchandise but can't afford it, reports Denise Kaluzna, the dealer's response is, "Host a party yourself and you can earn your Tupperware free."

Selling to Doctors and Hospitals

The version of the price objection that pharmaceutical sales reps most frequently hear from doctors these days, says Peter Pappas of CIBA-Geigy, is "I can prescribe the same product in generic form and save my patients money."

The running battle between brand-name and generic drugs is a continuing problem in the pharmaceutical business. The developer of a new drug must spend large sums to research and test it, and then after approval to advertise and promote it. The manufacturer gets an exclusive patent—usually for 17 years, although some of that time may be lost waiting for regulatory approval.

At the end of that time, any chemical manufacturer can make the identical drug, if approved by the Food and Drug Administration. Since the generic manufacturer has no research costs and much lower development and sales costs, it can sell the generic imitation for much less than the branded drug of the original manufacturer.

"But," says Peter, "the big question is: Are the generic tablets the same as the trade-name drug? An example of this is a vasodilator made by CIBA called Apresoline® (hydralazine), used for heart and hypertensive patients. The patent expired a few years back, paving the way for generic manufacturers to copy it.

"Because the product is sensitive to heat, light, and moisture, we must coat the active ingredient, which is white, with a coating that has the same color for all dosage sizes. The generic manufacturer may not coat his tablet. Without the protective coating, can one be sure that the effectiveness and safety of the generic will be the same as that of the original?

"CIBA makes Apresoline in four dosage forms, whereas many generic manufacturers make only the 25mg and 50mg sizes because there is less demand for the other two forms.

"Today we are accustomed to shopping for the lowest price, but will the bargain drug do the same? Will it dissolve correctly? Will it work in the body as long as the manufacturer says it will? Will you be able to get all dosage forms? Will the bottle of 100 actually contain 90 tablets and a spoonful of dust because the tablet wasn't manufactured correctly?

"So when the doctor says, 'I want the least expensive product for my patients,' it is incumbent upon the pharmaceutical rep to inform the physician of the differences and throw the question back to him: 'If you were the patient, Doctor, which drug would you prefer?'"

13
Closing

"Any conversation with a prospective buyer that does not end with at least one attempt to close the sale is not a sales call, it's a social visit."

That's another old cliché in the selling profession, but its importance is often overlooked. Some years ago, *Purchasing* magazine conducted a survey in which purchasing agents kept records of what happened when salespeople called on them. One of the questions was, "After the salesperson had explained the product or service, what did he or she ask you to do?" In an astonishing 35 percent of all sales calls, the answer was "Nothing."

Reluctance to try for a close is understandable. The salesperson has invested some planning time, some persuasive conversation, and some psychic commitment into the presentation. If an effort to close results in a turndown, all that has gone down the drain.

If the sales rep actually writes down six or eight possible closing questions, it seems easier to ask one of them at the opportune time.

There are two kinds of closes:

1. An *action* close, in which the sales rep starts doing something, such as writing up the order or filling out an estimating sheet, which the buyer must stop if he or she is not ready to purchase.
2. An *oral* or verbal close, in which the salesperson asks some question which probes whether the objective of the call has been achieved.

The emphasis is on the word "question." A statement, such as "I'm sure you'll be satisfied with the product" or "We can get a shipment on the way to you immediately," is simply another piece of information the buyer can ignore.

It's interesting to present this problem to a group of salespeople:

"Suppose you're an automobile salesman. A prospect has come into your showroom, selected the model he prefers, taken it for a test drive, and asked a number of questions about it. Finally the prospect asks, 'How soon can I get one like this?' What's your response?"

Many salespeople will reply, "In about two weeks" or "You can drive this demonstrator model home right now." These are only statements; the prospect can say, "That's interesting. I'll think it over."

The closing-minded response is, "How soon do you want it?"

There are three types of closing questions:

1. Just bluntly asking for the order. "How does that strike you, Mr. Jones?" or "Are we in business, Miss Smith?" Not too sophisticated, perhaps, but miles better than no closing trial at all.
2. The "alternative choice," or "which-not-if" type of close. "Shall we ship you four dozen, or will three dozen be enough?" or "Would you prefer the Junior model or the Executive model?"
3. An open-ended question, such as "How many will you want for your initial order?" or "When do you want to receive your first shipment?"

Many salespeople distinguish between a "trial close," which "takes the prospect's temperature" without asking for a commitment, and an actual close, which triggers a yes-or-no answer.

A trial close would be, "Which color would you prefer?" The prospect is not forced to decide right now whether to buy or not; the prospect is merely asked the question, "(If you did decide to buy), which color would you prefer?"

When can the sales rep try for a close? One answer is, "Sooner than he or she thinks, usually." While doing sales consulting work, I have recorded hundreds of actual interviews between sales reps and prospects. When they listen back to the tapes, sales reps almost invariably comment, "I talked right past a couple of chances to close. I could have closed that sale a lot sooner."

There is no magic moment at which the salesperson must ask for the sale or forever lose it. The rep can try for a close at an opportune moment and, if the sale isn't closed, go on with the presentation and try another close later on.

Another cliché in sales training is the story of the younger salesperson who asked the veteran, "How often can you try for a close?" The veteran's answer: "One more time."

If the sales rep has a variety of possible closing questions on the tip of the tongue, one of them can be used at any one of these closing opportunities:

- When there is a "buying signal," indicating that the prospect is ready to buy and needs only a bit more reassurance. "Are you sure you can get this to me in time?" and "How reliable is your service?" would be examples.
- When the prospect agrees with the desirability of one of the benefits the salesperson has mentioned.
- When the prospect agrees with the sales rep's answer to an objection.
- When both parties have said all they have to say, have asked all their questions, and there comes a "pregnant pause."

If the sales rep does not encounter one of those four closing opportunities, the rep can create a closing situation in two ways:

1. By asking, "Do you have any other questions?" If the buyer says "No," a closing question naturally follows.
2. By summarizing the benefits. "So, as we've seen, this product/service will do this and that and the other for you. How soon would you want the first shipment?"

Selling to Business and Industry

Several contributors stressed the importance of making some effort to close on each call. The "close" may not be the ultimate order, for in many forms of selling the rep has to go through a whole cycle of events or people to make the sale. But each call should end with a request for some commitment that will move the process closer toward the goal.

Says Janis Drew of the *Los Angeles Times*: "There is not enough that can be said about the importance of closing. I have seen the efforts of intelligent preparation and expert delivery fail when in the last inning a salesperson was afraid to ask for the business.

"It's human nature to fear rejection, but the rep must overcome this fear in order to succeed in selling. If you believe your medium [read: product or service] is good for the prospect, remember that you are helping him become more successful. By investing in your medium, he'll sell more of his product, which is his goal.

"Before leaving, I always ask, 'So what do you think? Will you consider the *Los Angeles Times*? Can you appreciate its value?'

"Make it comfortable and easy for him to say yes. He expects you to ask for the business. Otherwise, what are you doing there?"

Similarly, John Heitzenroder of Occidental Chemical says, "I see many salespeople spending their time and effort 'creating goodwill' and forgetting that our main objective is to get the order.

"Today's marketplace is very competitive. We face stiffer and more knowledgeable competition. Therefore, I feel that for the sales call to be effective, I have to remember to summarize the benefits the buyer has accepted and ask for the order."

"Purchasing agents expect salespeople to ask for the order," adds Jake Kulp of AMP. "I have received orders over competition because I asked for them and my competitors just expected them.

"In my type of selling, I have to close many times to conclude a sale. I must first close with the design engineer, convincing him that my product will meet his needs. Next I must close with reliability engineering, convincing them that the product will work as specified, day in and day out. Finally I must close with purchasing, convincing them there is true value in the purchase. I consider each point a closing point, because at any of these cycles, the sale can be lost.

"Rejection is an everyday occurrence in selling, and you have to overcome the discouragement that rejection sometimes brings. But if it's fear of rejection that inhibits you from asking for the order—find another career."

"Closing is the most important part of the sale," says John Paul Jones of Monsanto. "This is what the sales rep is paid for. Unfortunately, few realize this until after many years in the field. Most new salespeople think that by becoming friends with their prospects, almost to the point of a family relationship, the orders will fall off the desk into their cases. Just 'social visits.'

"In my type of industrial selling, we are constantly closing with each call. I call it a commitment to proceed to the next step, or next phase of testing, aiming for ultimate product approval.

"Selling engineered thermoplastics is never accomplished on the first contact. The product is first introduced, along with backup technical data to show that it solves a problem or provides a benefit. When the sales rep senses that this has been done, he attempts a modified close by asking Purchasing or Engineering to proceed with the next phase of evaluation. This agreement means a willingness to spend money to test the product.

"This procedure can continue for anything from three months to a year. Each time the prospect is asked to spend more of his time and resources. And he may be testing competitors' products at the same time.

"When all the tests are completed, the real close would be simple if your product was the only one tested, or the only one to pass the test. Not so in many cases. Closing then becomes like selling other competitive products or services, the only difference being that you have a longer time to organize your thoughts and build your case.

"My close begins with a summary of what we have accomplished together, then follows with questions as to when production will commence and when we should be ready to ship our product."

Charlotte Jacobs of Pitney Bowes assumes from the start that the deal is going to be hers, and uses trial closes all along the way.

"A closing technique that has been very successful for me in preventing prospects from beating around the bush," she reports, "is to say at the end of the presentation, 'Mr. Prospect, I expect to *earn* the right to do business with your company. I don't expect to be given anything. Tell me, what do I have to do to get your business?'

"This blunt, straightforward approach seems to work for me. Then I summarize the prospect's response by saying, 'In other words, Mr. Prospect, if I do this and this, then I've earned the right to do business with you—is that correct?'

"I've had cases where I'd been bidding on business year after year without ever getting it. When I asked them about it, they sometimes told me they were happy with their present supplier and requested bids only because their company policy required it. I've found that it worked when I said, 'I've been bidding on this business year after year—what will it take for me to get your business?' They'll say, 'We like our present vendor because of—' whatever it is. Then I can say, 'If I can (in some way beat their present supplier in the area they mentioned), then do I have your business?' "

"In the cellular-telephone industry," reports Roland M. Charles, Jr., of GTE Mobilnet, Inc., "customers usually phone in for information and an appointment. This tells me two things: First, the customer wants to understand the product better, and second, he is in a buying mood.

"I go into an appointment believing that the product is sold and that the prospect just wants to be sure he or she is selecting the product that best fits the needs.

"I will continue to close until the prospect signs on the dotted line. However, the sale doesn't stop there; the rep has to keep selling to get the sorely needed referral business."

The selling of multimillion-dollar incentive programs to *Fortune* 500 companies is almost never a simple matter of sales presentation and close, says Bruce White of Maritz Motivation Company.

"In fact, a series of presentations is likely, perhaps starting with one prospect. The sales rep is simply trying for an endorsement and an opportunity to move up the chain of command to the next link in the sale. Most closes, in this case, are simply asking, 'Who do we show this to next?' or 'Can we proceed to the next audience with a more elaborate presentation?'

"When the appropriate audience, including the decision maker, is reached, it is evident that a purchase will be made and it's now a matter of selecting the supplier. Here's where an experienced rep uses his best closing tools.

"I've found the best technique to be a timetable for program implementation. This method assumes consent and proceeds to a discussion of deadlines for program operation. Once the prospective client is past the financial part of the presentation and into the timetable, you have an excellent chance of getting the contract. They may want to discuss it among themselves, but they'll be talking about 'when,' not 'which.' "

In preparing a complicated insurance proposal for a company, Bill O'Neill of Wausau Insurance Companies has to meet with the prospective buyer a number of times to collect information, determine needs, and make surveys.

"Closing is a process that goes on all through these calls," he says. "There are small closings each time I'm with the buyer, so that the final presentation is almost anticlimactic. The buyer and I both know that he is going to buy.

"There are times, however, when I have to pick up the phone and simply ask if the business is ours. I agree that there's a psychological reluctance to make this call, and inexperienced reps are the most reluctant of all. The only thing I can suggest is that if you don't ask, your chances of getting the sale are zero, but by asking you at least give yourself a 50-50 chance."

Selling for Resale

The Drackett Company, Rich Ziegler reports, uses a five-step presentation in selling its household products to retail stores: (1) attention, (2) interest, (3) benefits, (4) trial close, (5) close.

Drackett uses a very specific kind of trial close in a very specific way. It is not just a "temperature-taking" question like "Which color would you prefer?" or "When would you want it shipped?" It is a question designed to get the buyer's *opinion.* "How do you feel about this program?" or "What's your opinion about my proposal?"

If the response is negative, the question has unearthed an objection that must be overcome if the sale is to be made. If the response is positive, it leads into the close, which is a specific question like "Will you OK these quantities?" or "When do you want it delivered?"

Rich describes nine different closes which Drackett salespeople are trained to use as the situation dictates:

1. *Ask for it* (also known as the "direct close" or "direct question"). "May I have your authority to increase the total facings on Automatic Vanish from four to six?" "Will 20 cases be enough?"

2. *The order-form close.* The sales rep begins filling out the order form. "What is your store number?" "What is the address?" and at the end, "Just OK this"—never saying "sign this."

3. *The alternative, or either-or, close.* "Do you want the order delivered Wednesday or Friday?" "Would you prefer ten cases or 15?" "Do you want the section reset tomorrow or next week?"

4. *The "half-nelson" close.* This commits the buyer to an order if an objection can be overcome.

Buyer: I'm not sure this shelf arrangement you're recommending will make it easier to reorder.

Rep: Will you agree to the shelving change if I can show you it will?

5. *The "cautionary tale" or third-party close.* For example, the rep mentions another dealer who reaped a big sales volume with the recommended display or promotion.

6. *The lost-sale close.* When all else fails, the rep asks, "Where did I go wrong? Why did I fail to convince you?" This often brings out a hitherto unvoiced objection.

7. *The process-of-elimination close.* If the prospect refuses to buy, the rep asks, "Is it because of such-and-such reason?" No. "Because of so-and-so?" No. Thereby the rep identifies and eliminates the most common objections. In the end, the buyer either has no objection to ordering or reveals a hidden objection.

8. *The "I'll think it over" close:*

Buyer: I'll think it over.

Rep: Good. You wouldn't want to think about it unless you were interested.

Buyer: Yeah, I'll consider it.

Rep: So that you'll have all the facts in your mind while you're considering, what is it that I haven't satisfied you about?

9. *The final-objection close:*

Rep: If I understand you correctly, the only reason you're not buying is—

Buyer: That's right.

Rep comes up with some way around the objection, and closes.

"When I first began my selling career, the weakest aspect of my presentation was the close," confesses Dave Pitzer of Dr Pepper. "I was reluctant to ask for the order. Looking back on my first year of selling, I am sure I lost many sales because I waited for the buyer to say yes.

"I finally realized that there are two good reasons to close confidently: (1) the buyer expects it and (2) if your product will actually help the buyer, be proud to ask the buyer to use it.

"My personal belief is that if the salesperson has done his/her homework, determined the buyer's needs, and fulfilled those needs during the presentation, then the close usually follows naturally. However, since one rarely encounters 'textbook' sales presentations, we train Dr Pepper salespeople in seven categories of closes:

1. *Trial close.* 'Assuming you decide to switch to Dr Pepper, which brand would you replace?' We encourage trial closes at all times. In addition to possibly closing early, an added benefit is that they will uncover buyer objections.
2. *Assume assent.* 'When would you like us to install Dr Pepper?' You simply assume that the buyer will buy. The only risk is that the buyer may say, 'I never said I was going to buy.' Treat that as a trial close and go on.
3. *Offer a choice.* 'Would five tanks of Dr Pepper be okay to start or should we send you seven?' Neither choice is a no.
4. *Action close.* We typically begin filling out paperwork to establish the prospective account as a National Account.
5. *Inducement close.* This should be used only when all else fails, or when necessary to meet competition. If the buyer buys only because of an inducement, you will lose the account very soon. We sometimes use the inducement calls to get the buyer to say yes on the first call rather than requiring two or three callbacks. *Always* sell the brand first and position the inducement as secondary.
6. *Summary close.* Many times this technique is used before an action close. Most of our target-account slide presentations will include a *summary* slide and a *next-step* slide, which really is an action close.
7. *The balancing-act close.* Simply list the risks and benefits. Most decisions center around these two items. If I can help the buyer see that the benefits clearly outweigh the risks, it's easier for the buyer to say yes.''

Carl Unger of Zenith says he always tries to find some type of urgency working for him—a special floor plan, a special co-op advertising program, special prices to the dealer for a limited time.

''If you get your order in today, we could ship it this week and you won't lose any sales over the weekend. You'd like to think it over for a couple of weeks? Surely, you can do that, but a lot of the really good merchandise may be sold by then. Maybe we should work up your order now, while you're not too busy.''

Paul Sanders of Hewlett-Packard really doesn't have to close. "My dealers don't even place their orders with me. They phone our centralized order-processing location. I don't even know what they're ordering until later. But I know they wouldn't be ordering anything if they weren't getting help from me in training, merchandising, marketing—everything related to retailing.

"I'd been with an office-equipment firm before coming to Hewlett-Packard, and there I was really 'grinding' on people, so to speak, trying to get them to buy more. I found that if I used that same technique selling to PC dealers, they wound up being overstocked, and that created a whole host of other problems."

Closing is a rather simple, straightforward process to some of the contributors.

"Magic has nothing to do with closing a sale," says Bob Chargin of McKesson. "It's very simple, in fact. You know when it's time to close. One of the cardinal sins of selling is to wear out your welcome. I learned in my first few weeks of selling that you can kill a sale by elaborating too much."

"When your entire conversation with the retailer lasts only about two minutes, you don't have time for the luxury of trial closes and sophisticated closing methods," comments Ed Lahue of The Dial Corporation. "The sales presentation usually goes, 'Here is the deal, here is why I think it will sell,' and the close is usually, 'How many do you want?' or 'I'd suggest 50 cases.'

"Our company wants us to be consultants more than salespeople. 'Based on my knowledge of the product and what you've done in the past, I'd recommend 20 cases this time.' You don't have to oversell, because you'll be back there again."

A. R. Flores of Alberto Culver summarizes the philosophy of closing as follows: "There are two keys to closing the sale:

"One, make the first attempt at closing as soon as the conditions, benefits, and proposal steps are completed. Then *continue* to attempt a close after you have turned each objection of the buyer into a sales point.

"Two, *never* give the buyer a choice between 'Yes' and 'No' on a close. Always ask for a decision between two alternatives that result in an order: 'Which color do you prefer, the black or the yellow?' 'Will 12 gross be enough, or would you prefer 24 gross?' 'Will delivery on the 30th be ample, or do you need it sooner?'

"You presume that the buyer will buy and that it's only a question of color, amount, or delivery date. By using a 'choice' close, you refocus the buyer's attention from the buying decision to the subordinate choices.

"You've made the tough decision for him—whether to buy or not—now all he has are easy decisions such as color, quantity, or delivery date."

"I learned early in my sales career," says Cevin Melezoglu of American Greetings, "that by asking closing questions throughout the entire presentation I had nothing to lose and much to gain. By asking closing questions, not only was I able to increase my chances of getting the sale, but I was able to gauge the customer's response level as well.

"One of the most disheartening experiences occurred when a buyer had been responding positively throughout the entire presentation, yet when I asked a closing question at the end, he responded with a polite no. It became glaringly obvious that I had lost the buyer at some point, but at this late stage it was difficult to determine at what stage of the presentation I had lost him. If I had tried to close sooner, I would have been able to recognize the buyer's main objection earlier and shaped the presentation in a manner designed to overcome his specific concerns.

"In short, asking closing questions is an ideal way to measure the buyer's agreement level with you."

Jon Vitarius of Nabisco Brands, unlike many sales reps, likes to give the buyer a "breather" between the information part of the sales call and the close. "We generally use the close as a way of summarizing and clarifying the entire call," he explains. "It gives you the opportunity to make sure there is no misunderstanding as to variety, quantity, or delivery dates.

"After presenting the proposal, I usually step back and give the customer a chance to digest the information. After this lag time, I once again approach the customer to finalize the sale. On a recent sales call, the customer said, 'Jon, I thought it over and think 100 dozen may not be enough. Make it 200 dozen.'

"I can't overemphasize how important mutual understanding is to our sales reps. We pride ourselves on giving customers exactly what they want—no surprises."

One way to make the closing comfortable, says Pat Markley, also of Nabisco Brands, is to create enthusiasm for the product. "I try always to be enthusiastic about the product. It's easy to be enthusiastic about something you truly believe in yourself. Enthusiasm—not hokey enthusiasm, but real enthusiasm—is contagious.

The customer wants something he thinks is going to make him as happy as it has made you.

"One of the tactics I find effective toward the close is to mention how much one of the retailer's competitors took. Just a mention that Mr. Jones took X amount of the product sometimes will spur Mr. Smith into taking X-plus of the product.

"Another close that seems to work for me is to ask, after presenting the advertising campaign, 'How much of the product will you need to support this program?' I plant a doubt in his mind that maybe the order he was thinking of was too small to support the impressive advertising campaign I've described."

If a prospective new account is reluctant to take on the entire Cooper tire line, Bill Clark sometimes suggests, "Rather than ordering all our lines, why don't we start by just ordering this particular type?" Even with existing accounts, if it's difficult to sell a large order, he suggests that they purchase a particular type of tire, perhaps a current special. "It makes the dealer's decision easier, and it's a foot-in-the-door strategy for me."

To Larry Nonnamaker of Eastman Kodak, a close is neither something to be dreaded nor something that has to be done at a specific time in a specific way. Rather, it is a natural thing that is handled in a natural way.

"I do not go into a presentation with a set timing or a set closing method in mind," he says. "I've walked into a buyer's office and found that he had heard about our new product, done his own research on it, and was ready to buy. I don't get paid to give presentations, I get paid to sell, so if I can write up the order immediately, that's great.

"Most sales calls are not that easy. I use very simple and natural questions as trial closes to get a feel for where I am. A question like 'Wouldn't you agree, Mr. Jones, that this is a state-of-the-art camera?' will serve as a trial close. We get to know our buyers very well and can spot buying signals like nodding the head or reaching for a purchase order.

"The main thing is to ask for the order. If you don't ask, you'll never know if they want to buy, or are ready to buy more than you suggested. The key is to enjoy the presentation, ask questions, and when it feels right, go for it. If you don't get the order, go on looking for signs and try again. Eventually, if you're prepared, if you've done your homework and are determined to get the order, you will."

Selling to the Consumer

The close of a Mary Kay Cosmetics sale is the logical conclusion of a carefully planned sales procedure, which starts by inviting women to "give their opinion" at a demonstration (called an "appointment") usually held in one woman's home.

From two to six women are seated around the dining room table giving themselves a facial, following the instructions of the consultant.

"I start closing the minute I walk into the appointment," says Judie McCoy. "I plant the answers to all the common objections in my presentation, so the close is simply telling them about the various options in buying the product."

Judie takes each participant in turn off to a sofa in another room for the close. She doesn't do it in front of the group, she explains, because if a woman feels she can't afford the product, she will not admit that but will come up with some other objection as a subterfuge, and this would simply plant that objection in the minds of the others at the appointment.

"The first step in the close is to establish that they love the product," she explains, "but that's so simple, because everybody loves the product. I'll ask, 'What do you like the most about the product?' or 'What do you like about the way your skin feels right now?' "

She then explains that the cosmetics can be purchased in one of three ways:

1. The complete collection—"everything you need for a total glamour look."
2. The basic skin care plus basic glamour collection, "which will care for your skin and give you a quick makeover."
3. The basic starter set with no glamour. (No woman wants "no glamour," Judie explains.)

Most women tend to pick the price in the middle, so the consultant picks the range she thinks will sell and then offers one higher and one lower.

Judie asks, "Which would you rather start with—the complete collection, the basic plus basics, or the starter set with no glamour?" The usual answer is, "I'd really like the complete collection, but today I think all I can afford is the basic skin care plus basic glamour."

The Mary Kay firm has an "on-site delivery system," meaning that the consultant has a supply of products right there.

"I put the product she likes right in her lap, so she is holding it," Judie says. "The possession motive is strong. It's her product, in her lap, it has her name on it. That's real powerful.

"If the prospect says she can't afford it, I say, 'I can appreciate how you feel, because I know other people have felt that way, but we've found that by using creative financing, we can usually find a way for you to get what you want. Now let's think about this. How could we work it out so that you can take it home with you today?'

"And then we simply discuss options. If they say they can't afford it, it usually means that they don't want to pay for it all in one bite. So I'll split the cost and suggest that they give me part in cash and part by check. If they want to buy $150 worth of the product, I'll say, 'You know what I've found, if you pay $50 in cash, and $50 with a check, and put the rest on your Master Card, it doesn't hurt in any one area.'

"I started suggesting that about a year ago, and it's the best, because psychologically they're not paying one big sum."

Judie uses similar tactics in recruiting new consultants. After explaining the nature of the work and the earnings potential, she asks, "What excites you most about what I just told you?" If the prospective recruit mentions some aspect of the job, the closing question is, "Is there any reason why we can't order your case today and get started with your training?"

If the prospect has a full-time job and doesn't think she'd have time to sell cosmetics, the answer is, "Realizing that there is a way to work this into your schedule, as we discussed earlier, other than that, is there any reason . . ."

Another useful close is: "If I could teach you to do what I do as well as I do it, could you learn it? Are you willing to learn it? Is there any reason why we can't . . ."

Denise Kaluzna, with a somewhat similar assignment in recruiting Tupperware dealers, uses this close: "Could you see yourself with $50 or $100 extra every week to put away in a secret savings account?"

"I love to close," says Betty Cinq-Mars of Merrill Lynch. "I described earlier how I paint a word picture of the investment process, from the opening of the account through the monthly statements and my continuing service. This closing process is self-completing. If the flow is there, the close just comes naturally. I never, never, never push. It may take some clients a little longer, but walking them through all the ingredients in the process is just as natural as can be."

Gordon Wallace of Spitzer Dodge often closes with a qualified commitment, similar to what Rich Ziegler calls the "half-nelson close." The prospect raises some objection or asks some question. "If we could do thus-and-so," Gordon asks, "would we have a deal?" He then figures out a way to meet the requirement and closes. If the prospect brings up another objection, he reminds him, "Hey, I thought you said we had a deal if I could do thus-and-so."

"Our close is basically the assumptive close," reports David Van Tosh of Encyclopaedia Britannica. "When we've finished describing the product, we show the different bindings available and then say, 'There are several ways you can obtain it: cash, pay half down now and the rest later, or put it on a credit card. Which method would you prefer?' "

"An important point," adds Tom DeLaMater, "is this: Once you ask the closing question, shut up! The old saying is 'Whoever talks first loses.' But that phrase implies a win/lose attitude, so I explain to our trainees that the first person to talk at that point is usually the one who is going to buy: Either the prospect buys the set or the sales rep buys the prospect's statement that he can't afford it.

"We leave the buyer an owner's manual that sums up the delivery guarantee, the five-year replacement warranty against natural disasters, the library service, and a 15-day satisfaction warranty. If after 15 days they are not satisfied, they can return the set for a full refund less shipping and handling charges. This would be a weak close if the rep closed the sale on it, but it's a good button-up when used after the sale is made to reassure prospects who might be worried about whether they're making the right decision."

In selling real estate, closes that come too early can be disastrous, reports Suzanne DeNoyior of Coldwell Banker. A closing question is best used after the prospective buyer's expressions or comments indicate an interest.

The close should be in the form of a question, she points out. "This is a large sunny room, isn't it, Mrs. Jones?" If Mrs. Jones agrees, the next question might be, "That sectional sofa you seem concerned about would really look lovely around that fireplace, don't you think?''

If the prospective buyer seems impressed by the home, the agent starts asking the homeowner questions that would naturally be of interest to the buyer—questions about utility costs, the neighbors, the boundary lines. This encourages the homeowner to be friendly and communicative, although sometimes the seller will blurt out a more blatant closing question than the agent would have asked, such as "How soon are you able to sign the contract?''

An unusual type of closing in real estate is the escape from a negative situation. If the prospect's body language clues indicate that he is completely turned off by a home—the "curb appeal,'' the neighborhood, or the interior decor, layout, or roomsize—the close is, "Now I know what you don't like, and that is a great help to me. The next place you'll want to see is . . .''

In discussing exterminating service with a homeowner, Hal Kessler of Terminix finds that the simplest way to close is to ask, "How soon would you want to get the service started?'' The usual answer is "As soon as possible,'' although this does not necessarily commit them to Terminix.

John O. Todd of Northwestern Mutual uses a technique that can be applied in many other forms of selling: getting a commitment from the prospect before doing a lot of work "on spec.''

"In most major sales of life insurance,'' he explains, "there is quite a bit of work to be done before the sale can be closed. Therefore, as we come to that point, my usual understanding with the prospect is based upon an affirmative answer to this question:

'' 'Mr. Prospect, I will be very happy to study these matters for you without any expense to you. All I ask of you is that if, as a result of any ideas I bring you, you decide to buy life insurance, other things being equal, you will buy it from me. Does that sound fair to you?'

"When I come back with my suggestions, there are two wonderful ways to ask for a close,'' John continues.

"The first is to ask the prospect for a medical exam, like this: 'As you know, Mr. Prospect, in addition to paying the premium, in order to get life insurance, we have to satisfy the insurance company that you are in good health. Let me arrange for you to have an examination, and I will put this whole thing together for you, then you can make a decision after you see all the facts. When would be the best time for you to see our doctor?'

"This is like the tailor asking you to try on a suit 'for size.'

"After the examination has been made on a no-obligation basis, there is a second opportunity to close. Before the application goes in, you phone Mr. Prospect and say, 'Mr. Prospect, I've just seen your medical, and it looks fine. As I told you, we have not yet made a decision as to just how much you are going to need and want to buy, so I can send these papers in to the company, and of course there will be no insurance in force. However, I have an idea. It usually takes two to four weeks before the papers work their way through the process and a policy is issued. Under the law, if we were to put the insurance in force, you would have a 10-day free look. So we can put it in force—that means the company is on the risk and you can be covered free while you are making up your mind. Doesn't that look like a win-win situation?' "

Just the evening before sending in his contribution to this chapter, Jack Hallberg of Allstate Insurance had an interesting experience.

"I closed a very, very nice life sale on what was actually the fourth presentation I had made to this man," he reports. "Normally in our business, you close on the first call—there are so many other cherries on the tree that you don't make a lot of repeat calls on the same prospect.

"But in this case, each time I tried to close and failed, in the interval I asked myself, 'Why didn't I get him?' I thought it was a strange situation: The need was there, the ability to pay was there, but it finally dawned on me that this was a rather unique individual who knew he was going to buy, but was just going to see how long I would keep after him.

"So I went back and closed. If I had run into him 15 years ago, I might not have realized that he was just trying to wear me down, and I might not have closed him. The biggest thing in closing, or in handling resistances, is experience: When you do miss a sale, ask yourself why."

Selling to Doctors and Hospitals

"The close in pharmaceutical selling is different," explains Ralph Eubanks of the Roerig division of Pfizer, "in that we can't ask the doctor to buy anything or sign anything, but you can get a commitment that he'll use the drug with some of his patients. I found it easier to close vacuum-cleaner sales while I was in college than to sell drugs, because the doctor can say, 'Yes, I'm going to prescribe it,' and sometimes it's an evasive technique. You don't know until you check with a nearby pharmacist a few days later whether he has followed through on his promise.

"We have discovered what we call the 'commitment consistency law of psychology.' A doctor is bombarded with so many requests upon his time that many of them are never acted upon, but the ones that *are* acted upon are those in which a commitment has been requested. Once a doctor makes a commitment, he has such a sense of integrity that there's a good chance he will use that product.

"The one thing we've found to be very effective in closing is summarizing the benefits. We've found in our research that the doctor primarily hears the first part of the presentation and the last part. Often when you get to the fifth or sixth point, the doctor has forgotten about a couple of benefits that impressed him at the beginning. So we end with a rapid-fire summation of four or five of the benefits we've covered. The summary works, because the doctor may have tuned you out in the midst of the presentation. Sometimes during the summary, the doctor will say 'Hey, what about that?' and show some interest in a benefit he hadn't heard earlier.

"We often use a trial close before asking for a decision. Our philosophy here is that if you ask for a decision and the doctor says no, the human tendency thereafter is to defend and justify that no. So we take the doctor's temperature by saying, 'Doctor, how does that sound so far?' If he's hot, we continue with the close; if he's cold, we use a probe to find out if there's some problem we're not addressing. The close would be something like, 'In the light of these benefits, Doctor, would you be willing to evaluate this product with a few of your Type II diabetics?'

"After getting a commitment, we sometimes use the action close. For example, if we're selling our intravenous antibiotic for pneumonia, we may say, 'Doctor, do you have someone in the hospital right now who may not be responding to therapy the way you'd like them to? Maybe they're spiking a fever, or maybe you have someone in there with some renal impairment and you may be having to treat them with an antibiotic that has some nephrotoxicity. That patient could really benefit from the advantages of our antibiotic.'

"If he has a pneumonia patient, chances are he has one with symptoms like that. Once you paint a picture of one of his patients, you come across basically as one who feels 'I'm interested in you.' It's an empathetic way to get some action. You're not asking 'Will you please phone the hospital and change all your patients to our Antibiotic X?' That sounds as if you're asking him to do something for you.

"It's a more empathetic, consultative approach to paint a picture of one or two situations that could very likely happen to most physicians who treat a lot of serious illnesses. Sometimes the doctor will say, 'I do have a patient with poor kidney status, and I'm going to make your day,' and pick up the phone and call the hospital. That's one way of getting some action on an intangible type of selling."

Peter Pappas of CIBA-Geigy stresses the importance of closing, pointing out that "without an attempt to close you don't know where you stand, or how your product might fit into the armamentarium of drugs the physician is using." Like Ralph Eubanks of Roerig, he usually closes by reviewing the product's advantages to the patients and then asking for a commitment to try the product on X number of patients. The attempt to close gives him an indication of the doctor's interest and a starting point for his next call on the physician.

"When the physician asks a question like 'Is it already stocked in the drugstores?' or 'Is it on the market yet?' or 'Is it FDA approved?' you know that his interest is strong and that it might be the time to close—the quicker the better, but not so quickly that he doesn't know all about your product and might prescribe it incorrectly.

"A question about his opinion is usually the best way to find out how much interest the physician has in your product. If it's a new and unique product, with definite advantages over what is already available, he is usually quite interested. If it's a product that has no advantage over products already available—what we call 'me-too' products—he usually conveys his lack of interest verbally or nonverbally and you know your work is cut out for you.

"I often ask, 'How many sample packets will you need to try on your patients?' This is a trial close that will elicit a response indicative of his interest. Normally when a physician uses a drug on his patients, he will use the samples given out by the various drug manufacturers. If he's interested, therefore, he will ask for the number of samples required to give it a good trial. Physicians today usually don't ask for samples unless they are getting good results with a drug—otherwise their offices would be wall to wall with samples.''

14
Handling Stalls

A "stall" is an attempt to postpone the buying decision. It's not the same as an objection or sales resistance. The objection says "I've decided not to buy your product/service because . . ." while the stall says "I'm not going to make up my mind right now because . . ."

Most salespeople encounter the same old stalls again and again, and work out their own ways of handling them. The stall comes in two varieties: (1) the prospect has the authority to make the decision but wants to defer it; (2) the prospect does not have the buying authority.

When the prospect can make the decision. Making a decision, especially when it requires a choice between two alternatives of almost equal value, requires mental effort. It's only human nature to postpone the decision—if there is no penalty for the postponement.

The sales rep has no right to ask the prospect to *buy* unless the rep can convince the prospect that the benefits outweigh the costs.

The sales rep has no right to ask the prospect to buy *now* unless there is some benefit in making the decision immediately, or some potential penalty for postponing it.

Advantages of an immediate decision might be the existence of some special offer or buying opportunity of limited duration, or simply the opportunity to enjoy the benefits starting right now instead of at some future date. Penalties for postponing the decision might be a possible price increase, unavailability of the product/service at some future date, and so on.

The standard response to the prospect who says "I want to think it over" is something like this: "By all means, think it over, Mrs. Murphy. Let me know what it is you want to think about, so I can give you any additional information you need." (This is really a way of smoking out an unspoken objection.)

In selling to consumers, the wife (husband) will often say she (he) wants to talk it over with her husband (his wife). A common response is "I'm sure your husband (wife) will appreciate your going ahead and making the decision—and we can always cancel it if he (she) doesn't agree."

A classic response is attributed to an Electrolux salesman. After he had demonstrated to a housewife how well his machine could pick up all kinds of dirt from the livingroom carpet, she told him, "I'll have to talk it over with my husband."

"Fine!" replied the salesman. "I'll be happy to come back and demonstrate this cleaner to your husband—what day does he do the housework?"

When the prospect cannot make the decision. There are circumstances in which the prospect simply does not have the purchasing authority. Typical instances are the buying committees which make major decisions at chain-store headquarters, or executive committees that approve major industrial investments.

In this case the salesperson will try, first, to be given the opportunity of personally making the presentation to the buying group, or, second, to get the prospect to agree to recommend the purchase to the group, and then to arm the prospect with persuasive visual and printed evidence.

Selling to Business and Industry

Michael Ciarcia, who sells million-dollar projects for the Turner Construction Company, stresses the importance of respecting the buyer's position. What looks like a stall to the sales rep is, in the buyer's perception, a logical procedure.

In response to the "think it over" stall, Mike uses questions that are much more specific than "What is it you want to think about?" He'll ask the prospect, "How do you feel about the schedule? The cost? The team we've assigned to the project?"

"If this person is not the final decision maker," he says, "you must first sell him on your involvement and then arm him to sell your involvement to his management. Since we are selling large projects to major corporations, this is usually a group decision. We must sell one person at a time, never proceeding to the next level until we know where the secondary decision maker stands. If he's in your corner, he can be your best ally. If he's against you, he can make life miserable.

"Don't be afraid to put the buyer under obligation to you. To a buyer who owed me a favor I once said, 'How can you *not* give me a chance to perform for you?' I got the chance, we did perform, and we got the contract."

To avoid the I'll-have-to-talk-it-over stall, Charlotte Jacobs of Pitney Bowes, early in the contact, asks questions like these:

"Is there anyone else in your company we should be talking with?"

"Is there anyone else along with you, Mr. Prospect, who will be involved in this decision?"

"If we meet all your criteria, can you sign the order?"

Questions can be direct without being objectionable, Charlotte observes.

To avoid sheer procrastination on the part of the decision maker, Charlotte asks, on her first call, "Just to make sure I'm working within your time frame, what sort of deadline do you have for making this decision?"

When many decision makers and influencers are involved in a major decision such as the purchase of a mainframe computer, says Nick Debronsky of Unisys, the best strategy is to get to the top man. There are many ways of doing it, he says.

"One route is the social route, but everybody else is doing that," he observes. "If you know your product and have the experience, other people in the company will realize that you know what you're talking about, and they'll help you get to the top man.

"I'd worked for months trying to sell one large school system without meeting the superintendent, but one day I happened to bump into him in the elevator ["Accidentally?" some readers will wonder], and we hit it off. From then on, he spent quite a bit of time with me discussing the computer installation. Everybody in the school system knew I had a close relationship with the superintendent, so I was practically walking on water."

Stalls aren't often a problem for Bill O'Neill in selling Wausau

Insurance Company policies, because there's usually an existing policy with an expiration date. To discover whether the prospect really has the buying authority, Bill asks, somewhere along the line, "How many copies of my final proposal will you need?" If the buyer asks for more than one, it's a clue that others will be involved in the decision.

John Heitzenroder of Occidental Chemical uses three different tactics:

"If it's a minor excuse, I acknowledge it and go right on with my presentation. Sometimes the excuse is forgotten before I get to the end of my presentation.

"If the buyer says he's too busy, I ask for an appointment at a later time.

"If the person I'm talking with doesn't have the final authority, I offer to make a joint call with him to explain my proposal to the decision maker."

Roland M. Charles, Jr., of GTE Mobilnet, Inc., says stalls can occur either because the prospect isn't the actual economic or "money" buyer for the company or because the person does have the authority to make the decision but has some questions that need to be addressed.

"In the first instance," he says, "the salesperson must find the economic buyer, possibly using the first contact as a 'coach' or 'rabbi' who is on your side. In the second circumstance, I review the benefits of the cellular telephone service. Since it will increase the productivity of the prospect's company, the quicker the decision is made, the faster the company will enjoy that increased productivity."

"You're always going to have stalls in space sales," says Janis Drew of the *Los Angeles Times*. "Sometimes the fiscal planning year is off, or the key decision maker is out of the country, or your product is new to them and they don't want to take the risk.

"Whatever the excuse, listen carefully and never degrade the client's or agency's viewpoint. Just persist. Don't let the call end without a thread or link to the next step. Invent a question that needs an answer from your research department. Make a luncheon date, or say you'll send an article on a subject you have discussed. The point is to keep the relationship going until there's a plausible opportunity for the buyer to say yes.

"In extreme cases, where you're getting a raw deal or a runaround, try another route. Call on another individual. If that's not possible, find a different method or style of approaching the same individual.''

In selling incentive programs, Bruce White of Maritz Motivation Company occasionally comes upon a decision maker who has the authority to buy but simply can't decide.

''He seems torn with indecision, and seemingly no amount of persuasion will get him off dead center. I had a client who was notorious for *not* making a decision, especially when it came to selecting an incentive travel destination. He would waver back and forth between two destinations until we finally forced a decision by telling him we were about to lose our option on hotel space at one of the destinations. In the future, we submitted only *one* destination that had been selected by his staff.

''The toughest stall to handle in selling major programs requiring significant investments is the postponement. They're going to buy but not now, for a number of reasons—a strike, an unprofitable quarter, a new product line, a new man at the helm, ad nauseum. They're still excuses.

''The sales rep can only reinforce the immediate benefits of the program. There are few penalties for not buying now—any 'penalties' you can dream up will be 'give backs' by a competitor.

''My advice is to hang in there, *cheerfully*—you'll get the business eventually. Buyers hate cry-babies and whiners, so don't make a stink. Make it easy for them to do business with you next time.''

Stalls are common in the purchase of engineering thermoplastics, reports John Paul Jones of Monsanto. ''They can result either when the prospect does not have complete authority to make the buying decision, or wants to alert my competitors in an attempt to gain additional benefits.

''I make it a rule of selling to determine the ultimate buying authority on the second visit. During the first call I avoid questioning the prospect's decision-making level to avoid losing his attention and concentration.

''Then, when scheduling the second call with him, I review the key points of the initial presentation and suggest that if testing and technical approvals are going to be necessary, we should try to include on this second call all those who will be involved in the selection process. The number present at that second meeting is sometimes an indication of how much authority the original contact has.

''The 'technical stall' is widely used in my business. This may mean that the buyer doesn't have the authority, but he can always say that the engineers are too busy to test the new materials, lab time costs money, UL and FDA approvals take time. Unfortunately, there is very little one can do to circumvent these delays except to offer to participate in the tests and share the costs.''

Selling for Resale

''The stall tactic is one of the most frustrating obstacles a salesperson must overcome,'' confesses Dave Pitzer of Dr Pepper. ''In many cases, a stall by a buyer occurs because of an objection that has not been discovered or overcome by the seller. This relates back to the importance of thorough fact finding before the call.

''One of the keys to overcoming stalls is pre-call planning. Rather than being surprised by a stall during your sales presentation, plan for it and have answers ready.

''For example, Dr Pepper has had enormous success with coupons offering the food-service operator $50 for placing Dr Pepper on the fountain equipment. We use the coupons not only as an added incentive for the operator to buy our product; we also use them as a reason to buy *now* rather than later. Therefore, the customer's stall might cost him or her $50.

''Another vehicle that I have used successfully in handling stalls is the offer of a 'no-risk trial.' Although we do not have a policy guaranteeing the success of Dr Pepper in food-services outlets, we do have a lot of confidence in the brand's strength. Therefore, if it appears that the buyer is sold on the product but wants to postpone the decision, I will make it easier for him to answer yes. I simply promise the buyer that if the product does not perform up to expectation, I will cover *all* costs associated with reinstalling the brand that was removed for Dr Pepper.

''Since the local Dr. Pepper bottler will back me up on the commitment, there is very little risk to the buyer or to the Dr Pepper Company. The key, though, is that I have never had a customer come back to me and take me up on the offer. Confidence in *what* you sell provides a lot of flexibility in *how* you sell it.''

''Stalls are handled by explaining the benefits of buying now,'' says Bob Chargin of McKesson Drug. ''Make your customer aware of incentives such as discounts, promotional periods, and 'dating' which will not be available in the future. 'Dating,' in the wholesaler drug business, is a form of deferred billing or special financing available at various times during the year.''

When a tire dealer tells Bill Clark of Cooper Tire that ''I'll think it over and let you know on your next trip,'' Bill's response is, ''Fine! And why not take this one item on this trip, so that when I get here on my next trip, it'll be in stock and I can show you how to set up a display and merchandise it.''

If the chain-store buyer says he or she will have to take up your proposal with the committee, suggests Rich Ziegler of The Drackett Company, ask, ''How do you feel the committee will receive it?'' In that way, the rep can arm the buyer with answers to the objections likely to be raised by other members of the committee. ''Taking it to the committee'' is sometimes a mere stall, but in some accounts a strict procedure.

''When I encounter a stall,'' reports Larry Nonnamaker of Eastman Kodak, ''the main thing I want to find out is whether there is a legitimate reason for delaying the decision, or whether this is merely an excuse from a buyer who does not have the courage to say no.

''If it is an objection, I want to deal with it then and there. If there is a legitimate reason for postponing the decision, I want to leave something in writing so the buyer will have a reminder of the benefits when he is making his decision.

''I also like to pin him down as to when I can expect an answer from him, or should see him next. In the case of special buy-ins with a deadline, I'll phone him a few days before the deadline to ask for the order. The longer you go without getting a decision, the less likely you are to get the order. I like to get the decision made while I am there if possible, but if I can't, I know I'll have to stay on top of it or lose it.''

Selling to the Consumer

The simplest answer to a stall was given by Gordon Wallace of Spitzer Dodge. When the prospective car buyer says he wants to think it over, Gordon asks, ''What is there to think about?''

When a prospective Tupperware dealer says she has to talk it over with her husband, Denise Kaluzna's response is, ''If he were sitting in that chair right there, what do you think he would say?''

Usually, if Denise has done a good job of selling the benefits, the answer is, "He'd say 'Give it a try.' "

Often a wife will ask Hal Kessler of Terminix to make his inspection and proposal during the day and will be eager for the exterminating to be done, but is afraid to sign a contract without her husband's approval.

"In that case," Hal says, "I'll write up the proposal with the price and say, 'Mrs. Jones, if you want to wait for your husband to make the decision, let's do this. Why not sign the contract—we'll make the initial service COD so you don't have to give me a check— and if you husband decides he doesn't want the service, you can phone me any time within the next three days to cancel the contract and that'll be the end of it.' Most of the time the woman will sign it, and 99 percent of the time the husband will approve it.

"If she doesn't sign it, I leave her a copy of the proposal with our brochure. Then that evening, or the following evening at the latest, I stop by after dinner to talk with the husband. Usually I close the sale. If they want to think it over, I give them time to think it over. I don't believe in being pushy—people don't like pushy salespeople, and I do very well in my mild-mannered way."

Encyclopaedia Britannica avoids the "I have to talk it over with my husband/wife" statement by insisting that both parties attend the presentation; so-called "one-legged" presentations are avoided.

"If they then say that they have to think it over," says David Van Tosh, "we really don't have a bona fide one-call close. We can't say that the supply is limited or that the price will increase tomorrow.

"We offer them discounts of up to 66 percent on other merchandise, such as a bookcase, dictionary, or atlas, if they will give us the order tonight. That seems somewhat backward: They say they can't afford it and we reply, 'Here's how you can spend even more money.' But it works."

Suzanne DeNoyior of Coldwell Banker encounters two kinds of stalls in selling real estate: (1) from the seller who hesitates to give her the listing, and (2) from the home buyer who can't make a decision.

In getting the listing in the first place, she stresses the importance of finding out, before the call, who the real decision maker is going to be, and making sure that that person will be present when she calls. If the homeowner wants to delay giving her the listing, her response is:

"Mr. Homeowner, why would you hesitate listing your home with me, with Coldwell Banker, when you know that I can do the best possible job for you, in the fastest time, with the least inconvenience to you?"

This requires an answer that may uncover an objection. If the homeowners say they intend to talk to other brokers, Suzanne says, "Mr. Homeowner, promise me one thing. Promise me that you will not agree to list your home with anyone else until you speak to me again. I would like to know what these other agents have said that I may have neglected to tell you." Mr. Homeowner is then put on the top of her priority list for follow-up calls.

For the home buyer, the greatest potential penalty in postponing the decision is the possibility that someone else will come along and buy the house. To the hesitant buyer, Suzanne says, "If you're not ready to make an offer today, promise me that you won't blame me if the house is not available tomorrow."

"This comment alerts the prospect to the fact that this home is special and must be acted upon immediately. Or, if it does not produce action, then I know that I may be wasting my time on a not-too-serious buyer. This I can't afford to do; my other buyers need me more than this prospect does."

The staller is the most difficult obstacle the life insurance salesperson must deal with, says John O. Todd of Northwestern Mutual. Different kinds of stalls are encountered in selling personal insurance and corporate insurance.

In selling individual policies, the most frequent stall is "I want to talk it over with my wife." John's answer to this common objection is:

"Mr. Prospect, it is certainly true that she is the person most affected by how much insurance you have. However, men tell me that this is the one decision that it really isn't fair to ask her to make because, you see, it puts her in a very difficult position.

"In the first place, she just doesn't even want to think about the possibility of your death. In the second place, she probably doesn't fully realize what an awful lot of capital it would take to produce an income comparable to what you are now earning. Finally, she may be very reluctant to say, 'Buy more insurance today so I will be better off if you die.'

"Those are the reasons why most men who think about it agree with me that this is the one decision they have to make for themselves. And I might tell you out of my own experience, when I discover the need for more life insurance, I go ahead and buy it and then come home that night and say to my wife, 'Honey, I bought some more insurance today, and I want to tell you why.' ''

In persuading corporations to buy life insurance policies on their key executives, the stall takes the form of multiple layers of authority through which the sales rep has to plow. Large corporations, John points out, operate under the principle of management by exception, which means "if it works, don't fix it."

His work in this field was made more difficult by the fact that most graduate schools of business administration teach that any major corporation can invest its money more profitably in ways other than buying permanent, cash-value-accumulating life insurance on their executives.

"To change this kind of thinking and reach the top decision makers means working through a maze of management levels," he says. "Top decision makers don't have the time personally to investigate the proposals made by a sales rep. Nor are they willing to run the risk of accepting the sales rep's advice without verification from the staff (whose job depends upon looking at things from the viewpoint of the company's best interests) or from outside consultants who are presumed to be unbiased.

"So the sales rep must either have attained the complete confidence of top management to the extent that he or she will ask the staff to investigate (with the staff knowing that the boss looks with favor on the proposal), or the rep must find someone lower on the totem pole who has the authority to make the decisions on the rep's recommendations.

"When I first broke the ice in establishing what is now virtually a household word, called COLI (Corporate-Owned Life Insurance), it was possible because over a period of years I had gained the confidence and friendship of the top man in one of the largest privately held companies in the United States.

"He was a brilliant man, and he understood it when I showed him how insurance on his upper-level profit makers could, through the principle of the Inevitable Gain of Permanent Life Insurance, not only protect his company from the loss inherent in early death, but would create a gain for the corporation at the policyholder's ultimate death, no matter how long the insured survived. He had the power to say yes—and he did.''

Selling to Doctors and Hospitals

Stalls are rarely encountered in selling pharmaceutical products to doctors, says Peter Pappas of CIBA-Geigy, since the doctor is not being asked to buy something for himself at the expenditure of his own resources. He will usually be candid about his interest in, or concerns about, the product and will make a decision.

When J. M. Garcia was selling computers to doctors and dentists, a stall like "I want to think it over" was usually met by reminding him that postponing the decision would merely result in additional time being spent on paperwork, additional delays in billing. If the prospect said he or she wanted to talk it over with the accountant or attorney, his answer was:

"I can certainly understand that in making a major investment like this, you would want the opinion of a third party. My only concern is that you would be asking them questions outside the realm of their expertise. For example, as crazy as it may sound, you would not get a podiatrist's opinion on oral surgery. If you want reassurance about the purchase of a computer, you would ask a computer expert, not an accountant or an attorney.

"In order to give you peace of mind, tell me—which is your major concern, financial or legal?" Suppose the answer is financial.

"Good. Let me offer you two options: I'll prepare a proposal based on the financial considerations he'll be looking for, or I'll make a presentation to him based on the financial aspects of the purchase."

Either choice eliminated the stall.

Part Four
After the Call

15
Getting Referrals

It's an odd quirk of human nature that, if you want to make a friend of somebody, you don't do that person a favor—you let that person do you a favor. Perhaps we're slightly embarrassed by being under obligation to those who have done a favor for us, but feel somewhat superior to—or at least more comfortable with—those for whom we have done a favor.

Which means that you have the opportunity of making all your customers and prospects feel more friendly toward you by letting them do you the favor of referring you to other potential customers.

Referrals are, for most salespeople, the best source of leads, not simply because they provide the name of a prospect, but because the referrer's name can be used in making the appointment, and in adding credibility to your presentation when you do see the new prospect.

Most people find it difficult to come up with names if you simply ask them, "Who do you know who might be interested in my product/service?" In selling to consumers, the better way is to prompt them by suggesting specific categories of acquaintances:

"Who do you know in this block that might . . . ?"
"Who do you bowl or play golf with that might . . . ?"
"Who in your company might . . . ?"

The same principle works in selling to businesses and industries. "Who do you know in this industry who might . . . ?" "Which of your suppliers might . . . ?"

Selling to Business and Industry

The importance of referrals varies from very high for some of our industrial salespeople to very low for others.

"Referrals are essential to a successful sales rep," says Roland M. Charles, Jr., of GTE Mobilnet, Inc. "I view referrals as 'kiss me' sales, because more often than not the existing customer has already sold the referral customer on the product or service.

"When I sell a customer, I use a high degree of professionalism, and I assure the customer that any referral given to me will receive the same kind of professional treatment. If you provide a superior product or service and use a high degree of professionalism, you will get your share of referrals."

"We are continually asking our present customers to suggest other dealers who might handle our line," reports Bill Clark of Cooper Tire. "To get his suggestions, we use a bit of flattery: 'Do you know of anyone else who runs his business as well as you do, who might be interested in our line?' or 'You're running a sharp business. Do you know of anyone else who might do as good a job on our line as you do?' Sometimes we ask for referrals just as a personal favor: 'Can I ask a personal favor? Would you suggest . . .' Often they know of many other good dealers but don't realize that it's important to us to know who they are."

"Most of my referrals come from satisfied project managers and engineering groups referring me to other prospects within their own companies," says John Paul Jones of Monsanto. "Do a good job for Engineer A, and he will usually refer you to Engineer B, who is working on an application where my material might produce a good result. Rather than just give me a name, he will often introduce me to the new prospect on that same sales call."

Although referrals are not needed by Paul Sanders of Hewlett-Packard, whose entire territory consists of four major retailers, he nevertheless agrees with the strategy of letting the customer do you a favor. "I found that out on a previous job," he recalls. "I had a boss who was always trying to do favors for his customers. When he found out one day that I had let one of my customers do me a favor, he almost went off the deep end. This became my biggest customer; he liked me a lot because he had done something for me."

Also agreeing is Mike Ciarcia of Turner Construction.

"Be like a politician," he adds. "Always be in a position of owing someone a favor. I also believe that people are turned on when you ask their opinion or advice; this is a key ingredient in developing a close relationship. Don't be afraid to ask for opinions. In pursuing a project, I may ask six or seven different architects, all competing with one another, what they think about what I'm doing.

"In selling construction services, I may be asked for a reference from someone who is a competitor of the prospect. Do I ask for the referral? Absolutely! It's a form of flattery to the first client. Also, this forewarns the first client that the referral prospect may contact him.

"Whenever I invite a client such as a real estate developer to a ball game or a dinner, I always suggest that he bring along an architect or a financial man or a prospective tenant. This becomes both a referral and an endorsement. Don't be afraid to ask!"

Bill O'Neill of Wausau Insurance Company finds that if he gives policyholders the best service he can, they will volunteer referrals without being asked.

"Since people are the source of our sales," says John Heitzenroder of Occidental Chemical, "I maintain good relations with all people, not just customers but also consumers, distributors, even competitors.

"You make the buyer's life easier if you work hard for your company in such areas as availability of material, good service, correct invoicing, on-time deliveries, product quality, complaint handling, accuracy of information, personal punctuality. With that approach, I find purchasing people more than willing to help me become more successful by supplying me with names of prospects for our products.

"At various purchasing/sales functions they tell others what a good job you are doing for your company; you end up with a good reputation in the industry."

"Referrals take another form in selling space," says Janis Drew of the *Los Angeles Times*. One way of letting a client do you a favor, she suggests, is to ask for a testimonial.

"For instance, if an airline pulls very well from the *Los Angeles Times* travel section, ask the airline's VP marketing to put it in writing. Send out a photographer to shoot a picture of him and produce

a testimonial ad for your publication. You can then use this in selling to other airlines, since members of most industry groups watch
what other members of the industry are doing."

Nick Debronsky of Unisys rarely asks a customer for names of
possible prospects. He does, however, refer prospects to satisfied
customers as a form of third-party testimonial. "Of course," he
points out, "you always get the customer's permission to use him
as a testimonial, and you check frequently to make sure he's a satisfied customer—if a prospect phones him while his computer system is down, you're not going to get a very glowing testimonial."

Since she deals with a limited number of national accounts,
Charlotte Jacobs's referrals are usually to other possible users in
other departments of the same company.

"I also work closely with our service department," she says,
"because they can give you tips on whose equipment needs replacing. Customers will often talk to a service person more openly than
they will to a salesperson. I occasionally take a service rep out to
lunch, or take them along with me on demonstrations so they can
answer technical questions."

Selling for Resale

"In selling Dr Pepper to restaurants in the Midwest and North-
east," reports Dave Pitzer, "there is no problem finding potential
customers. There are countless opportunities. Therefore, we actively
try to secure the help of our current customers in selling to new
customers. We do this in two basic ways.

"One, we ask our current customer to provide us with a testimonial supporting his/her rationale for using Dr Pepper. Two, we
ask our current customer for percentages of soft drinks sold. For
example:

XYZ BURGERS

Soft Drink Brands	% Soft Drink Sales
Cola	54%
Dr Pepper	16%
Diet	13%
Lemon Lime	12%
Flavor	5%

"This localized type of support for the product lends credibility to our sales presentation.

"If you think about it, every company in the sales business will most likely have some type of literature telling customers why they should use its product. The soft drink business is no different. Both cola companies have literature telling restaurant operators why they should be using their products. They also have literature telling restaurant operators why they should not buy Dr Pepper.

"Therefore, when selling Dr Pepper, I will always *sell my source of information* before selling my product. If the customer understands why I am using a particular source, he/she will be more likely to believe the information I present.

"Also, after showing the customer information developed on a national basis, I will narrow it down to a local basis and use the information gathered from operators in the same area.

"In summary, we use our existing customer base to develop information to help sell additional customers."

"At American Greetings we often use testimonial letters from accounts for prospecting," says Cevin Melezoglu. "The best way to collect these letters is to select an opportune moment with a satisfied buyer, such as after a particularly profitable holiday sell-through or after handling some special request for the buyer. My technique is to come straight out with 'Mr. Jones, I'm collecting testimonials from my accounts on their experiences with American Greetings. Could you please jot down a few sentences outlining your business rapport with our company?' After the retailer puts in writing how pleased he is with American Greetings, I ask him if any of his colleagues in the business might benefit from learning more about what AG has to offer."

"If you treat your customer well, he'll reciprocate," says Bob Chargin of McKesson Drug Co. "My customers, over the years, have become my best allies. They have set up golf dates and dinners, even made appointments with potential customers. Why? Because I have serviced them well and they know I'll do the same for their friends. To me, this is the supreme compliment.

"Several years ago my sales manager wanted me to transfer to another state. He felt that my small territory, which was producing only $50,000 a month, didn't have enough potential for me.

"I didn't want to move and persuaded him to give me a little more time to build the territory. Today I have one of the top territories in the United States, billing more than $1 million a month.

"There's no magic in being a good salesperson as long as you honestly like people and aren't afraid to work."

Carl Unger of Zenith simply explains to one of his dealers that he'll be calling on a prospective new dealer in another city. "Do you mind if I use your name and suggest that he phone you?" Carl asks. Usually, he says, his dealers are happy to be of help in any way they can.

Referrals are uncommon for Larry Nonnamaker of Eastman Kodak, as he works primarily with an established dealer network. Once in a while, however, a Kodak dealer will be approached by someone completely outside the photo industry, asking about how he or she could sell cameras or film. Dealers refer these inquiries to Larry, and follow-up calls often produce new channels of distribution.

Selling to the Consumer

In many types of consumer selling, repeat business from the same customer is either long deferred (as in autos) or practically non-existent (as in encyclopedias). Hence prospecting is the cornerstone of the selling process.

Prospecting has been developed to a fine art in the life insurance business, and one of the leaders in that development has been John O. Todd, CLU, of Northwestern Mutual.

"When I first came into the life insurance business," he reports, "my boss used to say, 'Prospecting is like shaving: If you don't do it every day, you're a bum.' I never really liked prospecting by cold-canvassing methods, and I think that although it may be necessary in the early phases of any selling job, the only intelligent thing to do is to get to other methods as soon as there is any referral or client base from which to work.

"I have found no better method of getting good references than to have a satisfied customer. The salesman who walks away from such a customer without giving that customer the opportunity to pass him on to others is walking right past the 'gold in them thar hills.'

"However, getting such references is difficult unless the salesperson nominates people to whom the customer can relate. For example, instead of asking 'Who do you know that might benefit by the use of my product (or service)?' I would ask, 'Who are your company's biggest suppliers?' or 'Who is your doctor?' or 'Who is your lawyer?'

"You can go on with questions like these that can only elicit a specific answer. By talking about people who sell or provide services to your client, you will be getting 'power leads.' As soon as you have a name in front of you, then your client or customer will easily answer further questions that you will ask to learn something about the individual.

"Often a successful technique that I have used, after getting the name and enough information to determine that the person in question is indeed someone who seems to me would be a prospect, I will say, 'He sounds like someone I would like to know. Would you be willing to introduce me to him by writing a brief note on the back of my business card?' Then I will say, 'I want to tell you just how I will use that card. I will say to him when I call, "Mr. Smith, I told Bill when he wrote that nice note on my card that I didn't want you to feel in any way that you should be influenced by it to do business with me. He just thought that I might be able to help you as I have had the pleasure of doing for him." ' Then I reach over and tear up the card. This dramatically reassures my present prospect that I am not going to continue to use the card as a means of influencing the new prospect."

"Water seeks its own level," remarks Betty Cinq-Mars of Merrill Lynch. "Chief executives of major corporations associate with people of that same class. If I do a good job in managing the assets of the president of a major corporation, he'll tell his friends about me.

"How do I get him to do that? By doing the best possible job for him in (a) making money and (b) servicing his account, making him feel that he is important to me and that I am here to achieve his objectives. I never let him feel that I am in a subservient position. He phones me at 8 A.M. because he knows I am busy. Interestingly, it's the busy people who are considerate about other successful people's time. He knows, from word of mouth, that I am very successful, work hard, keep long hours, and am in tremendous demand.

"For the people I don't work with very closely, I send out cards and *ask* for referrals. When a new client says he/she got my name from a customer, I write that customer and thank him for mentioning me. When a new prospect—Mr. Jones, let's say—tells me, 'Jim Smith said I should call you because you do such a good job for him,' I tell Mr. Jones that I appreciate the referral. That message will encourage Mr. Smith to send me more referrals and let Mr. Jones know that I like referrals."

"Referral business accounts for well over 50 percent of all real estate transactions," reports Suzanne DeNoyior of Coldwell Banker. "That's why successful people remain successful, and it also may be the reason why so many agents leave the field prematurely—they simply haven't given themselves enough time.

"I rarely have to ask for referral business—it just naturally comes my way—but I do train new agents to ask for it. I think the best possible approach is to do a wonderful job, and just expect that both buyers and sellers will tell everyone about you.

"I've had very few dissatisfied prospects. I always work like a dog with a bone: never let go. Keep on top of the sellers; keep the buyers so busy they have no time for anyone else.

"Bring about a meeting of the minds, and those minds will tell the world! And then it's time to nonchalantly hand out a few extra business cards and suggest that they give them to anyone who needs the services of a real estate agent."

Referrals built a whole new industry for John O. Todd of Northwestern Mutual.

"As a result of the successful installation of a large split-dollar life insurance program for the major closely held company mentioned earlier," he reports, "I was called to New York City to help solve a compensation problem for a major *Fortune* 500 company. I was sure the problem could best be solved by the use of permanent life insurance.

"Talk about delays, stalls, reversals! It took six years to prove to all levels of management that permanent life insurance was the best solution. This initial referral sale mushroomed into so many sales that in 1970 I was joined by a number of other Northwestern agents to establish the John O. Todd Organization to handle the huge administrative load of servicing what by now has become more than 200 corporations.

"There is no way to copyright an idea. We knew there would soon be many competitors, but competition is one of the highest forms of flattery. Other practitioners have turned the idea into such a trend that today COLI (Company-Owned Life Insurance) is in the public domain. Therefore, we all do better than we could have done by ourselves, but it does mean that in order to maintain our position as leaders, we have to work smart enough to earn it."

Selling to Doctors and Hospitals

Referrals and prospecting are nonexistent to the pharmaceutical sales rep, who makes regular calls on a known universe of doctors and hospitals. There is, however, one form of referral system reported by Ralph Eubanks of Roerig.

"Our hospital reps, who contact the medical students, interns, and residents, fill out a card giving the address where the new physician will open his practice, as well as what products he is currently prescribing in the hospital. These cards go to the rep in the territory, who not only calls on the new doctor but sometimes sets up a little introductory party with other physicians."

16
Maintaining Customer Relations

Maintaining good relationships with existing customers is important for a number of obvious reasons: (1) it prevents or minimizes competitive inroads, (2) it provides a source of leads, (3) it creates the opportunity for additional sales to the customer, and (4) it provides a testimonial, third-party endorsement, or even plant visits. As several contributors pointed out, "If you lose a customer, you need to capture two new ones if you want to grow."

Selling to Business and Industry

"Customer service is vitally important," says Steven Rand of Dun's Marketing Services. "However, it's not just the actual service that must be done and done well. Equally important is the client's perception of, and your communication of, that service.

"All clients like, and some insist upon, lots of attention. Never give insufficient attention to a client. They're human, and you must constantly stroke their egos. They must know not only that you appreciate their business, but that they as persons are important to you.

"In the last ten years I've forgotten that lesson twice and lost two key clients as a result. Although they were getting adequate service from my customer-service reps, they believed that I personally was not paying enough attention to them. I was out of rhythm with these accounts. They had the impression that I was too buy elsewhere and not spending enough time thinking about them, their needs, their problems. And they were mostly right! When problems came up, I wasn't there fast enough or didn't even learn about it until it was too late.

"In order to never allow myself to lose a client again due to 'service' or the lack of it, I've developed the following safeguard procedures, which I follow religiously:

1. I write up an outline defining the objectives of the project and define what results are needed to constitute success.
2. During the course of a program, I make daily or at least weekly phone calls to the decision maker and to each person or department involved in the project. These are in-person visits if required.
3. I provide weekly or monthly service status reports, with copies to all appropriate parties. The report includes the number of orders processed, delivery time frames, problems and solutions, participants' comments, and remaining or future actions to be taken.
4. After the project is completed, I deliver a follow-up report on results, good or bad. If it's bad news, I want it to come from me, along with recommendations on what we learned from our mistakes and how to avoid them in the future."

"In print sales, as in all sales," says Janis Drew of the *Los Angeles Times*, "your customer is your number-one priority. The relationship you have worked to develop with him or her can be maintained only by care and attention. The business is so highly competitive that you could lose it if you do not constantly reaffirm the relationship."

"Make it your priority to service your client," advises Bill O'Neill of Wausau Insurance Companies, "and do it! I use entertainment only after the prospect has been sold and a relationship has been established. Generally, entertainment for me is a luncheon with a buyer who is now a friend. I rarely discuss business as such; the purpose is to solidify a business relationship. It is relaxed and casual, no pressure—the buyer can let his or her hair down.

"Quite frankly, I don't entertain prospects very often. I don't feel that it conveys the right message. I want to sell the prospect on my professionalism and product, not my entertainment. I know some account reps who use entertainment very effectively with prospects, but it's just not my style."

Paul Lentz of ADP feels that the degree of after-sale commitment is what determines the difference between a good sales rep and an excellent one.

"Plan regular meetings with your support group, both during and after conversion, to ensure that nothing is overlooked," he advises his salespeople. "Stay in touch with each of the client's departments affected by the conversion. Just one squeaky wheel can kill a deal.

"If you start getting frustrated at dedicating so much time to post-sale activities, just think how much effort was required to find that one account who was ready to buy. When those commissions start rolling in, it tends to ease the pain."

"Service after the sale is the most important part of my business," says John Paul Jones of Monsanto. "I have probably gained 50 percent of my business over the last 20 years as a result of marginal follow-up and service by competitors.

"Some say the hardest order is the first. Not true. What makes the difference between a one-time order and a regular customer is the follow-up attention to product quality, on-time delivery, changing prices, and suggestions for improving productivity.

"I consider follow-up the most important part of my job—not only for order and shipment status but, most important, for the comments and promises resulting from conversations during an in-person or telephone visit.

"Remember, the sales rep is the only link between the two companies, and he must not only carry the message but also ensure that the job is done. We are really lawyers for both parties.

"*Complaints should be given top priority.* They must be handled with concern and interest, with immediate investigation and prompt reporting, no matter where the fault. Prompt action in every case, in addition to satisfying one customer, may prevent broad-scale problems in other areas.

"Entertainment is part of the job. I try to use it to break the ice on an account where the press of business provides little time to get to know the people, also at times to say thanks for a good relationship."

"After I close a computer sale," says Nick Debronsky of Unisys, "I really become a consultant to that account. Not only do you get involved with the installation of the system, but from then on you have to keep up with the customer on state-of-the-art concepts and solutions, and recommend those solutions to the customer."

"You don't drop the customer after the sale," says Charlotte Jacobs of Pitney Bowes. "You provide follow-through, or what I call 'customer care,' because that's how you get referrals and possible additional business from the same customer.

"After closing a sale, I always send little handwritten thank-you notes or silly little cards, something to let them know I really appreciate their business. When I buy tickets to a concert, I sometimes buy a couple of extra ones to send to a customer."

The sales rep should play a key role in the installation or implementation of a new product or service, says Greg Deming of American Express Travel Management Services.

"Many salespeople like to close the sale and move on to other things, letting someone else in the company supervise the implementation," he explains. "Unfortunately, for new clients, the implementation phase determines whether or not they actually get what they were promised, and if they begin to feel the least bit insecure, you can bet your program will be stalled.

"Salespersons who are truly concerned about their company's image, their own professional reputations, and delivering on their promises will not allow anyone else to control this last step in the sale."

John Heitzenroder of Occidental Chemical stresses the importance of making a personal follow-up call when a prospect asks for a sample or a quotation. The call, he points out, gives the rep a chance to uncover needs, offer additional support from his or her company, clarify misunderstandings, or perhaps even alter the proposal.

John, like other contributors, feels that a complaint, if properly handled, can make the customer relationship stronger than ever. "There's only one way to handle a complaint," he says, "and that's to visit the customer. Find out what happened. Offer to settle the complaint any way the customer wants—usually he'll ask for less than your company would be willing to give. Explain why the fault happened and what steps are being taken to prevent it from happening again."

Entertainment is important in the chemical industry, he says, and such things as baseball or football games, a fishing trip, or dinner with the spouses build an in-depth relationship with the customer and sometimes lead to a lasting friendship. "But," he cautions, "if you assume that the prospect is going to do business with you just because you take him to lunch or baseball games, the business relationship will never get to first base."

In selling incentive programs, reports Bruce White of Maritz Motivation, "entertainment is a key client activity and can vary from lunches and dinner/theater outings or sports events (golf, football games, and the like) to checkout trips to prospective incentive travel destinations—which are never 100 percent business! The sales rep must match entertainment to the specific client, however, as some are offended even by an offer of lunch."

Another word of warning was sounded by Jake Kulp of AMP. "A basic rule of thumb," he says, "is to treat customers as you would want to be treated if you were in their place. But be careful not to cater blindly to every customer request. This may not lead to a long-term win-win relationship. You have a right to expect profits when you provide a high-quality product or service and the necessary support. Above all, it is imperative that you establish a relationship in which mutual respect and trust are shared."

Selling for Resale

"In our business," says Carl Unger of Zenith, "it's vitally important to maintain good communications with our accounts. Frequent personal calls are a *must*, and handling their problems is super important."

Although Jon Vitarius of Nabisco Brands and Larry Nonnamaker of Eastman Kodak are both selling to retailers, they have different attitudes toward mixing business with entertainment.

"As far as entertaining customers is concerned," says Jon, "I let my work speak for itself. Time can be better spent working with the customer than having a few drinks. I try not to mix my working relationships and social relationships."

"Establishing and maintaining good customer relations is critical to a company like Kodak that depends heavily on repeat business and an established dealer network," comments Larry. "We expect a great deal from our dealers, and they have a right to expect certain things in return.

"Follow-through is critical in maintaining good relations. Our dealers must be able to rely on us to come through on our promises. I like to go beyond the commitment if possible; this lets the dealer know how important his business is to us.

"Entertaining is also a very large part of good customer relations. It may be a simple lunch, a very formal dinner, a good round of golf, or a trip to the Indianapolis 500. We all know that we have to take care of business first, but after the business is behind us, I like to enjoy the informal relationships with the many friends I have established through business. I believe this personal touch separates Kodak from many of our competitors.

"I also believe, however, that you have to justify the expenditure from a business standpoint. Is the money you are spending reflected in the business you are receiving? If not, you have to reevaluate your entertainment. A great deal of business is done outside of corporate walls. Often, in fact, due to excessive interruptions, I will use lunch or dinner as the main place to transact business."

"I like to get new customers away from their place of business by inviting them to breakfast, lunch, or dinner," says Bob Chargin of McKesson Drug. "It gives me a chance to get their undivided attention.

"I also like to entertain my regular customers simply as a way of saying 'Thank you.' The entertainment should fit the customer—instead of a restaurant, it might be a round of golf or a day at the races. Entertainment, by the way, should not cut into your working day.

"One thing to watch very closely when entertaining is the consumption of alcohol. I have seen a sales rep lose a good account because of something he said when under the influence. I'm not against drinking, but I do pace myself."

Sometimes little things can help cement customer relations. "I would never think of walking into a buyer's office without a carton containing eight or ten different boxes of Nabisco Brand cookies," says Pat Markley of Nabisco Brands.

"Also, in writing up a promotional program, I include the store's logo in it. It's a nice personal touch, making the customer feel that he or she has been given special consideration in preparing the program.

"I always try to have something new and different in every program—a new format, a new product, a new idea. If I have two new products, I'll build one into this month's proposal and save the second one for next time. I don't want buyers to get the idea that my proposals are ever the same old things."

"Some PR work is always necessary," says Carl Unger of Zenith. "Our entertainment usually consists of buying the client a meal, although sometimes the client offers to buy. Some dos and don'ts on meal entertaining:

- Do not order a drink unless your client does.
- Do not order a meal that will tie up too much of your client's time.

- Do not order a meal considerably more expensive than what your client orders.
- Do not embarrass your client by leaving an inconsiderate tip.
- Be considerate in choosing the type of restaurant and the type of food that your client might enjoy.''

Selling to the Consumer

Betty Cinq-Mars, Vice President of Merrill Lynch in Kalamazoo, points out that since investing is an ongoing activity for her clients, maintaining a good relationship with them is the crux of her business. She lists six things she does regularly to cultivate her existing clients:

1. I mail out updates on stocks whenever there is an opinion change or any significant news on a stock a client owns. My clients appreciate the fact that I am keeping an eye on their stocks.
2. I mail out birthday cards to my IRA clients, since I have the record of their birthdates. Many clients appreciate this personal touch.
3. Whenever a client's CD becomes due, I send a notice of the amount due together with current CD rates and a request that the client phone me. The client may wish to purchase something else instead of renewing the CD. Either way, this is a revolving source of business and a very important one.
4. I remember people's names and voices. People always like to think that they count as individuals, not just as account numbers. This is one advantage we have over banks, and my clients are always impressed with the fact that I remember their names and account activities despite the large volume of business I handle.
5. Periodically I run a computer list of clients who have large sums in money market accounts, and suggest that they invest some of it in securities with a better return.
6. I encourage my clients to sit down with me occasionally to evaluate their positions. Many older clients have securities they purchased a long time ago which have lost much of their value. Or they may have stocks which have appreciated greatly, and it may be a good time to take a profit. Either way, I can help them keep their portfolios up to date.

"There must be systematic, ongoing programs to generate a steady flow of business," she concludes. "You can't sit back and wait for clients to come in with their bags of gold. Many investors just sit on their money and even forget what they have. It's our job to remind them of profitable changes."

"In casualty and life insurance," says Jack Hallberg of Allstate, "we are dealing in a world of constant change, so I send periodic mailings to my entire book of business to inform them of changes they should be aware of, and to let them know that my office staff and I are always available to them, never farther away than their telephone. I let them know that if they have a question, it's not an inconvenience to us, it's part of our business to keep them informed of change.

"If we're in sales, we have to like people, we have to enjoy the function of maintaining good customer relations. The sale doesn't end with the sale, especially in the insurance business, where repeat business is so important.

"Sometimes customers bother you with foolish questions, but just keep reminding yourself that every time a customer pays a premium, you're making money, and answering his questions is one way you're earning it."

Selling to Doctors and Hospitals

Peter Pappas of CIBA-Geigy says that entertaining is a good way to get to know physicians, but is difficult because of their busy schedules. What his company occasionally does instead is to invite a group of physicians to a dinner at which the guest speaker is an out-of-town physician who is well known in some specialized area.

"Physicians generally like this type of program," Peter reports, "because they can come directly from their offices, relax over dinner, and hear about the latest state-of-the-art way of treating a particular disease. Although I'm aware of the fact that you can't do business over a bar, this does give me an opportunity to get to know my physicians."

17
Time and Territory Management

Every sales rep is a manager. The rep manages two valuable assets:

1. The rep's own time—a priceless and perishable asset.
2. The territory—a portion of the company's market, whether defined geographically or in some other way, from which the company expects the rep to generate maximum profits.

Territory Management

Most sales executives will agree that the sales rep is managing the territory effectively when

- The rep knows what is there. He or she knows where the existing and potential customers are, what their needs are, and what they are purchasing from whom. The rep also knows the activities, strengths and weaknesses of the competition.
- The rep has established sales targets, by product lines and by customers, usually for one year into the future, with monthly or quarterly milestones.
- The rep allocates precious selling time in the most productive

way among customers and prospects of various types and sizes.

The salesperson's results depend on the management of three variables. The equation looks like this:

$$R = N \times Q \times A$$

where R = results

N = the number of calls made. Obviously, ten calls will produce more results than five calls, all other things being equal. What many sales reps resent is the fact that their company measures *only* the number of calls—because that's easy to measure—without taking into consideration the quality of the calls. They are fond of quoting a whiskery old anecdote about a salesman whose boss insisted he make 20 calls a day. When the boss criticized him for making only 19 calls one day, the rep replied, "I would have made 20 calls, except that last guy asked me what I was selling."

Q = the quality of the call. Five effective, well-planned calls will naturally produce more results than five off-the-cuff, here-I-am-again type of calls.

A = the allocation of calls. Is the sales rep dividing his or her time in the best way among customers and prospects, big ones and little ones? A very large number of very well handled calls cannot produce maximum results if they are made on the wrong people.

To allocate selling time effectively, the rep needs to *classify* customers in some way, usually into A, B, and C groups depending on present sales and future potential sales. Then a *call frequency* needs to be established for each group.

In selling to retailers, customer classifications are fairly stable. A rep can categorize the customers, assign call frequencies, lay out regular routes, and make only minor revisions every month or so. This is known in the trade as the "milk run" type of routing. In some companies, itineraries are so stable that if a manager wants to meet a rep at 11 A.M. on a Wednesday, he or she checks the rep's planned itinerary, goes to Store 4 on Day 3, and there's the rep.

In classifying customers, many companies and sales reps follow the Pareto principle. Pareto, an Italian economist, pointed out that in most collections of unlike objects, the most important 25 percent produced 75 percent of the results, while the less important 75 percent produced only 25 percent of the results. Twenty-five percent of the products account for 75 percent of the sales volume, 25 percent of the sales reps (sometimes) produce 75 percent of the sales volume, 25 percent of each rep's customers (usually) produce 75 percent of the sales.

So reps classify the top 25 percent of their customers—on the basis of potential as well as present volume—as A customers and call on them twice as frequently as on the other 75 percent (or B) customers.

If a rep has a large number of customers, call allocation can be improved by following a refinement of the Pareto principle, developed by Dr. J. M. Juran. He found (see Figure 17-1) that in many cases, the top 15 percent of the customers produce 65 percent of the sale, the next 20 percent produce 20 percent, and the remaining 65 percent produce only 15 percent of total sales. Juran refers to this as the principle of the vital few and the trivial many—or, as I prefer to state it, the important few and the unimportant many.

It's a fairly simple matter for the rep to rank his or her customers by present and potential future volume and see if the Juran principle applies. If it does, a good time allocation is to call on the A's twice as often as the B's, and the B's twice as often as the C's. For example, the rep might see each A customer or prospect every week, each B every other week, and each C every fourth week.

Time Management

Face-to-face selling time with the customer or prospect is the main opportunity for sales reps to apply all their knowledge and skills. Time management, for the salesperson, consists in spending as much time as possible with customers, and minimizing the time spent on nonselling chores and/or handling them outside selling hours.

Most sales reps are familiar with these basic ways of conserving selling time (although they don't always follow them 100 percent):

- Reducing traveling time by planning effective routes and by doing as much travel as possible before or after selling hours.
- Knowing when each customer is available.
- Phoning ahead to make sure the customer will be in, which

Figure 17-1. The "Juran principle" of the important few and the unimportant many.

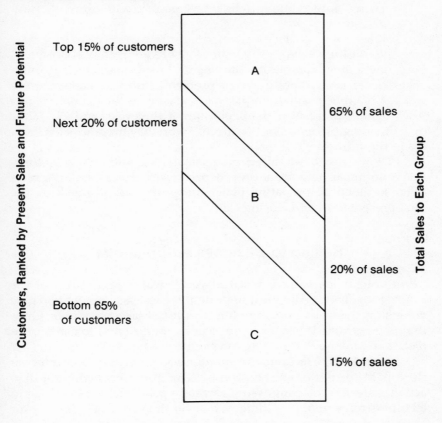

Used by permission of J. M. Juran.

not only avoids the "not in" call but also reduces waiting time when the customer is in.
- Using waiting time to catch up on paperwork or necessary reading.
- Handling other paperwork outside selling hours.

- Using lunch hours and even coffee breaks for customer contacts.
- Using entertainment, like ball games and dinners, judiciously.

The sales rep selling very expensive or very technical products, involving a long, complicated buying cycle and many buying influences, faces an entirely different problem. Priorities change every week. "A" time is spent on prospects at or near the decision stage, "B" time on those near the beginning of the cycle, and "C" time on cultivating prospects or "suspects" who may become active buyers in the future.

In some cases, the salesperson can allocate selling time by functions—so much time spent on prospecting, so much on initial sales calls, so much on preparing plans and proposals, so much on the final presentation and closing call.

Selling to Business and Industry

"Run your business or it will run you," warns Janis Drew of the *Los Angeles Times.* "The most important tactical assignment you give yourself is the task of determining your list of target accounts. Once that is determined, you use your sales expertise and experience to dictate the methods for going after these accounts.

"In general, I recommend spending 80 percent of your time on the top 20 percent of your business. Remain in control of your day, acting instead of reacting. Work toward a goal and be careful not to let others rob you of your time. Whatever time it takes to make your sales quota, that's the time you should take. In most cases this will mean longer hours than many of those around you, but to excel is to go beyond what everyone else is doing."

When Charlotte Jacobs of Pitney Bowes was just getting started, she avoided zigzagging from one end of her territory to the other by concentrating on one section of the territory each day and following the "3-3-3" plan: three cold calls on prospects, three follow-up calls, and three closing calls each day.

Sales representatives of Maritz Motivation Company, says Bruce White, use the pie-chart method of allocating time (see figure 17-2). The rep develops a 90-day action plan, which determines the amount of time the rep will spend with each major customer and the type

Figure 17-2. **Maritz Motivation's "pie chart" method of time allocation.**

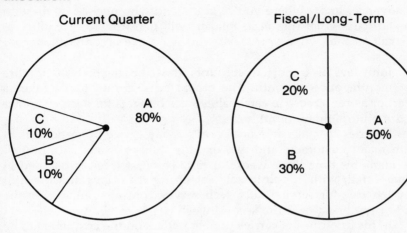

Current Quarter

Fiscal/Long-Term

80%—Customer A
Product-Support Program
Machine-Sales Program
Engine-Products Support Program
Engine OEM Sales Program
1987–1988 Program-Development
   Meetings
10%—Customer B
1988 Travel Program

10%—Customer C
Others

50%—Customer A
Product Support
Machines
Engines
Other Programs
Dealers

30%—Customer B
Multiple-Line Program
Corporate/Region Programs
20%—Customer C
All Others

Courtesy Maritz Motivation Company

of sales activity, from initial-familiarization calls to formal presentations to follow-up service calls.

"The larger accounts take more initial development work," Bruce says, "but the incentive programs they run take the same amount of service time and effort as small-volume accounts. So it pays to develop one or two large accounts and stick with them."

"The best way to use your time wisely," says John Heitzenroder of Occidental Chemical, "is to plan ahead. Make appointments in advance, know where you're going and who may be going with you, discuss what role each 'player' will perform. Keep control of the call so that when you leave, you will have accomplished your purpose."

John sees his important accounts, those buying $50,000 or more per month, once a month. The others he sees four to six times a year, or as required. He establishes sales budgets for each customer and monitors them monthly.

He tries to make five or six calls a day, three by appointment with major customers and two or three "fill-in" calls with others. He plans his time three weeks ahead. The first week is planned in some detail, with appointments set up for four days and the fifth day left free for service calls, tech service, or emergencies. By the end of the first week, the second week has been filled in.

In his briefcase he carries the file folders on the customers to be seen that day. If he has to wait a few minutes before seeing the customer, he uses the time to review important points for the upcoming call, or to write up his report on the preceding call.

"We try to keep paperwork short and simple," he says. "Get it in on time and be sure that it includes only important market information or important requests for support, such as price or freight-rate information, or preparation of a quote or contract."

Jake Kulp of AMP agrees that "time is your scarcest resource."

"One must prioritize it and allocate it carefully," he comments. "I use this simple classification of tasks:

Those I must do.
Those I want to do.
Those I don't have to complete, but will if time allows.

"Factors influencing the classification of tasks are:

- The dollar amount involved.
- The critical nature of the problem: Does it threaten a product-line shutdown or merely a revision in the catalog?
- The deadline: Do I have two weeks to respond to an RFQ (Request for Quotation) or only five days?
- The degree of cooperation available from those involved.
- The time required in relation to the potential return."

"Twenty-three years in the business have not made this writer an expert in time and territory management," comments John Paul Jones of Monsanto. "My present territory, approximately 90,000 square miles, is covered on a five-week cycle. That is, I try to be at the same account every fifth week, plus or minus a day.

"Currently I am working about 32 average-size accounts and eight which are considered major accounts. In addition, I rely on my distributor to provide coverage on many small accounts I was responsible for before 1983.

"I visit the average account once a month, with telephone contacts in between. I visit the majors twice a month, also with telephone follow-up. Barring customer problems, I try to spend at least one hour with the average account and usually allocate half a day for the majors.

"Reduction of travel time is almost impossible in my area. All travel is by surface; the territory is divided into four quadrants.

"Calling time, on both average and major accounts, is always divided into three segments: first to Purchasing as a courtesy, and to determine if orders and deliveries are correct; second to Quality Control and Manufacturing to make sure the product is running satisfactorily; and third to Engineering to see if improvements are needed and learn what's new.

"Regarding paperwork and making the best use of time: I learned many years ago that most reports should be written the same day instead of waiting until the weekend or month-end rush. I spend waiting time making notes on the previous call, to be finalized that evening. My first stop next day is usually at the post office to dispense with some of the burdens of the previous day."

Flexibility is the key to time management in a job like Bill O'Neill's with Wausau Insurance Companies.

"Because of the nature of my business," he explains, "it is impossible to define customer categories for establishing call frequencies. Almost every phone call I get is a priority to the policyholder, and usually I have to be able to respond immediately. Therefore, the only priority I can establish is that my present clients come first and new business or prospect calls come second. I really can't anticipate what my clients' needs will be on a daily basis, so flexibility is important.

"Nevertheless, even though I'm on 24-hour call (my wife can attest to the 5 A.M. or midnight phone calls) to respond to my policyholders' needs, I *do* have a plan in which I allocate 50 percent of my time to service and (ugh!) paperwork, and 50 percent to pursuing new accounts. Of course, more often than not I have to abandon the plan to take care of other priorities. But the important thing is that I always have a plan that gets me up every morning with a direction for the day.

"One other priority—perhaps more of a personal goal with me—is that I return all phone calls the same day I get them, and make every effort to satisfy my customers' requests the same day they ask them. So many businesspeople don't return calls, don't follow up on requests, that they make anyone who is halfway professional look better than he or she really is.

"I am always amazed when people thank me for returning their calls. I've even asked some of my clients, 'Why are you thanking me? That's what I'm here for.' They tell me, 'You have no idea how many people *don't* return calls.' Can you imagine salespeople not returning calls? Wow! I can remember early on when I would pray just for one call a week! Even now, when I sometimes get thirty calls a day (all of them emergencies, naturally!), I never complain, because I remember when there were none.

"A bit of general advice: highest and best use of time: Do something! Don't just stand around; it will kill you."

Selling for Resale

Contributors in this category generally used the classification and time-allocation procedures discussed in the introduction to this chapter.

For example, Bob Chargin of McKesson Drug, whose territory is large for a wholesale drug rep, calls on each client every two weeks, scheduling his calls geographically. He has standing appointments with each customer at a certain time every other week, and spends about 1½ hours with an independent drug store and three hours at a chain. (Instead of calling on smaller customers half as often, he spends half as much time per call—a sensible method of time allocation when covering a large area.)

"Since the customers know when to expect me, they're usually available," he reports. "If the client is busy, there are three things I can do: (1) check problem areas in that store, (2) catch up on my own paperwork, or (3) take care of recalls.

"If the client is going to be busy longer than the time I can allot, I leave. Fortunately that doesn't happen too often. Occasionally I'll reschedule all my calls on a given day to better suit one customer—provided it doesn't inconvenience another customer.

"I can't cover my territory in an eight-hour day. I'm often on the road shortly after 6 A.M. and seldom get home in time to have dinner with my family.

"My advice on making the best possible use of one's time is simple: work. My brother-in-law owns a couple of cocktail lounges. He says a lot of his daytime business is from salesmen, many of whom come in every day and spend from two to six hours. You're not going to make many sales sitting on a bar stool—unless you're selling liquor."

Carl Unger of Zenith makes weekly calls on accounts buying more than $100,000 a year and on new accounts needing sales training. If a buyer is tied up, he looks for a retail salesperson he can take aside for a bit of sales training.

Cevin Melezoglu of American Greetings developed her own unusual priority-setting and control system to manage her time effectively and achieve a balance between her work and her personal life.

"First of all," she reports, "I would place all projects and paperwork into four separate baskets labeled 'Priority A' through 'Priority D.' Next, I followed the guidelines I had established for each priority:

- Priority A: I could not go to sleep that night until everything in this basket had been completed. Needless to say, not many projects ended up in this basket.
- Priority B: I could not go out that weekend until this pile was empty.
- Priority C: This was work that needed to be done but had no special deadline.
- Priority D: This was a catch-all for tasks that could be put off indefinitely. Often, Priority-D tasks became obsolete before I wasted time on them, but sometimes they got bumped up to a higher rating.

"I attribute the success of this system to the integrity of its application. Rarely did I violate my own self-established guidelines.

"Basically, I would suggest avoiding the trap of spending time on tasks that you enjoy in order to spend more time on tasks that are really the most important, even though they may be less enjoyable.

"Another tip: To reduce travel time, plan your itinerary so that you're always driving against the traffic. Map out your day so you're never going with the rush-hour traffic."

Pat Markley of Nabisco Brands finds that she saves valuable time during sales calls by mailing descriptions of the forthcoming promotion programs to the buyers two or three days before her call. "If you come at the buyer cold with a lot of information," she says, "it not only takes up a lot of time, but the bombardment of information causes the buyer to turn you off."

Jon Vitarius, also with Nabisco Brands, stresses the importance of maintaining a consistent schedule in calling on retail accounts. He sees his important A accounts three times a week, on Mondays, Wednesdays, and Fridays, trying to see each account at approximately the same time of day. The more important accounts, he says, should be seen early in the day and early in the week, less important ones later in the day or week.

Nabisco Brands classifies accounts as follows:

- A: Customers, major food chains (high volume).
- B: Customers, major food chains (low volume) and independent food chains.
- C: Prospects, high potential.
- D: Prospects, low potential.

Jon, like most Nabisco Brands sales reps, has seven major food chains and eight independents. Nabisco Brands sales reps spend 80 percent to 90 percent of their time concentrating on existing accounts. Jon blocks out his week as shown in figure 17-3.

"The time-and-territory-management aspect of selling is becoming more and more important," reports Larry Nonnamaker of Eastman Kodak. "There are so many demands on one's time that it would be easy to forget your main objective: selling.

"Kodak has recently taken four divisions and combined them into the United States Sales Division. This consolidation has made time and territory management a major priority if one is to be effective.

"Kodak's sales territories vary greatly in terms of geography, dealer size, and total dollars. The key, regardless of territory, is to be well organized and to use your time as effectively as possible.

Figure 17-3. A schedule for calling on four categories of accounts.

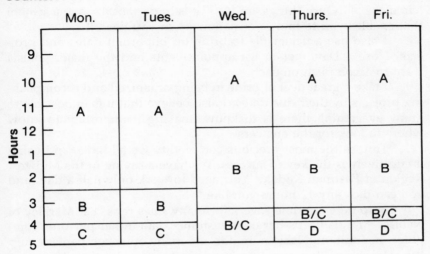

We have weekly call reports which force us to plan two weeks in advance. We also receive many computer-generated reports which tell us how we are spending our time. This lets us know how well we are allocating our time among dealers of various sizes.

"However, it still falls back on the sales rep to plan effectively and make sure all dealers have the appropriate call coverage. As a national account coordinator, I spend about 50 percent of my time with two national accounts—25 percent on administrative duties and paperwork, 25 percent on actual calls. The other 50 percent is spent with other dealers.

"It is very important to prioritize your projects. I list all goals and projects in the appropriate order and never go from one to another until the more important one has been completed.

"Mail and paperwork are sometimes overwhelming today. I use the 'A-I-R-WB' filing system for filing my mail:

A: Action required.
I: Information needed for sales calls.
R: Reading on the market or the photo industry.
WB: Wastebasket.

"They don't make file cabinets big enough to hold everything. It is critical to know what needs to be saved and what goes in the 'circular file.' Once things are filed, it is important to have a system that enables you to find information when you need it.

"I also use a tickler file to bring up important dates and projects. I use a Daytimer to list appointments and the major goals I want to accomplish on each.

"I take a great deal of pride in being organized and accomplishing projects by their due dates. I also believe that it is impossible to know everything there is to know, making it important to know where to look for the answers.

"Time is the most precious commodity we all have, and using it effectively is the key to success. We have a saying in the Midwest Region of Eastman Kodak: 'You need to work only half a day, and you can pick any 12 hours you like.' "

Computers are time savers for many sales reps. Pat Markley of Nabisco Brands keeps her own customer data in her personal computer. In addition, Nabisco Brands and many other companies equip the sales rep with a computer modem that enables the rep to network with the company's mainframe computer to get information on each customer, such as purchases, type of programs favored, planned call frequency, and date of last call.

Carl Unger of Zenith finds that there are "morning people" and "afternoon people," and takes this into consideration in scheduling his calls. In order to lose as little time as possible, he also lets his dealers know when to expect him.

Selling to the Consumer

John O. Todd of Northwestern Mutual explains that "I can't comment on territory management, because the world is my territory," but submits the following analysis of "time control for salespeople":

"Even though we all have a product or service to sell, *time* is the most important ingredient that any salesperson has.

"There are just 24 hours in every day, and if eight hours are for sleep, then each of us has exactly the same number of hours to work or play. We often say 'I didn't have time,' but what we mean is that there was something else we thought was more important to do.

"So setting priorities is the key.

"Production in any sales position is a product of a very simple but absolute formula, as follows: *number of attempts to close × percentage of closing efficiency × size of average sales = production.*

"Ahead of this phase of the equation must come: *the number of calls × the percentage of interviews required to produce a qualified prospect.*

"Of course, it is essential that records be kept by the salesperson if these formulas are to do any good. To start with, for a new sales rep or for anyone who has not kept such records, it is possible to assume certain ratios and then to correct the assumptions as records of actual performance become known.

"So now let's look at a sample of how production can be established as virtually a known quantity, fully under the control of the salesperson.

"Assume that the objective is to earn $100,000 in commissions in the next 12 months. We look back on last year's production and discover that over the past year, the average sale has produced $400 in commission. To make $100,000, therefore, we need to make 250 sales. If we plan to be working for 50 weeks, that's five sales a week, or one a day.

"Next, we find that it takes four new calls or interviews to find two qualified prospects, and that we make one sale for every two closing calls. So now we know what a good day's work consists of. We must make four prospecting calls and two closing calls each working day.

"Now let's look at the formula:

> 4 suspects × 50% = 2 qualified prospects
> 2 attempts to close × 50% = 1 sale
> 1 sale @ $400 × 5 days a week = $2,000
> $2,000 × 50 weeks = $100,000

We can see that if we fail to recognize each factor in this formula, the whole chain breaks down. Furthermore, we note that if we increase our efficiency in any one of the factors, we increase the end results. But most important of all, we know that a good day's work includes all of the factors and is not limited to a day when we happen to close a big one.

"Furthermore, we must know that, whether we are aware of it or not, *all sales are preceded by the factors we put into the formula.* So why not take control?

"Time control and the willingness to adhere to it will guarantee success in sales. Lack of it leads to confusion. Confusion wastes time, but definiteness puts an end to confusion."

Because those selling to consumers can often set their own hours, says Jack Hallberg of Allstate Insurance, the rep should decide how many hours a week he or she wants to work, and then actually put in that many hours.

"Many sales reps," he points out, "aren't working as many hours as they think they are. It's like a fellow on a diet. He says, 'I've been on this 1,000-calorie diet for a month, and I still gained three pounds.' But if he started keeping a record, he'd find that he'd actually been consuming 1,500 to 2,000 calories.

"If a sales rep actually kept a record of his time for a while, he might discover that he's wasting time without even realizing it. The 15-minute coffee break takes half an hour, the five minutes spent scanning the sport pages stretches to 20 minutes, the one-hour non-business lunch absorbs two hours. Some people think they've worked eight hours just because they put in the time from 9 to 5, but if they kept a log and found out how few hours they really worked, they'd realize that their paycheck represents a pretty good rate of pay per hour actually worked.

"There are only so many hours, and you do have a responsibility to your family, to your church, to your community, and certainly to your business. One of the criteria for success is to realize that you have only X amount of minutes in the day to devote to your job, and to make sure that in those X minutes you're giving the job 100 percent of the best you can possibly do. You have to make sure that in the time for work, you're working; in the time for play, you're playing; in the time for sleep, you're sleeping—just make sure you don't mix them all up."

One way Jack expands his selling time is to persuade customers to come to his office and see him. In that way he can see six or seven clients personally and handle many others by phone—far more than he could contact by driving all over the Chicago area.

"We have a handy office location just off an expressway," he explains, "and I can get 90 percent of the prospects to come see me. I explain to them, 'Later on we'll be able to handle most of our business by phone, but I want to meet you just this one time. I want to have a picture of you, and I want you to have a picture of me and the staff.' "

An important time saver, he adds, is to put together a staff that can handle most of the paperwork. He has two assistants who follow up constantly on requests to other departments of Allstate. If a request hasn't been answered within two weeks, a computer printout reminds the staff of that fact and they follow up by phone.

"Another time-saving tip," he adds, "is to keep a record of the names of everybody you talk to in other company departments, or even in outside agencies like the Assigned Risk Program. It's amazing how things get done when people know you've asked for them by name."

"We teach our salespeople to use their time effectively by making appointments," says Dave Van Tosh of Encyclopaedia Britannica. "Since we must see the husband and wife at the same time, 99 percent of our appointments are in the evening.

"We also teach them to overlap their appointments (see chart below). Instead of making appointments at 6 P.M., 7 P.M., and 8 P.M., they make their first appointment for 'between 6 and 8,' the next for 'between 7 and 9,' the third for 'between 8 and 10.'

	6 P.M.	7 P.M.	8 P.M.	9 P.M.	10 P.M.
First appt.	————————————————				
Second appt.		————————————————			
Third appt.			————————————————		

"Let's say you start with the 6 P.M. appointment. If Mrs. Jones says, 'Mr. Jones is stuck at the plant tonight—can you come back some other time?' you can go to your 7 o'clock appointment and then to your 8 o'clock appointment. Or, if you make a presentation at the 6 o'clock appointment and finish in an hour, you can still get to your second appointment. If the 7 o'clock presentation takes two hours, you still have time to make the 8-to-10 appointment.

"By overlapping your appointments you have the best of two worlds: You're never late and you always have enough time. There's nothing worse than sitting in your car because you don't have time to make another call without being late for the appointment after that."

"Telephone, telephone, telephone—it's the best tool you have," says Hal Kessler of Terminix. "Car phones aren't available in my district, but I wish they were. If I'm driving down the street and see a tree stump loaded with termites, there's a good chance the house on the property has termites as well. I hate to drive in the driveway to make a cold call, but with a car phone I could go 50 feet down the street and telephone for an appointment."

Hal makes the most of his selling time by working on lists of prospects at home in the evening. Like many salespeople, he gets into the office an hour earlier than he is supposed to—at 7 A.M. instead of 8 A.M.

Selling to Doctors and Hospitals

"Call frequency is the key to success in pharmaceutical selling," reports Peter Pappas of CIBA-Geigy. "The sale is usually not generated by the first call on a physician and perhaps not by the eighth call, but with persistence we usually get the business. Since the physician is not making a purchase for himself but instead is prescribing for his patients, he will not make a commitment to use our product until he is sure it will fit his practice.

"We try to see the high-prescribing physicians and cardiologists at least eight times a year. If you spend ten minutes with a doctor eight times a year, you can really get to know him and to know how and why he prescribes what he does.

"Because of the size of my territory and the number of accounts it contains, it would be absolutely impossible to cover it without a planned itinerary. I look at each city and town and consider the volume of our major product sales in that area, and the number of high-prescribing physicians. From this I can determine how much time to spend in each city to see the important doctors every six weeks. Once the itinerary is made up it must be followed exactly, so that neither too much nor too little time is spent in each part of the territory."

Biographies of Contributors

Bob Chargin, retail account manager, McKesson Drug Company, Sacramento, California. BS in Business, Sacramento City College, 1966. Salesman of the Year six times; member of the McKesson Ring of Excellence.

Roland M. Charles, Jr., major account executive, GTE Mobilnet, Inc. (cellular auto telephone services), Houston. Attended Butler County Community College in El Dorado, Kansas, University of Houston, and Columbia College in Columbia, Missouri. Former positions included program coordinator and administrative aide for the city of Wichita, Kansas; Yellow Pages advertising salesman for Southwestern Bell Telephone in Wichita and winner of their Objective Achievement Award; account executive for MCI; with GTE Mobilnet since August, 1984.

Michael C. Ciarcia, director, business development, Turner Construction Company, New York City. Bachelor's degree in Architectural Engineering from Penn State University, 1972. Went into sales in 1978. Now sells construction services ranging from $1 million to $300 million to corporations, institutions, developers, governments; networks constantly with architects, engineers, brokers, bankers, public officials, and corporate executives.

Betty Cinq-Mars, vice president and financial consultant, Merrill Lynch, Kalamazoo, Michigan. MA in French, University of Massachusetts, 1972; MBA, Western Michigan University, 1976. With E. F. Hutton in New York for two years before joining Merrill Lynch in Kalamazoo 11 years ago. No. 1 among all Merrill Lynch brokers in number of IRA accounts, among the top 100 in total production. Has received Circle of Excellence, Champions' Circle, and other awards.

David F. Clark, sales representative, Simmons USA, Stone Mountain, Georgia. MBA, Georgia College of Milledgeville, 1983. Sales rep for Toyota Central before joining Simmons. Won Toyota Sales Award, 1979; Simmons All-American in 1985 and 1986; member of Simmons Million Dollar Club.

William J. Clark, regional sales manager, Cooper Tire and Rubber Company, North Brunswick, New Jersey. BS, 1957, Seton Hall University, South Orange, New Jersey. Cooper is an independent tire manufacturer selling replacement tires rather than original equipment. Won Salesman of the Year award before being promoted to management; selected as Regional Sales Manager of the Year many times. Conducts workshops on selling for the American Management Association; volunteer lecturer at Rutgers (NJ) State University.

Nick Debronsky, account executive, Unisys Corporation, Denver. BS in Business, California State College, Los Angeles, 1971. Served in 98th Data Processing Unit, U. S. Army. Sells mainframe computers, peripherals, and software. Rookie of the Year with Honeywell in 1972 and with Sperry in 1974.

Thomas W. DeLaMater, staff assistant, Encyclopaedia Britannica USA, Atlanta. Psychology major, State University of New York, Albany, 1964. With Encyclopaedia Britannica since 1968 except 1981–1982, when he sold business telephone systems for ITT Terryphone in Miami. Work with EB has included sales trips to Labrador, Cuba, and the Panama Canal Zone and selling Great Books of the Western World in five eastern and southeastern states. National Man of the Month several times; Phoenix Ring Winner, 1973.

Gregory A. Deming, director of sales, American Express Travel Management Services, El Segundo, California. BS in Business Administration from California State University in Fresno, 1975. Sold American Express credit card acceptance to restaurants and retailers, 1977–1980; sold American Express Corporate Card to businesses, 1980–1984; now with American Express Travel Management Services, directing the sales activities of 17 field personnel in California, Arizona, New Mexico, Texas, and Louisiana. Winner of American Express Sales Excellence Award.

Suzanne DeNoyior, manager, Huntington (Long Island) office of Coldwell Banker Residential Real Estate. BS, psychology major at

Suffolk Community College. Became a New York State Licensed Broker in 1983 and currently is Treasurer of the Long Island Board of Realtors. Former multimillion-dollar producer, now managing Coldwell Banker branch with a staff of 40. Awards include President's Club, Three Million Club, and Marketing Specialist.

Janis Drew, Eastern magazine manager, *Los Angeles Times Magazine*. Educated at Miami University, Oxford, Ohio; Bachelor's degree in 1973 and Master's in 1975. Salesperson for the *Los Angeles Times*, 1976–1979; awarded Suburban Salesperson of the Year, 1978. Moved to *Los Angeles Magazine*, a division of ABC Publications, in 1979 and was responsible for automotive, fashion, and liquor advertising. In 1982, was hired by *Omni Magazine* and promoted to Los Angeles manager for *Omni*. Returned to the *Los Angeles Times* in 1986 and is now headquartered in New York as Eastern magazine manager of *Los Angeles Times Magazine*.

Ralph C. Eubanks, manager of training and development, Roerig Division of Pfizer, New York City. BA, Tampa University, with majors in both business administration and psychology. Member of Vice President's Club for Consistent Sales Performance; Regional Managers Award, 1980; runner-up as Representative of the Year in 1981, many regional and district awards. Promoted to district hospital representative, 1982; manager of training operations, 1984; manager of training and development, 1986.

Anthony R. Flores, national sales manager, Household Products Division of Alberto Culver, Naperville, Illinois. BA in Business Administration, Pierce College, California, and Youngstown (Ohio) State University, 1965. With Lever Brothers from 1966 to 1982 as sales rep, account manager, area sales manager, market manager of Foods Division, market manager of HBA (health and beauty aids) Division; one year as field sales analyst at national headquarters. Regional manager with Celloplast U.S.A., 1982–1983; joined Alberto Culver in 1983 as regional manager, promoted to national sales manager in 1985; vice president, sales, with Merkt Enterprises in 1987.

J. M. Garcia, program manager, employee development, General Electric Medical Systems Business Group, Milwaukee. BBA, Southwest Texas State University. Western Region sales trainer for Quaker Oats in Chicago; national sales training manager at Estech General Chemical and Norwich Eaton Pharmaceuticals; human relations director responsible for training in sales, service, and management at Diacon Computer Systems; currently responsible for customizing and administering training programs for a GE division that makes imaging equipment for hospitals.

Jack Hallberg, senior account agent, Allstate, Chicago. Joined Allstate as sales representative in 1968. Responsible for selling and servicing more than 5,600 accounts comprised of casualty, life, group life and health, and commercial insurance. Has the largest number of life accounts of any of Allstate's 14,000 agents; one of four agents awarded Allstate Life Millionaire designation for 17 consecutive years; seven-time winner of Allstate Gold Record Award as No. 1 life insurance underwriter in the 13-state Midwest Zone; largest book of casualty accounts of any Allstate agent in Illinois.

Douglas Haynie, account manager, Baxter Travenol (division of American Hospital Supply), Atherton, California. BS in Business, University of Florida, 1971; MBA candidate, Golden Gate University, San Francisco, 1972. Was No. 1 in commission increase nationally 1975, 1976, 1985; over 110 percent of profit plan 11 years in a row; No. 1 in sales, gross profit, and commissions in 1984, 1985, 1986; President's Award, 1984, 1985; Sales Excellence Award for California, all 13 years; Premier Club, 1984, 1985, 1986 charter member.

John Heitzenroder, Jr., account manager, Occidental Chemical Corporation (formerly the chemical division of Diamond Shamrock Chemicals Company), Hockessin, Delaware. BS in Marketing, University of Delaware, Newark, 1969. Sells industrial chemicals (sodium hydroxide, potassium hydroxide, chlorine, solvents, silicates, chrome chemicals) in carload and truckload quantities to refiners, manufacturers of chemicals, pharmaceuticals, food products, and so on; and distributors for customers buying in smaller quantities. Salesman of the Year, Philadelphia branch, 1981; President's Inner Circle (one of five), 1985.

Charlotte Barrett Jacobs, national account manager, Pitney Bowes, Cincinnati. BS in Office Administration, Miami University, Oxford, Ohio, 1978. With Pitney Bowes nine years. Sells mailing systems, shipping systems, electronic inserters, copiers, and mailroom furniture to a limited number of key accounts. Member of Sales Leadership Club seven consecutive years; director in 1983 and 1984; nominated for 1986 Salesman of the Year Award.

John Paul Jones, sales account manager, Monsanto Chemical Company, Greenville, South Carolina. BA, The Citadel, 1954. With Monsanto for 30 years, 23 in sales. Sells thermoplastic resins, nylon, ABS, and modified styrene acrylonitrile products directly to converters for use in electronic, textile, automotive, and appliance industries. Winner of four Master Sales Awards, Monsanto's top award; General Manager's Achievement Award; contributor to book *The Master Salesman* written in 1984 by winners of the Master Sales Award; won the Go for the Gold Award in 1980 as one of two individuals in the Plastics Division who exceeded all budgets during the recession.

Denise Kaluzna, unit manager, Tupperware Home Parties. BA in Early Childhood Education, National College of Education, 1972. Joined Tupperware in 1980 as part-time dealer, promoted to manager in 1984. In 1986, her team of 70 people was No. 2 nationally in the first quarter and No. 1 in the remaining three quarters. Her personal sales in 1986, $112,000; her unit's sales, $660,000. Has developed 14 managers and brought 112 people into the business; has won autos, diamond necklace, color TV, trips, many other prizes.

Hal Kessler, sales representative, Terminix International, Fairfield County, Connecticut. Two years college. Developed a distribution center shipping sugar packets to wholesale grocers and built it to $9 million volume in four years. Sells monthly pest control service and termite treatment to residences and businesses. Won Terminix Salesman of the Month Award for 10 months in a row.

John H. ("Jake") Kulp, promoted during preparation of this book from senior sales engineer in Texas to industry manager, Federal Systems Business Group, AMP, Inc., Harrisburg, Pennsylvania. Started with AMP one week after graduating from Bloomsburg (PA) State College with BS in Marketing in 1979. One year as assistant to marketing manager, six years as salesman. AMP Man of the Year and Man of the Southwest District, 1985. AMP is the world's largest ($1.9 billion) supplier of electric and electronic connectors.

Edward J. Lahue, senior key account supervisor, The Dial Corporation, Edwardsville, Illinois. BS in Business Administration, Southern Illinois University in Edwardsville, 1985; recently earned MBA in Marketing on part-time basis. Started in retail sales rep for Armour-Dial, Inc., selling and merchandising 170 retail accounts in St. Louis area; promoted to key account supervisor responsible for the independent wholesaler account. When Armour-Dial merged with Purex to form The Dial Corporation, was given responsibility for all products sold to the National supermarket chain, representing $2 million in sales annually. Products include Dial Soap, Tone Soap, Pure & Natural Soap, Purex Bleach, Purex Detergent, Armour canned meats, and others. Top Sales Representative, West Central

Region, for May/June 1986 in recognition of success achieved with St. Louis Division of National supermarket chain.

Frank Paul Lentz, national account district manager, Chicago Region, Automatic Data Processing. AB in Political Science cum laude, Miami University, Oxford, Ohio; diploma in French language and linguistics, Sorbonne, Paris, 1976; BA in French and Spanish, Northern Illinois University, DeKalb, 1978; career-related course work in math and electronics at Harper College and Elgin Community College in Northern Illinois. Taught French at Northern Illinois University and University of North Carolina. Technical writer in three languages for Contec Controls, Elgin, Illinois, 1981; major accounts sales representative, Lanier Business Products, 1982–1983; district manager, ADP, 1983–1984. As ADP national account district manager in Chicago, is responsible for marketing integrated payroll, human-resource, and tax-filing systems to companies with more than 500 employees. Completed fiscal 1986 as No. 1 salesman in the nation in both dollar volume and percentage of quota; set new record for total sales in one year.

Patricia M. Markley, promoted during preparation of this book from sales representative to account manager, Specialty Sales, Nabisco Brands, Inc., New York Metro Area. BA from Hofstra University, specializing in technical theater, 1972. Joined Nabisco Brands in 1975. Took over a Long Island territory, selling Nabisco Brands products such as Oreo cookies, Fig Newtons, Premium crackers, Ritz crackers and Chips Ahoy! In her new position, she calls on national and regional headquarters in the New York metro area of all chains, other than food chains, handling Nabisco Brands products: K-Mart, Woolworth, drug chains, and so on. For five years responsible for preparing her division's brochure used at annual sales meeting; trained many new reps.

Judie McCoy, executive senior sales director, Mary Kay Cosmetics, Waukesha, Wisconsin. Became consultant for Mary Kay Cosmetics in 1976. Has built up staff of 1,000 consultants and directors with sales in 1986 of $3 million. Was No. 1 Mary Kay director nationwide three times, No. 2 director twice, member of Half Million Dollar Club eight times, on Director's Queens Court of Recruiting. Awards won include pink Cadillac, full-length mink coat, diamond ring and pins, trips.

Cevin Melezoglu was promoted during her contributions to this book from sales training specialist, American Greetings, Cleveland, to manager of sales training for the 250-person sales force of American's recently formed subsidiary, Carlton Cards of Dallas, Texas. BS in Marketing and Business Administration, University of Maryland, 1983. Started as sales representative for American Greetings in Baltimore; after 17 months made sales training specialist in 1985. American Greetings is in the social expression business, manufacturing and distributing greeting cards and related items; has developed theme characters like Care Bears, Ziggy, Strawberry Shortcake, and Popples; Carlton Cards is a relatively new venture targeted at the specialty gift shop market.

Larry C. Nonnamaker, national account coordinator, Eastman Kodak Company, Cincinnati. BS in Business Administration, Bowling Green State University, 1981. Joined Eastman Kodak in 1982; was made national account coordinator in Cincinnati for the newly formed U.S. Sales Division of Kodak in 1984. Member Kodak's 110 Club (top 10 percent of sales reps, measured by sales vs. quota), 1984 and 1986. Sells Kodak film, cameras, processing services, paper, chemicals, and batteries to retailers, wholesalers, and photofinishers.

William L. O'Neill, Jr., sales representative, Wausau Insurance Companies, Belmont, Massachusetts. BA, University of Pennsylvania, 1972. Sells and services business insurance, including workers' compensation, property, general liability, surety, auto, and business life insurance. Sales Quota Buster Award in nine of his 11 years with Wausau; four Leadership Sales Conference Awards. Consistently in top 5 percent of sales force in new business written while maintaining a renewal percentage of more than 90 percent every year.

Peter C. Pappas, professional sales representative, CIBA-Geigy Corporation, Pharmaceutical Division, Albany, New York. Associate's degree in Science, Dean Junior College, Franklin, Massachusetts, 1960; BS in General Education, State University of New York, Albany. Sold pharmaceutical and medical supplies for ten years before joining CIBA-Geigy ten years ago. Calls on physicians, pharmacists, and hospitals in the Albany area to gain specifications for his product line. The CIBA-Geigy Pharmaceutical Division specializes in cardiovascular products for patients with hypertension (high blood pressure) or heart problems. Peter is a three-time winner of CIBA's Distinguished Performance Award, winner of the Circle of Excellence Award, and two-time winner of the Circle of Merit Award.

Walter W. Patten, Jr., account manager, *BusinessWeek* magazine, Boston. BSME, Cornell University, 1949. Joined Publications Division of McGraw-Hill Corporation in 1954 as space salesman for business publications *Petroleum Processing, Purchasing Week, Electrical World, American Machinist.* Joined *BusinessWeek* in 1985; 33 years with McGraw-Hill.

J. David Pitzer, vice president sales, Northern Region, Dr Pepper, Columbus, Ohio. BS in Business Administration, Ithaca College, Ithaca, New York, 1977. From 1977 to 1980 sold industrial foods for Procter & Gamble as sales rep in Boston and as zone manager in Dallas. From 1980 to 1982 with Pepsico as district sales manager, Food Service Division, and national account manager, Columbus, Ohio, selling to Wendy's. Joined Dr Pepper Food Service Division in 1982; 1986 was his fourth straight record-volume year; led U.S. in percentage over quota in 1983. Responsible for sale of Dr Pepper fountain syrup to all locations selling fountain soft drinks.

Steven Rand, senior account executive, Dun's Marketing Services, northern New Jersey. BA in Liberal Arts and MA in Marketing, Fairleigh Dickinson University, 1973. Dun's Marketing is the business-to-business marketing group of Dun & Bradstreet, compiling and selling business and executive name mailing lists, providing lead services to field and telemarketing sales forces, and building marketing-information data bases. A leading account executive for DMS for more than 18 years, he has been particularly successful in establishing ongoing dealer support programs to carry out a manufacturer's cooperative and national lead-generating advertising programs. Multiple winner of Dun's President Citation Award, sales contests, Circle of Excellence, and Salesman of the Year. Top salesman for the last two years and in the top five every year for the past ten years. Charter member of Dun's Presidential and Direct Mail Advisory Councils and member of its New Product Development Board.

Gary Rucker, sales training manager, Kitchen Products, Whirlpool Corporation, Benton Harbor, Michigan. Attended University of New Orleans. Marketing manager for Kalvar Microfilm Corporation before joining Whirlpool Corporation in 1977 as builder territory manager for the New Orleans Sales Division. In 1981 was selected as Builder Territory Manager of the Year for the New Orleans Sales Division and also earned the Hall of Fame Selling Award. In 1985 promoted to sales training manager, Kitchen Products Division, and relocated to Benton Harbor. In 1987 promoted to field sales manager in Charlotte, North Carolina, at the Charlotte Sales Division, which covers North and South Carolina.

Paul Sanders, sales representative, Hewlett-Packard Company, San Francisco. Associate of Arts, Modesto (CA) Junior College, 1966; BA in English Literature, California State University, Turlock, 1968; candidate for MA in English Literature, Simon Fraser University, British Columbia, 1973. Sales rep for Polygram Records in British Columbia for three years; outside sales rep for San Francisco office-equipment dealer for three years. Joined Hewlett-Packard in 1981, selling personal-computer products to major retailers, primarily by supporting their retail sales efforts. Rookie of the Year award his first year; awards every year for exceeding quota; charter member of Hewlett-Packard's President's Club, 1986.

Gourdin E. Sirles, recently retired division sales manager, AT&T, New York City. Responsible for protecting and growing, on a worldwide basis, several million dollars of AT&T revenue from ten of the nation's largest international insurance and financial-services customers. While supervising a sales force, continued handling the tough sales assignments.

John O. Todd, CLU, insurance company salesman, Evanston, Illinois. Known as "a legend in his time" because of his many innovations and contributions to others in the life insurance industry. He still puts in a full day's work in his 85th year, is the only person on earth to *qualify* for the Million Dollar Round Table (MDRT) for 52 consecutive years (others have been members that long, but no one else has sold at least $1 million in insurance every year for more than half a century). Even more remarkable, for the last 12 years, since Top of the Table was founded (calling for approximately six times the MDRT qualifications), he has qualified each year. Born in Minneapolis, Minnesota, 1902; AB, Cornell University, 1924; earned his CLU from the American College in 1933. Started in the insurance business in Minneapolis in 1926 with The Equitable. Left Equitable in 1928, and after 3 years as an independent broker, joined Northwestern Mutual, with which he has been associated ever since. In 1938, having an opportunity to enter the larger Chicago market, he moved his office to Chicago and his home to Evanston. Several of his innovations have subsequently become major breakthroughs for uses of permanent life insurance. For example, he wrote his first insured pension plan in 1941, a year before the federal pension law was enacted. In 1947 he designed one of the first major split-dollar life insurance plans for the management group of Cargill, Inc.; then, in 1969, the first executive compensation plan based on permanent life insurance for a major publicly held company, General Electric. Other Northwestern agents joined him to form the John O. Todd Organization, which has designed, installed, and administered plans for more than 250 major public and private companies. It has offices in 17 cities. He served for 21 years as Trustee of the American College, one of a very few to be honored by the College as Life Trustee. In 1978 he received the College's highest award, the Huebner Gold Medal, for his "contribution to education and professionalism." In 1969 he received The Golden Plate Award from the Academy of Achievement, as well as the top award in the insurance industry, the John Newton Russell Award of the National Association of Life Underwriters. President of the Million Dollar Round Table in 1951, President of the MDRT Charitable Foundation in 1971, and President of the Association for Advanced Life Underwriting in 1964. Author of *Ceiling Unlimited*, an inspirational and how-to book for insurance and other salespeople, published by Lexington House, Inc., of Lexington, Kentucky, and now in its fifth edition.

Carl J. Unger, Fremont, Indiana, distributor sales representative selling Zenith color TVs and VCRs and Admiral appliances in 11 counties in Indiana and Michigan. Attended Indiana University and Tri-State College. Starting right out of college, with little sales experience, has sold $40 million worth of Zenith merchandise in 29 years. Winner many times of the Zenith Sales Captain's Award and Zenith Top Performers Award.

David Van Tosh, executive vice president, sales, Encyclopaedia Britannica USA, Chicago. A string bass player, he won a music scholarship to the University of Miami, graduating with AB in music in 1960. Desiring a broader education than learning to play an instrument, he enrolled at the University of Miami law school. In the middle of his second year, he started selling Britannica part-time, was soon earning $600 to $700 a week, which was good money in those days. When he learned in 1963 that the new Law School Dean, the highest paid Dean on the University faculty, was making only $25,000, he dropped out of school to sell encyclopedias full-time. Built the new Orlando district from 0 to 12 salespeople, with sales of 70 sets a month. District manager in Miami 1967–1974, three-time winner of "Brown Doiby" award (so named to avoid title conflict with the Hollywood restaurant) for best district out of the 120 in the nation. Division manager in Houston 1974–1980, winning seven quarterly awards and one annual President's Cup Award for best of the 34 divisions. In 1980 moved to Chicago headquarters as one of three sales vice presidents with 11 divisions reporting to him; 1982–1986 regional vice president in Atlanta; since January 1986 executive vice president, sales, with six regional vice presidents reporting to him.

Jonathan Joseph Vitarius, sales representative, Nabisco Brands, Parsippany, New Jersey. BS in Marketing, Fairleigh Dickinson University, 1983. "Uneeda Boy" award for sales excellence, 1985.

Gordon D. Wallace, sales representative, Spitzer Dodge, Columbus, Ohio. Operated his own service station for nine years, managed a Shell station for four years. Joined Spitzer Dodge four years ago. Won Certified Oil Company's Salesman of the Year Award in 1979 for selling more tires, batteries, and accessories than any other station in that chain; Salesman of the Year Award from Shell in 1982 for selling more TBA than any of the 500 stations in his zone; No. 1 in sales in his zone for Chrysler Corporation. Awards: No. 2 for Certified; No. 1 for Shell.

Bruce White, senior account manager, Maritz Motivation Company, Peoria, Illinois. BFA in Theater, Illinois Wesleyan University, 1965. Was sales rep with Connecticut General Insurance, Texaco, and Honeywell before joining Maritz in St. Louis in 1971, later working out of Milwaukee and Peoria regional offices. Maritz is a full-service motivation agency selling performance improvement programs that feature communications, training, and incentives such as travel, merchandise, and recognition awards. Calls on *Fortune* 500 firms to sell these programs; coordinates an internal team of artists; writers; travel agents; production, research, and administrative staff personnel. Candidate for Leadership Award in 1973; four-time nominee as Man of the Year.

Richard A. Ziegler, senior sales training specialist, The Drackett Company (Bristol-Myers Company), Cincinnati. BS in Education, Miami University, Oxford, Ohio, 1973. Joined Drackett in 1975 as field sales representative in Columbus, Ohio; in 1977, promoted to district manager in Syracuse, New York, managing Syracuse and Albany markets. In 1981 joined human resource development department as sales training specialist; promoted to senior sales training specialist in 1985. Drackett manufactures a number of household products, including Drano, Windex, Vanish, O-Cedar, Renuzit, and Endust.

Index